A Guide to

MID-ATLANTIC GARDENS

Detailed Descriptions of Over 100 of the Mid-Atlantic Region's Finest Public View Gardens

text and photos by
JACK DEMPSEY

CAROLINA CONNECTIONS • KILL DEVIL HILLS, NC

This book was first published in 1994 by Carolina Connections, PO Box 2408, Kill Devil Hills, North Carolina 27948

ISBN 0-9640307-0-5

First Printing: February, 1994

Printed in the U.S.A.

... even Solomon in all his glory was
not arrayed as one of these.

Matthew 6:29

Table of Contents

List of Photographs

Indoors at Longwood Gardens (PA)

The Lewis Ginter Botanical Garden (VA)

Indoors at Brookside Gardens (MD)

A lush border at Leaming's Run (NJ)

Fall at Ladew Topiary Gardens (MD)

Sandhills Community College (NC)

Hershey Gardens (PA)

A panorama at Nemours (DE)

Dumbarton Oaks (DC)

Spring at UNC-Charlotte (NC)

Indoors at the Norfolk Botanical Gardens (VA)

The parterre at Tryon Palace (NC)

Indoors at Phipps Conservatory (PA)

Agecroft Hall (VA)

Handicapped-accessible at Frelinghuysen Arboretum (NJ)

The Biltmore Estate (NC)

cover: The Enid A. Haupt Garden (DC)

TWO ERRATA
The bottom photo facing page 104 is correctly identified
as the Bryan Park Azalea Gardens. The garden on page
146 is correctly identified as the PA Horticultural Society

Dedications
and
Acknowledgements

To the Creator, who tried (unsuccessfully) to give man a Utopian place in which to live--the *Garden* of Eden.

To all the volunteers and persons in garden clubs, historical societies and other voluntary associations who have given of their time, talents and personal fortunes to present the viewing public with a marvelous set of mid-Atlantic gardens.

To the scientists and managers and workers in those gardens who toil endlessly for the enjoyment of others.

To all those who helped me with my research, either on-site at a garden or by phone.

To Judy, my wife, who graciously accepted my endless trips away from home and my pre-dawn writing habits.

To Mary, Karen and Peter at Carolina Connections who were always there.

To the two seniors whose conversation I overheard at the Norfolk Botanical Garden.
First Senior: "Do you know what they say about old gardeners?"
Second Senior: "No, what do they say?"
First Senior: "They say, 'Old gardeners never die, we just go to seed.'"

To old gardeners and to all those who find new places to visit in my guidebook.

Jack Dempsey

Chapter 1
Introduction to
Mid-Atlantic Gardens

A year ago I embarked on one of the most enjoyable missions ever undertaken by a human being: to find the hundred finest gardens in my region; to savor their delights to the limits of my capacity; and to describe them for the enjoyment of thousands of kindred souls I will otherwise never meet.

Think of it. A year devoted to gardens--the highest form of beauty, the pinnacle of art, the closest approximation of paradise. Is there *any* other way to spend a year more enjoyably?

Too much of a good thing?

Man is known to require diversity to avoid boredom, even in life's most enjoyable pursuits--filet mignon at every meal would soon become tedious. Would there be enough diversity in the gardens I visited to keep the year as continuously stimulating as the occasional change-of-pace visit to one of my favorite places? Or would a year of wonder slowly decay into just another ... job?

Interestingly, no one could have fully advised me on this at the beginning. I have talked with at least one person at each of the gardens described in the chapters to follow and, without exception, even these professionals possess an incomplete knowledge of mid-Atlantic gardens beyond the most famous ones region-wide and the less publicized ones in their immediate vicinity. (I am assuming that the average reader has visited fewer than a half-dozen public view gardens.)

The mid-Atlantic region, it turns out, is blessed with one of the largest and most diverse sets of gardens in the world for its size. Probably the Region's most internationally reknowned display is at Longwood Gardens (PA) where dazzling, constantly changing indoor extravaganzas exhibit the world's most exotic plants complementary to an outdoor collection of stunning gardens, fountains and music unrivaled in the country. Imagine the largest and most beautiful garden in your neighborhood, multiply it by a thousand, and you *may* approximate Longwood Gardens in *one* of its seasons.

Further south in North Carolina, The Biltmore Estate distributes over thousands of acres Italian, English-walled and naturalistic gardens, each of which projects a different type of botanical beauty. In between, Virginia hosts the largest collection of famous historical gardens such as George Washington's Mount Vernon or Thomas Jefferson's Monticello or the incomparable grounds at Colonial Williamsburg.

There are one-stop gardens such as the U.S. National Arboretum in

Washington, D.C. which contains acres of just about anything that interests you; the lucky tens of thousands of visitors in a single spring day hope that you confine your interests to needlepoint. The Norfolk Botanical Garden (VA), an awesomely diversified garden complex, offers acres of roses, a tropical plant pavilion, my favorite gift shop, garden tours by foot or by boat or by tram, fountains, plants from Asia, seasonal beds, a reference library, statuary, ample parking, masses of camellias, dozens of educational events, plant sales, assorted groundcovers--for starters.

New Jersey offers the public the largest set of county-owned and managed gardens of quality in the Region. The Frelinghuysen Arboretum and Deep Cut Gardens, for instance, offer a full set of beautiful gardens with the added mission of helping the homeowner take back home some ideas for the yard. New Jersey also has the largest assortment of specialty gardens, the best known of which is Leaming's Run Gardens; just about everyone has planted marigolds or zinnias or pansies or some sort of annual at one time or another, and Leaming's Run has specialized in it. It has been recognized as the largest annual garden in the country and has even been recognized internationally. It sits by itself on the southern Jersey coast, but is well worth going out of the way to visit.

North Carolina has the bragging rights in the Region for university- and college-based gardens of quality; it has nine. Duke University's Sarah P. Duke Gardens has been reknowned for its terraced beds since the 1930s. UNC-Charlotte is still gaining recognition for its azaleas and rhododendrons on the outside and its orchids and tropicals on the inside.

Special gardens exist for special tastes. If you prefer the more subtle appeal of naturalized gardens, you can begin and end your search at incomparable Winterthur (DE), which almost defies description. Even more natural is UNC-Chapel Hill which specializes in natural plant habitats. If you like aquatic plants, go to Lilypons in Maryland or Kenilworth Aquatic Gardens in Washington, D.C. If you like irises, go to Presby Memorial Iris Gardens (NJ). If you like bird-attracting gardens, go to Wing Haven (NC). If you like topiaries (ornamentally shaped hedges), go to Ladew Topiary Gardens (MD). If you like immense live oaks draped with Spanish moss, go to Orton Plantation. If you like herbs, go to Well-Sweep Herb Farm. If you like ornamental grasses, go to Delaware Valley College (PA). If you like gardens that emphasize the interrelationships among all living systems, go to the Virginia Living Museum. If you like rock gardens, go to the Leonard J. Buck Garden (NJ).

If, on the other hand, you want a well-rounded garden that tastefully offers a wide selection of gardens, go to Hershey Gardens (PA), the Elizabethan Gardens (NC) or the Morris Arboretum (PA).

If you want to integrate yourself into national societies, go to River Farm (VA--the American Horticultural Society). If you like religious gardens, go to the Washington National Cathedral or Franciscan Monastery--both in D.C. If you like roses, go to Colonial Park (NJ). If you like regal French gardens, go to Nemours (DE). If you like trees, go to Tyler Arboretum (PA), Georgian Court

College (NJ), Cora Hartshorn Arboretum (NJ) or dozens of other places. If you like high society gardens, go to Hillwood Museum (DC). If you like college campuses that are total arboreta unto themselves, go to Haywood Community College (NC) or Swarthmore College (PA). If you like gardens on top of mountains, go to Skylands (NJ). If you like English Tudor-era gardens, go to Agecroft Hall (VA). If you like espaliered fruit trees, go to Hagley (DE).

That's about 40 gardens and, hopefully, the litany demonstrates the marvelous diversity the mid-Atlantic gardens offer the viewing public. As a set, they offer a national treasure to be cherished.

But are there a hundred quality gardens?

The principal problem I encountered in my odyssey proved not to be boredom and not to be padding my list to reach a hundred; it proved to be *limiting* it to a hundred. Even narrowing my definition of "garden" for acceptance or rejection of candidate gardens helped very little.

Very early in my search for candidate gardens, I encountered my first dilemma regarding acceptance or rejection. I turned off the road to see what the sign, Eternal Gardens, referred to. It turned out to be a cemetery, and a very beautiful one at that. It was a veritable sea of brilliantly white edifices with rose-covered arbors, azaleas, perennial borders and ornamental trees. Unfortunately, its purpose was to commemorate the departed rather than to delight visitors who otherwise would have no reason for being there. So I excluded the entire class of cemeteries, even though many are fine works of botanical art.

I excluded zoos, even though many have gone far beyond the minimal botanical habitats the resident animals require to survive. Like cemeteries, the missions are different plus something else. If a rare wildflower by the side of the road had a choice, I believe it would choose to be transplanted to a caring garden where both it and the caring humans shared the same goal--to realize its maximum healthy growth and to reproduce for the following year. A caged habitat for animals is still a cage and few would choose to be there voluntarily. Zoos are necessary and educational, of course, and many animals unable to survive in the wild are given a second chance there, but still there is an element of unnaturalness that detracts from the purer dedication to beauty in a botanical garden. "Zoological gardens" contains two words that fit each other imperfectly.

A different mission also excludes some beautifully landscaped corporate headquarters. I know a few that would easily qualify for the top 25 gardens in this Region on their merits. But if they became known as such and hordes of visitors descended on the parking lot and grounds, many would either downsize the gardens or erect barriers to exclude the public. It seems better to let them keep their gardens in relative anonymity.

My saddest exclusions were of unkempt gardens, fortunately few in number. It is a terrible, terrible experience to arrive at a respected garden only to find trash everywhere, unweeded beds, unclipped hedges and no evidence that anything has been pruned in years. I excluded three for this reason, one with a proud tradition. Very sad.

I was not quite sure what to do about commercial establishments. Many commercial nurseries, retail outlets and florists are truly works of beauty. Indeed, there are so many of them that they seem to warrant a book of their own. Only a few of them, however, have display areas for public enjoyment and educational programs, so I have included only those few.

A most unusual experience clarified for me some nagging uneasiness I had been feeling about "botanical" gardens. My wife and I were driving to one of our favorite gardens, took a wrong turn and happened upon some attractive display beds and collections of shrubs, and there seemed to be much more further back. It turned out to be a university's field botanical research station. Being Sunday, no one was there and we took an undisturbed tour of the facility, finding in one of the greenhouses a fine, healthy, large collection of potted crab grass. Botanists, this experience reminded me, are interested equally in all plants. From a scientific point of view, a set of crab grass beds with poison ivy borders would constitute a "botanical" garden. But it's not what I had in mind when I undertook my mission.

Botanical scientists also are interested in completely natural areas and some might delight in studying the growth of non-flowering aquatic plants in a mosquito- and snake-infested swamp. Also not what I had in mind.

It strikes me that "horticultural" is the better word, its two roots meaning "the cultivation of a garden." This would exclude purely natural areas, which are important enough and numerous enough to warrant a guidebook of their own. Yet, interestingly, only the gardens at Sandhills Community College, Fairmount Park Horticulture Center and the Pennsylvania Horticultural Society use "horticultural" in their titles whereas many use "botanical."

Also perplexing is the use of the term, arboretum. Strictly speaking, arboreta are collections of trees and, unless the intention is to display trees for their beauty, arboreta would not qualify for acceptance. In practice, however, many gardens use "arboretum" as a general term for a highly diversified set of horticultural attractions that include trees as one of the features. The arboretum at North Carolina State University is a good example. One could visit it and enjoy the many non-aboreal attractions without looking at a single tree in the excellent collection of them. (The arboretum is sponsored by the *horticulture* department.)

Because of the non-specific way many people use terms to describe various botanical entities, I have found it useful to shift my vocabulary to characteristics of the visitor, rather than characteristics of the horticultural entities. My sub-title refers to "public view" gardens. The general public expects a garden to be a work of beauty for the sake of beauty, usually with at least some cultivation and usually with some flowering plants and usually in a tastefully landscaped area. This excludes purely natural areas and many collections of non-flowering plants. It does not exclude naturalized landscapes nor does it exclude some cul-

4

tivated gardens in which degree of flowering is of secondary consideration, such as many herb gardens.

"Public view" also excludes gardens that only tolerate public visitation. I found a few gardens that open to the public only a day or two a month; several communities (especially historic ones) and one state (VA) feature a weekend or week a year when large numbers of private gardens participate in a common "open house"; a few places have no regularly scheduled openings, but will accept group tours by prearrangement only. All of these are excluded. This does not exclude places such as Duke Gardens (NJ) and Nemours (DE) that require appointments to control the number of visitors at any given time for the guided tours--that's just good management for your convenience and their sanity.

An entire class of accept/reject decisions revolves around sites where the gardens share the spotlight with other attractions, frequently being the secondary attraction. This is true of many recreational complexes that also include gardens. This presents no problem for first class gardens such as Brookside Gardens (MD) which occupies one corner of the enormous Wheaton Regional Park, because all the garden components are together. In places such as Hamilton Veterans Park (NJ) and Tanglewood Park (NC), however, the gardens are distributed throughout the complex, which has a dilution effect on visitors with time limitations or physical impairments. I decided to include them, however, when the garden areas, if combined in one place, would qualify for my guidebook.

A much more difficult decision presents itself when a garden shares the spotlight with historical attractions, such as a mansion, a plantation complex or a civic landmark. In well over half of such cases, the garden is either subordinate in importance to a principal attraction or is just one element in a larger constellation in support of a period of history (e.g., Old Salem--NC) or the lifestyle of a dignitary (e.g., William Trent House--NJ).

The nature of historic gardens complicates the decision, with the degree of difficulty increasing with the age of the garden. Colonial gardeners, for instance, had a narrow selection of species available to them; modern hybrids with longer bloom periods and greater hardiness were not available; maintenance equipment was primitive; pest control technology was limited; general botanical knowledge was infinitesimal compared to today. Although some dignitaries-- Washington at Mount Vernon (VA), Jefferson at Monticello (VA), Paca in Maryland--still managed highly significant gardens, as did public grounds (Tryon Palace--NC), many historically significant gardens simply do not cater to modern tastes or expectations.

Add to this the complication of how the historic gardens have been managed. Some (e.g., Mount Vernon) were acquired by history-conscious associations early enough to *preserve* at least some of the original gardens; some (e.g., Monticello) have been *restored* to the original *design* with *period* plants; especially in the absence of original plans, some (e.g., Tryon Palace) have *created* a garden typical of the period in design and plant composition; and all combinations of the underlined variables. If you had room for one more garden in

YOUR guidebook, how would you choose between the following two? The first consists of a rather anemic garden--by historic and modern standards--that belonged to an immensely important forefather, and it has been faithfully (and anemically) preserved or restored in period design and plants. The second was originally an anemic garden but, in tribute to the significance of the forefather and his otherwise majestic estate, has been replaced with a beautiful, modern garden that anyone would delight in visiting. Which would you include, historical integrity or embellished brilliance?

These dilemmas are of no small moment because the mid-Atlantic region contains the nation's finest set of historic gardens, a national treasure to be cherished and a very large proportion of gardens to be seen. So large, in fact, that all cannot be included in a guidebook that limits itself to the hundred top gardens in the Region.

In the absence of a mathematical, mechanical or other objective approach to decision-making, I resorted to my "Leaming's Run Criterion." If I felt that any garden was worth going out of one's way to see for any reason--historic or face value or other--I included it unless it disqualified itself for the reasons above or was displaced by sheer numbers of similar gardens.

For a working definition of garden, therefore, I accepted places that offered the public a cultivated work of botanical beauty that was significant enough in size or composition or uniqueness or historical significance to warrant going out of one's way to see. This excludes places with limited public access, purely natural areas, unattractive or unkempt botanical entities, corporate headquarters, zoos, cemeteries, most commercial outlets, stands of trees without a cultivated undergrowth or complementary display areas, and fine gardens that simply were outnumbered by others in their class.

In spite of these exclusions, I still had difficulty limiting the number to a hundred and, in fact, ended up with a dozen more. These include diversified and specialized gardens; formal, informal and naturalized gardens; sole-attraction and shared-attraction gardens; modern and historic gardens; religious and secular gardens; public and private gardens; indoor and outdoor gardens; well-established and brand new gardens; seasonal and all-season gardens. In spite of the exclusions, the variety is still so great that only a cumbersome, multi-dimensional classification system such as the above can do it justice. Boredom has never been a problem.

My original intent was to search for the 20 best gardens in PA, NJ. VA, and NC and 20 in DC/DE/MD combined--these three together approximate the other states in landmass and population. A glance at the table of contents reveals that I met or reluctantly exceeded that in every case. And I could have included many more: it was very difficult to draw a line and stop *somewhere*.

West Virginia posed a dilemma. Some do and some do not consider it to be a mid-Atlantic state. Upon investigation I found that the State considers itself a national leader in natural areas and rural park systems, in contrast to formal gardens, and it really belongs in a guidebook with that focus. Still, Greenbrier,

6

just over the border with Virginia, is so unique that I have included it in the set of Virginia descriptions.

How does one find gardens?

Actually, it's difficult not to. I went through my final list and found that I identified gardens in ten different ways. First, of course, there were the ones I already knew about. Next, other directories were partially helpful; none focused exclusively on the mid-Atlantic region; most were incomplete for the Region; and all were outdated, missing the new gardens and including some that had closed. (For instance, one Maryland estate garden closed for financial reasons and one North Carolina garden had been obliterated by a hurricane.) Road signs led me to places like the Virginia Living Museum and the Lewis Ginter Botanical Garden (VA). Fourthly, magazine ads and articles led me to places like Stratford Hall Plantation (VA). Personnel at places I visited directed me to places like Sayen Gardens (NJ) and the Enid A. Haupt Garden (DC). I found Airlie Gardens on a map when I was plotting my exit from Wilmington, NC and went to see if it was a cemetery or a garden. Just ask a lot of people: friends I was visiting in southern Maryland informed me of Sotterley. If you drive around long enough, sooner or later you just bump into places like the Raleigh Municipal Rose Garden. Finally, read between the lines: I purchased a book on colonial architecture and found a curious reference to the Adam Thoroughgood House in Norfolk; I went to see it on a hunch and found a delightful garden.

They are everywhere. Unfortunately, I am still finding more and feel quite badly that I cannot include them all.

Source material for the garden descriptions.

Each garden description in the chapters to follow draws on three sources of information. First and foremost, direct observation--this is not a piece of library research. Secondly, published pamphlets, brochures, books and other materials. Thirdly and last in temporal sequence, a telephone interview with someone identified by the director of the garden. (This mainly consisted of the director, a botanist, a landscape architect, a horticulturalist, a groundskeeping supervisor, an owner, someone in the public affairs office.) The three sources of information were then integrated and expressed in standard format, one by one. There is no "plot" to this book: each description of each garden stands by itself, related to the other gardens only in terms of state residence.

The standard format for each garden description begins with basic identifying information--name, address, phone, hours.

Next comes the overview which briefly summarizes the principal dimensions of the garden, which usually include its size, dominant garden features, other attractions on site, ownership and (when relevant) principal viewing seasons.

The directions first orient you to the general location of the garden and then lead you to it on your most likely route. *Please use an up-to-date map* as an adjunct to my description. If you are traveling from an unusual direction, you should still be able to adapt my detailed directions to your best route on the map.

The historical profile provides developmental and opening-to-the-public dates, sometimes land-use histories, sometimes garden development milestones, and sometimes biographical data on significant individuals. Obtaining historical information was the most frequently difficult part of my data collection.

The description occupies the largest block of text and elaborates on the overview. The intent is to be more comprehensive than detailed here--what are all the viewable attractions and which are the most significant? Shared attractions are mentioned, but not in detail; at a recreational complex such as Greenfield Park (NC), for instance, I mention boat rentals and other recreational opportunities without elaboration.

Garden-related activities are also mentioned without great detail; workshops, lectures, annual plant sales, etc. change significantly from year to year in dates and composition, and there are many annual additions and deletions to the list.

A few gardens seemed to pride themselves on their garden-related activities as much as the gardens, so I created a Special Features section for those few.

Finally, there is a terminal section called "Personal Impression." In the interest of objectivity, my writing style is mainly journalistic in nature. A steady flow of objectivity, however, can become rather dull, so I loosen up in this section and say "wow!" if I want to.

This is the standard format for each garden so that visitors can quickly find the information they need, especially when one hand is on a steering wheel.

Data boxes.

A large data box insert accompanies the narrative for each garden, providing cursory information on 21 characteristics of each facility. The frequent visitor to gardens may quickly locate in the same space for each garden information of immediate relevance such as, "Is there food there?" or "Do they have restrooms?" As needed, I footnote information in the cells.

Ownership. Official ownership is rather straightforward and is nearly always public (Federal, state, county, city) or private (non-profit or commercial). Management of publicly owned gardens, however, may be complex because it may be completely delegated (privatized) to a private group or shared collaboratively, with many shades in-between. When this occurs, the arrangement is explained in a footnote.

Pet on leash. No garden welcomes pets in the garden, for obvious reasons, but some do permit pets on leash. Others tolerate leashed pets and most prohibit them. I indicate the policy as yes (leashed pets permitted), no or tolerated/discouraged.

Brochure. Yes or no--gardens either do or do not have a brochure, at least part of which describes the garden.

Size. This usually refers to the landscaped area, but clarification is offered in a footnote when the landscaped area is just part of a much larger area. It is intended to help readers decide how long it will take to view the garden.

Weddings. Many gardens allow weddings and/or wedding pictures on-site, frequently for a fee. A few also cater receptions. Since policies in these regards seem to change frequently, call for details as far in advance as possible.

Educational programs. I usually indicate only yes or no here because the precise nature of the educational programs changes constantly. Unusually numerous and/or diverse programs are described in the text.

Rest rooms. Obviously, either yes or no. Bear in mind, however, that many restrooms are located indoors, and those facilities may have shorter hours than the grounds.

Sell plants. Yes, no or occasionally. Yes refers to those gardens that have a good, year-round selection (e.g., Washington National Cathedral) or a good selection throughout the growing season (e.g., Elizabethan Gardens). "Occasionally" usually refers to those gardens that sell plants once or twice a year at special events.

Special events. Usually yes or no. A yes means you should call for an up-to-date calendar of events. Amplification, when needed, is offered in the text or in footnotes.

Pay phone. Yes or no. If you have an emergency, garden managers are understanding and will allow you the use of a desk phone, but a pay phone is helpful if no one's there.

Membership. Usually yes or no for paid membership in a society with benefits such as free entrance to gardens, discounts for special events or in the gift shop, receipt of a newsletter, invitation to limited-access events, etc. Costs are usually graduated from student level to benefactor with many shades in-between. Some gardens have a vehicle for receiving gifts, but have no benefits; this is described in a footnote.

Labeling. Personally I find labeling a major feature when viewing gardens and I was pleased to find that so many places were in process of improving this. Usually yes or no.

Visitor center. This refers to *any* sort of official point-of-entry, from a sign-in desk in a hallway to a complete, real-life, full-size, separate structure. A place where you can ask questions and get a brochure.

Gift shop. Like visitor centers, these come in all shapes and sizes. When the garden is the principal feature on the property, there usually is a strong horticultural offering. When the spotlight is shared with other features, usually historical structures, the gardening component of the shop may be weak; large facilities such as Mount Vernon and Monticello are the exceptions. Gift shops and plant sales are generally physically separated.

Volunteers. Without volunteers, many gardens would cease to exist or, at least, suffer serious reductions in quality. Usually my entry here is yes or no, with footnoted amplification when necessary.

Fees. Most of my entries here are yes or no, but this is too important to be left at that. See separate section on fees that immediately follows this section.

Off street parking. This is self-explanatory except that available off-street parking does not guarantee you a space. Attendance at special events in peak season may consume all nearby spaces. Call if this presents a problem for you.

Library for public. There are facilities that have no library, that have a library for members only, that have a library with a gardening emphasis, that have a library requiring advance notice, and all combinations of the above.

Ext. photo limits. There are few restrictions on taking a couple of photos when you visit a garden. The exceptions, however, are sufficiently complex that I have included a separate section on this immediately following the section on fees, which follows this section.

Garden clubs active. In the same way that individual volunteers have become indispensable to many operations, organized groups such as garden clubs, historical societies and various other voluntary associations contribute variably from total ownership to an annual plant sale. These associations have profoundly impacted on the availability and quality of public-view gardens in the Region.

Food. Should you eat before you get there? Even if I indicate that food is available, bear in mind that its availability may diminish or disappear before and after the peak season. Call to make sure.

The handicapped. I took note of handicapped access during my visits to each garden, especially wheelchair access, and decided against including my observations in the data box. The recent passage of the Americans with Disability Act has at least a third of the gardens making plans to improve access and services. Since many of them have extremely limited budgets, it is difficult to project when they will complete planned improvements. Therefore, call in advance to determine whether a given garden can accommodate at that time a family member with a particular type of handicap. I found restroom access to be the most frequent limiting factor.

Fees.

Garden-viewing may be the most economical form of recreation in the United States. Roughly half charge no fee at all for the gardens. Many leave the amount of a nominal donation to your discretion.

Of those that do charge fees, the vast majority charge $3-$5 for the grounds per adult. Nearly all discount children under a certain age or allow them free admission; many discount seniors; some discount groups; a few discount military personnel. A few offer annual frequent-visitor packages.

There may be separate fees for weddings, commercial photography, guided tours, transportation through the gardens, parking and especially access to non-gardening attractions such as a historic house.

I have inviariably found food, when available, to be reasonably priced. It generally is light fare, but I have found gourmet buffets at places such as Winterthur, and at a reasonable price. Similarly, gift shop prices are invariably reasonable.

Fees vary so much over time and vary according to what you want to do so much that I have not provided the dollar amounts I paid. If it's the end of the month and you are short on cash, call first to find out precisely what the current fees are.

I like the fee-structure at Tryon Palace because it graduates the fee according to how many attractions you want to see. When I visited it, the fee for the grounds was $4, the fee for the grounds and Palace was $8, and the fee for the grounds, Palace and surrounding historic district was $12. At the Biltmore Estate, however, I paid one handsome fee for everything, even though I had time enough to see only the gardens. Plan your trips carefully to get the most for your money.

Courtesy and visitor restrictions.

Mid-Atlantic gardens impose amazingly few restrictions on visitors mainly because they don't have to. People who visit public view gardens are among the best-behaved groups in our society. Nonetheless, there are some formal restrictions and some informal "preferences" worth discussing, and most of these are related to courtesy.

Indoor smoking is almost routinely prohibited as a courtesy to other people and to plant health, as well as to reduce litter and prevent fires, especially in old, historic structures. Outdoor smoking is discouraged because the butts add little to the beds.

Unleashed pets are always discouraged or prohibited. Leashed pets are sometimes excluded, sometimes tolerated, and never enthusiastically welcomed--for obvious reasons. If possible, leave Rover at home.

I was surprised to find so many gardens expressing concern about children, although only a few of them explicitly require a certain ratio of supervisors to children or exclude unaccompanied children below a certain age. Stomping on flowers, cutting blooms, gouging antiques, stealing or switching labels, defacing restrooms--all of these occur with intolerable frequency. The Botanical Gardens at Asheville (NC) recently experienced severe vandalism. One university professor said that, given a choice, he would leash the children and let the pets run free--they do less damage. Three gardens come to mind as seriously considering the abandonment of labeling because they were unable to keep up with the pilfering. Parents and teachers, please supervise the kids.

Photographic restrictions are tied overwhelmingly into considerations of courtesy. Indoors, cameras are frequently excluded because picture taking impedes the normal pace of guided tours; tripods are more frequently prohibited because they gouge the floor and furnishings, and impede the flow of visitors; flash guns are frequently prohibited because they irritate some visitors and may cause an accident--imagine being momentarily blinded while descending some stairs. Outside, rarely does one find restrictions on cameras or flashes, but tripods are increasingly wearing out their welcome.

Most restrictions pertain to commercial photography, both indoors and out. If you want to bring massive equipment in, you will probably be required to do so during low visitation periods. If your only interest in the garden is as a backdrop for a product you are selling (e.g., a car), you will probably have to pay a fee. On the other hand, if you are as unobtrusive in your picture taking as the average visitor, you usually are requested only to provide a courtesy notice of use so that they can keep track of the type of publicity they are getting. That's entirely reasonable. Check the brochure for restrictions before you go.

Overall, however, garden managers allow you to enjoy yourself in any sensible way--just use courtesy and common sense.

Some lessons, conclusions and suggestions.

Above all, *call ahead*, especially if you will travel any distance to see a garden. I drove all day to the other side of the Region to see a garden I had missed during my first trip; it had been closed almost a week while a ruptured water main under the street was being replaced. I drove some distance to another state to see a public garden, which had closed to commemorate a state holiday not observed in my state. I drove to a university garden one Saturday afternoon only to find thousands of raucous visitors attending a homecoming football game; I never did find a parking space. Please call ahead.

And when you do, have them send you their brochure and other free literature, and read it. You are undoubtedly intelligent enough to read a brochure and walk through a garden at the same time, but you probably won't. So you will miss all the little insights and understandings that are not self-evident to the eye. Please call ahead.

And when you do, verify any information in this guidebook that you deem important. I have been amazed at how quickly things can change--telephone area codes, mailing addresses, fees, hours open, availability of food, policies on pets and weddings, even management.

Two major, municipal gardens privatized over the past year. To those who think positively, this and other changes offer opportunities for sidelight enjoyments. In a larger context, I found a much-larger-than-expected number of publicly owned gardens that delegated or shared management with private associations-- e.g., the Reeves-Reed Arboretum (NJ), the Daniel Boone Native Gardens (NC), the Cylburn Arboretum (MD), the Botanical Gardens at Asheville (NC), Phipps Conservatory (PA), Greensboro Beautiful (NC). I hope to find the time to study this more intensely in the future.

Similarly, I hope to study the role of volunteers more carefully. At the beginning of my odyssey, I completely underestimated the importance of volunteers to the operation of over half of the Region's gardens--dedicated individuals, garden clubs, historical societies and other associations. Garden workers, receptionists, gift shop workers, historical researchers, tour docents, managers, technical consultants, fund raisers, special event sponsors, bookkeepers, drivers, office workers, librarians, even owners--volunteers do it all. I estimate that at least 15% of the Region's gardens would close immediately without volunteer individuals and organizations, and another 30% would suffer significant reductions in garden quality, hours open and scope of activities. I hope to refine these estimates in the future because I think they are too low.

Please take a survival kit with you that includes at least insect repellent, a compass and a AAA or other auto club card. (My car's alternator died at dawn on Sunday on top of a remote New Jersey mountain--what a nightmare.)

Take film with you during prime viewing seasons because they sell out fast.

If possible, visit on weekdays. Parking is easier, crowds are smaller, technical people are on-site to answer questions.

Check my guidebook before you get there for restroom and food availability.

Take your checkbook, credit cards and ample cash. The average gift shop at places that have one offers distinctive merchandise that is difficult to find elsewhere. You can provide much-needed support for the gardens and do your gift shopping simultaneously.

Take a close look at the plants for sale at places that have sales. They tend to offer hard-to-find species and varieties in order to avoid competing with (and alienating) local commercial outlets. I recently purchased an Old Blush rose plant like the one I saw at Tudor Place (DC); heritage roses typically have shorter bloom periods than modern hybrids, but are much more fragrant and are next to impossible to find at commercial outlets.

While you are there, ask questions. My wife and I have *never* experienced discourtesy or curtness from garden staff--they genuinely enjoy being helpful. The gardeners at Hershey Gardens (PA), Mount Vernon (VA) and the Elizabethan Gardens (NC) come to mind as being particularly receptive to questions.

I invite you to join me in expressing appreciation during visits to those who overcome enormous problems to offer us dazzling gardens--voracious deer (Morven Park--VA; Acorn Hall--NJ; Gunston Hall--VA; probably two dozen other places), recession-induced public budget cuts (Rutgers University--NJ; Paca House--MD; many others), dogwood blight and Japanese beetles and plant diseases (dozens of places), hurricane and other weather damage (Wing Haven--NC), and on and on and on. Those beautiful gardens more frequently result from agonizing problem-solving than from unrestricted creative expression.

And, oh yes, don't forget to enjoy yourself. I did. Wow!

Chapter 2
D.C., Delaware and Maryland

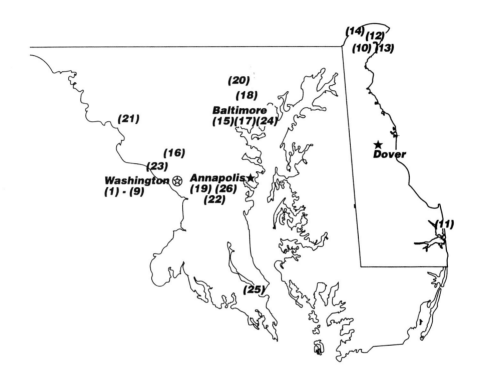

DC (1) Dumbarton Oaks
  (2) Enid A. Haupt Garden
  (3) Franciscan Monastery
  (4) Gardens of the Washington
      National Cathedral
  (5) Hillwood Museum
  (6) Kenilworth Aquatic Gardens
  (7) Tudor Place
  (8) U.S. Botanic Garden
  (9) U.S. National Arboretum

DE (10) Hagley
  (11) Homestead
  (12) Nemours Mansion &
      Gardens
  (13) Rockwood
  (14) Winterthur Museum,
      Garden, and Library

MD (15) Baltimore City
      Conservatory
  (16) Brookside Gardens
  (17) Cylburn Arboretum
  (18) Hampton Nat'l Historic Site
  (19) Helen Avalynne Tawes
      Garden
  (20) Ladew Topiary Gardens
  (21) Lilypons Water Gardens
  (22) London Town Publik
      House and Gardens
  (23) McCrillis Gardens & Gallery
  (24) Sherwood Gardens
  (25) Sotterley
  (26) William Paca House and
      Garden

DISTRICT OF COLUMBIA

There is some clustering of gardens in the District of Columbia. The U.S. National Arboretum and Kenilworth Aquatic Gardens are across the Anacostia River from each other, east of the Capitol. The U.S. Botanic Garden and the Enid A. Haupt Garden (Smithsonian Institution) are within walking distance of each other along the Mall west of the Capitol. Dumbarton Oaks and Tudor Place are within walking distance of each other in Georgetown (western part of town), and the Washington National Cathedral is a short drive up Wisconsin Ave. from them. Hillwood Museum is a modest drive north from there. Only the Franciscan Monastery sits by itself in the far northeastern part of town.

(1) Dumbarton Oaks

1703 32nd St., N.W.
Washington, D.C. 20007
(202) 342-3200
Hours: the grounds are open 2-6 daily, April-Oct., and 2-5 daily, Nov.-March; museum collections open 2-5 daily except Mondays; the Rare Book Room opens 2-5 weekends. Closed major holidays and for inclement weather.

Overview. Dumbarton Oaks, site of the planning of the United Nations, contains 10 ingeniously landscaped, highly diversified, carefully maintained garden acres--one of the premier gardens of the Region. Administered by Harvard University, the expanded estate mansion houses several art and rare book (including landscaping history) collections of high reknown.

Directions. Locate Georgetown on a map of D.C. directly north of Theodore Roosevelt Island in the Potomac River. Take Wisconsin Ave. northwest to R St., turn right and proceed a block. At the intersection of R St. and 32nd St., the entrance to the walled grounds is on R St. and the entrance to the Museum is on 32nd St.

Historical Profile. Robert and Mildred Bliss, a wealthy heir/heiress couple, purchased this hilly, 53-acre farmland in 1920, naming it after the on-site great oaks and the Rock of Dumbarton in Scotland. The c. 1800 mansion was remodeled and enlarged to include the library and collections which now occupy the entire building. Landscape gardener Beatrix Ferrand introduced a multi-level set of terraces for the gardens, which today comprise 10 of the property's current sixteen acres and incorporate elements of traditional French, English and Italian gardens. In 1940, Mr. and Mrs. Bliss donated the 16 acres to Harvard University and, in 1944, internationally attended meetings there produced the principles that later were incorporated into the charter of the United Nations.

Description. Less creative landscapers never would have chosen the grounds north and east of the mansion for cultivation because the terrain slopes so steeply away from it. However, Mrs. Bliss and landscaper Ferrand met the challenge with an ingenious employment of multi-level terracing that is unique in the mid-Atlantic region. The multiple levels allowed the creation of highly distinct garden segments, each with its own design. This multi-level segmentation dominates the panorama.

Although the creators of the garden represented the overall design as eclectic and progressively informal as one proceeds down from the mansion, the very formal upper gardens, the sharp demarcation of the levels and the extensive use of non-botanical features provide a distinctly formal, European ambience. Throughout are extensive ironworks, stone steps and walkways, sculpture, mosaics, 10 pools and 9 fountains. The surface proportion of non-botanical material is probably unsur-passed in the Region.

Ownership	Pet on leash	Brochure
private[1]	no	excellent
Size	**Weddings**	**Ed. programs**
16 acres	no	no
Rest rooms	**Sell plants**	**Spec. events**
yes	no	no
Pay phone	**Membership**	**Labeling**
no	no	some
Visitor center	**Gift shop**	**Volunteers**
yes	yes	no
Fees		**Off street parking**
yes		no
Library for public		**Ext. photo limits**
yes, call		commercial
Garden clubs active		**Food**
no		no

[1] *Harvard University*

The self-guiding tour brochure identifies 18 stops at various garden segments and features. The Orangery in the mansion houses terrace container plants in winter. The Star Garden just outside the mansion features astrological motifs and a relief of Aquarius surrounded by a white azalea hedge. The paved Arbor Terrace features a wisteria-covered 16th century-styled arbor on the west side and serves as a "tub garden" in summer--gardenias, lantana, citrus. The Rose Garden contains c. 1000 plants in highly formal arrangement. Irish yews flank the ends of an elongated English-style herbaceous border, which presents a seasonal procession of tulips, annuals, perennials and mums. The Fountain Terrace harbors two lead fountains with seasonal borders.

This set of garden segments describes less than half of the cultivated areas which, *in toto,* present an enormous variety of white and black oaks, magnolias, beeches, cedars, dogwoods, flowering cherries, maples, oleanders, peonies, lilacs, azaleas, forsythias and *much* more. The plantings are usually dense and meticulously groomed in one of the most labor-intensive gardens in the Region. The total effect on the visitor is one of awe.

Proceeding around the corner to the Museum, one finds the Byzantine Collection (c. 1939), the Pre-Columbian Museum (1963), the Garden Library (1963), and the Music Room (1929). (Igor Stravinsky performed his Concerto in E Flat here, more widely known as the *Dumbarton Oaks Concerto*.) Call for a brochure describing the collections and exhibits.

Personal Impression. The landscaping here truly constitutes an artistic creation, and the meticulous care of highly diversified plantings and artwork makes this one of the Region's premier gardens. Don't miss it.

---

(2) The Enid A. Haupt Garden
(at the Smithsonian Institution)
1000 Independence Avenue (main entrance)
Washington, D.C. 20560
(202) 357-2700 (general Smithsonian information)
Hours: the Garden is open at 7 a.m. daily, year round, except Christmas; the closing time from Memorial Day through September 30 is 8:00 p.m., and from October 1 to Memorial Day is 5:45 p.m. The visitor center in the Castle opens 9-5:30 daily, year round, except Christmas.

Overview. This 4.2 acre, formal exhibition garden in the Nation's Capital, adjacent to the Smithsonian Institution's original building (the Castle), sits atop an underground museum complex and features a very large embroidery parterre and two international gardens that complement the on-site National Museum of African Art and Arthur M. Sackler Gallery (Asian art). It is the most formal, all-seasons garden area in the 180 acres maintained by the Institution's Horticulture Services Division.

Directions. Locate on a map of D.C. the Mall between the Capitol and the Washington Monument. Independence Ave. runs parallel to it and just south of it; 1000 Independence Ave. is on the northern side of the Avenue, closer to the Monument than to the Capitol. There is limited street parking; call the number above to obtain by mail general trip-planning information, including the location of nearby parking garages and public transportation systems.

Historical Profile. Established in 1846 with funds from English scientist James Smithson, the Smithsonian Institution has steadily grown to its current 16 museums and the National Zoo, making it the world's largest museum complex. The current site of the Haupt Garden, beginning as a grazing field for bison, underwent numerous changes in use until a generous donation from philanthropist Enid Haupt made her namesake garden possible, opening to the public in 1987. The rectangular grounds are nestled among several Smithsonian buildings and provide a relaxing, contemplative atmosphere for the appreciative visitor.

Description. The Enid A. Haupt Garden occupies a 4.2-acre area bordered by Independence Avenue on the south, the famous Castle building on the north,

17

the Arts and Industries Building on the east and the Freer Gallery of Art on the west.

If, instead of entering the garden through the center gate on Independence Avenue, you walk around the garden perimeter next to the buildings, you would first encounter a row of small-leaved lindens on Independence Avenue, then gums along the Arts and Industries Building, then American hollies along the Castle, and finally a mixture of southern magnolias and darlington oaks by the Freer Gallery of Art.

Back where you started, if you now pass through the central entrance on Independence Avenue toward the Castle--the north/south axis of the Garden--you immediately encounter the very large parterre between you and the Castle, flanked on either side by saucer magnolias. Seasonally changing, ornamental plants are artfully patterned in the center. The parterre is the exact center of the geometrically designed Garden and, in all directions, red brick walkways match the surrounding red brick buildings, providing the entire complex with a sense of unity. Also in all directions are ornamental lampposts supporting seasonally changing flower baskets.

Ownership	Pet on leash	Brochure
1	guide dogs ok	yes
Size	**Weddings**	**Ed. programs**
4.2 acres	no	yes
Rest rooms	**Sell plants**	**Spec. events**
yes	no	yes
Pay phone	**Membership**	**Labeling**
yes	2	yes
Visitor center	**Gift shop**	**Volunteers**
yes	yes[3]	yes
Fees		**Off street parking**
not for garden		no
Library for public		**Ext. photo limits**
yes[4]		none
Garden clubs active		**Food**
no		yes[5]

[1]The Smithsonian Institution is an independent trust of the Federal Government.

[2]There are many types of Smithsonian memberships, but none is exclusively horticultural.

[3]Gift shops are in most of the museum buildings.

[4]Slides and books are available in the Arts & Industries Building by appointment only. Call (202) 357-1544.

[5]Cafeterias are available in many of the museums and fast food is available from street vendors. Picnicing is not allowed in the Haupt Garden, but is in the Ripley Garden.

To the right of the parterre on the cross-axis is the Fountain Garden, reminiscent of Moorish gardens of medieval Spain, northern Africa and the Near East. A centered, foot-level jet of water is enhanced by surrounding bubblers, rivulets, a chadar (a Persian water chute) and thornless hawthornes. Its theme complements the African Art Museum in the southeast corner of the Garden.

To the left of the parterre is the Island Garden, a central island with four bridges over a pool similar to the Temple of Heaven in Beijing. (One enters through a circular moon gate; in China, the circle is a symbol of heaven.) Its theme complements the Sackler Museum in the southwestern corner of the Garden.

Scattered throughout, in addition to seasonal bloomers, are roses, yews, wisterias, climbing hydrangeas and a good selection of flowering and exotic trees. And benches for the weary.

In spite of the highly numerous and diversified plantings, a feeling of openness pervades the Garden. Meticulous grooming enhances the formal, first-class ambience of the grounds.

As long as you are there, walk to the other side of the Arts and Industries Building to find the relatively small Mary Livingston Ripley Garden which connects Independence Avenue with the Mall. It contains a delightful collection of labeled plantings in predominantly elevated beds.

The Smithsonian Institution is intimidatingly huge and advance planning is strongly recommended. You may obtain a planning kit by calling the number above. The Castle serves as the visitor center for the entire complex and constitutes a logical starting point for any visit. The Institution offers a constantly changing set of educational programs, many of which are horicultural in nature. (Call 202-357-3030 for current information.) Group tours of the Garden are by prearrangement. (Call 202-357-1926 for information on tour requests.) Gardening literature is especially plentiful in the gift shops in the Arts and Industries Building next to the Garden and in the American History Museum across the Mall from it. The U.S. Botanic Garden is within walking distance.

Personal Impression. This is a thoughtfully designed, carefully groomed, all-seasons garden that also tastefully complements and integrates the surrounding, architecturally exquisite buildings. I have not found anything like it in the mid-Atlantic region.

(3) Franciscan Monastery
1400 Quincy St., N.E.
Washington, D.C. 20017
(202) 526-6800
Hours: the grounds are open to the public 8 a.m. to sunset, year round; the visitor's desk in the main church is open 9-5, seven days a week, year round.

Overview. This early twentieth century Franciscan Monastery, constructed on 45 wooded acres in northeast Washington, D.C., offers the public a view of many replicated shrines in the Holy Land, Rome and southern France. Many of the shrines reside in the magnificent, yellow-brick main church which is architecturally reminiscent of Hagia Sophia in Istanbul. The others are distributed throughout the 15 landscaped acres, the ample and well-tended gardens being intended to accent the principal religious theme. Although beautiful spring through fall, the grounds are considered to be most resplendent in May and August.

Directions. In the northeast quadrant of Washington, locate on a map Rhode Island Avenue which runs NE/SW. Exit onto 14th St. going north for about 10 blocks; the Monastery is on your right and off-street parking is on your left.

Historical Profile. Over 700 years ago the Roman Catholic Church entrusted the shrines of the Holy Land to the Order of St. Francis. In contribution to this trust, the Franciscan Monastery was constructed on what is now called Mount Saint Sepulchre in northeast Washington, D.C. The first friar to arrive in 1897 was Brother Isidore (St. Isidore is the patron saint of farmers and gardeners); the cornerstone was laid in 1898; the main church was dedicated in 1899; finishing work and landscaping 15 of the total 45 acres continued to c. 1920 when the facility opened to the public in basically its current form.

In addition to its training and financial support purposes, the Monastery offers persons the opportunity to view faithfully replicated shrines they may otherwise never see. The original shrines reside in the Holy Land (which today encompasses Israel, Jordan, Egypt, Lebanon, Syria, and the Islands of Cyprus and Rhodes), Rome (the catacombs) and southern France (Lourdes). Many of these replicated shrines at the Monastery reside outside the principal structures, and the gardens are intended to complement and enhance the overall meditative ambience of the grounds.

Description. The grounds available to the public may be divided into the hilltop portion (more formal) and the valley portion (more natural).

From the parking lot across the street, one views the magnificent yellow-brick main church rising above the yellow-brick Rosary Portico which surrounds it and the hilltop grounds. The highly regarded rose parterres (c. 2000 plants) in those grounds compete for attention with a small Oriental garden in the northeast corner, considerable

Ownership	Pet on leash	Brochure
priv., relig.	yes	yes
Size	**Weddings**	**Ed. programs**
1	no	no
Rest rooms	**Sell plants**	**Spec. events**
yes	some	no
Pay phone	**Membership**	**Labeling**
yes	2	no
Visitor center	**Gift shop**	**Volunteers**
yes	yes	call
Fees		**Off street parking**
none		yes
Library for public		**Ext. photo limits**
no		no
Garden clubs active		**Food**
no		yes

¹Fifteen landscaped acres on 45 total acres.
²Donations are accepted.

20

religious statuary, well-tended shrubs and blooming borders, the artwork in the Rosary Portico, a chapel and the commanding presence of the church itself.

A steep, winding path to the adjoining valley ends at the centered Lourdes Grotto which is surrounded by the Grotto of Gethsemane, the Tomb of Mary, the Chapel of St. Anne, the Ascension Chapel and the peripherally distributed Stations of the Cross. Heavily wooded and densely undergrown with azaleas, rhododendrons and ivy, the combined effect of the shrines, the plantings and the solitude is unique in the Region. Seasonally blooming bulbs, lilies, perennials, crape myrtles, dogwoods and more add to the already compelling nature of the grounds.

The squarish interior of the church follows the lines of the Five-fold Cross; a simple altar centered beneath the main dome is surrounded by many peripheral altars and chapels, the position of honor at the east end being accorded to the replicated Tomb of Christ. Replicated catacombs also reside in the interior which, *in toto,* is an awesome work of religious art. Tours are conducted hourly; there are daily masses and confessions.

A gift shop is adjacent to the main church, and restrooms and a snack bar are available diagonally across the street in the Franciscan Center.

Personal Impression. One thinks of a monastery as a reclusive place that really does not cater to the general public. The Franciscan Monastery, to the contrary, does so and in a botanical and artistic atmosphere that uniquely enhances the central religious theme. It's well worth your time.

---

(4) Gardens of the Washington National Cathedral

Massachusetts and Wisconsin Avenues, N.W.
Washington, D.C. 20016-5098
(202) 537-6200
Hours: the gardens are open daylight hours, year round; the Herb Cottage (which also serves as a visitor center) is open 9:30-5 Mon.-Sat. and 10-5 Sun.; the greenhouse opens for plant sales 9-5 Mon.-Sat. and 10-5 Sun.

Overview. Historical landscaping virtually surrounds the massive, stately Washington National (Episcopal) Cathedral, a fourteenth century-style Gothic edifice in northwest Washington. Highlighted by the well-known and highly regarded Bishop's Garden, the voluntary All Hallows Guild oversees the formal and informal set of gardens, the Herb Cottage and the grounds as a whole. Biblical and medieval European gardening history are more completely represented here than in any other mid-Atlantic garden.

Directions. Locate on a map of D.C. the intersection of Massachusetts and Wisconsin Avenues in northwest Washington. The tall Cathedral is visible as you approach that intersection from any direction. The principal gardens are located on the Massachusetts Ave. side of the Cathedral.

Historical Profile. Originally owned by Joseph Nourse, the first Registrar of the Treasury under George Washington, the Cathedral property was acquired in 1898 by Henry Yates Satterlee, the first Episcopal Bishop of Washington. Under the guidance of Satterlee, landscape architect Frederick Law Olmstead, Jr. and Florence Bratenahl (1916 founder of All Hallows Guild), gardens began a near century-long evolution in the tradition of a 14th century Gothic cathedral "with plants of historical interest, plants of the Bible and Christian legends, and native plants." Keystoned by the impressive Bishop's Garden, scattered cultivated gardens, pathways and borders virtually encircle the Cathedral. Much of the original beech and oak woodland has been retained according to Olmstead's master plan.

Ownership	Pet on leash	Brochure
priv., relig.	discouraged	excellent

Size	Weddings	Ed. programs
57 acres	no	yes

Rest rooms	Sell plants	Spec. events
yes	excellent	yes

Pay phone	Membership	Labeling
yes	yes[1]	extensive

Visitor center	Gift shop	Volunteers
yes	yes	yes

Fees	Off street parking
[2]	yes[3]

Library for public	Ext. photo limits
no	none

Garden clubs active	Food
yes[4]	no

[1] *In All Hallows Guild.*
[2] *A donation is requested in the brochure.*
[3] *Parking is frequently a problem; be prepared to park some distance away; call to locate nearby public transportation systems.*
[4] *Particularly at the annual Flower Mart in May.*

Description. The Bishop's Garden occupies much of the slope south of the Cathedral and features: a lower perennial border (spring tulips, peonies, summer perennials); a yew walk (Irish yews); the hortulus (the predominantly herbaceous plantings surround the Carolingian baptismal font in raised beds and are selected from plant listings in ninth century Europe); a rose garden; an upper perennial border; and numerous intriguing features (sculpture, gates, archways, bas reliefs, a small pool, a medieval cross and even a twelfth century capital from Cluny, France, that serves as a birdbath).

Peripheral to the Bishop's Garden are: the Herb Cottage (also a gift shop) and surrounding garden; an open lawn and borders; a garden house designed by Philip Frohman; a woodland path; an equestrian statue of George Washington; a Japanese bridge; the Robert C. Morton Border (redbuds, viburnums, hydrangeas, etc.) by the ampitheater; and the Phyllis Nitze Garden (perennials and shrubs).

North of the Cathedral, one encounters a cloister garden (the Garth) and a generous scattering of viburnums, cotoneasters, a ginkgo, etc.

West of the Cathedral stands a native oak and beech grove by the West Portal Court entrance.

Dogwoods, hollies, azaleas, camellias, boxwood and a multitude of other species contribute to the lush ambience of the grounds without a feeling of over-crowding. Atlas cedars and fig trees trace their origins to Biblical times.

Docented tours are offered Wednesdays at noon. Group tours by pre-arrangement. The annual Flower Mart is held on the first Friday and Saturday of May. Serious gardeners may obtain a complete plant list from the All Hallows Guild. The greenhouse, specializing in herbs, also sells shade perennials, cacti, vegetable sprouts and seasonal annuals; the selection for sale is the largest I have found among the gardens listed in this book, and it is open year round.

Personal Impression. I found the pervasive attention to history quite impressive, and I strongly recommend your obtaining the excellent brochure at the Herb Cottage because there is much more there than meets the eye. Seemingly every stone step and birdbath has an interesting history behind it. How else will you know which of the plants were selected from ninth century lists prepared by Charlemagne and others?

(5) Hillwood Museum

4155 Linnean Ave., N.W.
Washington, D.C. 20008
(202) 686-8500
Hours: closed in February; for rest of year, Tue.-Sat., enter 11-3, gardens close at 4. Reservations are required for the 2-hour house tour (202-686-5807).

Overview. Hillwood, Marjorie Merriweather Post's home in northwest Washington, D.C., until her death in 1973, now houses a world-class collection of European decorative and fine arts on beautifully landscaped grounds that integrate formal, informal, Oriental and natural designs. Intended for Mrs. Post's personal enjoyment, the lavish grounds are now maintained as they were with some current restoration of plant composition that changed slightly after her death.

Directions. From the Capital Beltway (I-495) north of Washington, D.C., exit toward the City onto Connecticut Ave. for about 6 miles. Turn left onto Tilden St. (the two-syllable street names are alphabetized), then left onto Linnean Ave. and the entrance is almost immediately on your right.

Historical Profile. Marjorie Merriweather Post (1887-1973), cereal heiress (Postum Cereal Co., Ltd., later General Foods Corporation), purchased 25-acre Hillwood in northwest D.C. in 1955. She immediately remodeled the Georgian-style mansion (1920s) into a living museum for the fine and deco-rative arts, drawing especially from eighteenth century France and Imperial Russia. (The latter collection is considered unrivaled in quantity and quality outside Russia.) The gardens were redesigned with consultation from landscape

23

architect Perry Wheeler, a contributor to the White House Rose Garden. She willed the property to the Smithsonian Institution in 1973 which, in turn, deeded it to the Marjorie Merriweather Post Foundation of the District of Columbia, which opened the property to the public in 1977.

Description. Surrounded by heavily wooded Rock Creek Park and an established neighborhood with ample tall, stately trees, Hillwood's setting seems more rural Appalachian than urban. The entranceways into the estate continue this theme with informal, densely planted, meticulously groomed trees and shrubs, especially azaleas and rhododendrons. The feeling of lush growth pervades the estate, about half of which is hilly and natively wooded.

Ownership	Pet on leash	Brochure
priv., N.P.	no	yes
Size	**Weddings**	**Ed. programs**
25 acres	no	being planned
Rest rooms	**Sell plants**	**Spec. events**
yes	no, temporarily	yes[1]
Pay phone	**Membership**	**Labeling**
yes	[2]	being planned
Visitor center	**Gift shop**	**Volunteers**
yes	yes	yes
Fees		**Off street parking**
yes[3]		yes
Library for public		**Ext. photo limits**
[4]		no
Garden clubs active		**Food**
no		yes

[1]*Annual garden party in May.*
[2]*No society; financial support welcomed.*
[3]*A modest fee is charged for the grounds; the larger fee for the mansion tour includes the grounds.*
[4]*The library is not strongly horticultural.*

The more formal gardens lie to the west and south of the main house and are mostly contiguous. A large, formal French parterre is immediately adjacent to the house, enclosed by an ivy-covered fence and anchored by a centered pool and fountains at either end. The formal rose garden next to it features 14 varieties of florabundas and Mrs. Post's ashes are in the centered memorial. Next is the Friendship Walk, a 1957 gift from her friends that provides "a quiet lane with a picturesque vista." South of the house sets the Japanese garden on a steep slope; designed by Shogo J. Miyaida in 1956, it features a "tinkling" stream that spills over rocks and into pools crossed by stepping stones and quaint bridges. The 1930s greenhouses (c. 6500 square feet) east of the house contain a significant orchid collection); plant sales there have been suspended at this writing, but may be reintroduced in the future. There is a cutting garden and clusters of trees and shrubs everywhere. In every respect, the lavish style of the grounds matches the elegance of the mansion and the flamboyance of Mrs. Post's socialite lifestyle.

Although the mansion and its collections are the main attraction and require a reservation, the grounds and other structures (a Russian log house with collection, the Native American Building and the C.W. Post wing) do not.

Special Features. The merchandise in the gift shop is of the highest quality and includes many items of gardening interest. The on-site library features decorative arts, not horticulture. Guided tours by pre-arrangement. A new visitor center and an interpretive center are in planning now; a zoning change is being sought to expand parking capacity.

Personal Impression. Probably not a single reader of this book has experienced, or aspires realistically to experience, the affluent lifestyle of Mrs. Post. But a visit there tells us a little of what it must have been like.

---

(6) Kenilworth Aquatic Gardens
National Capital Parks--East
1900 Anacostia Dr., S.E.
Washington, D.C.
(202) 426-6905
Hours: the grounds are open 7-3 daily, year round--sometimes longer in summer; visitor center hours change seasonally--call to determine.

Overview. These 12-acre aquatic gardens, bordered by 44 acres of tidal marsh, are maintained by the U.S. Department of the Interior along the Anacostia River in eastern D.C. The dazzling bloom season occurs mainly in the summer months, June-August. Easily one of the more impressive specialty gardens in the region.

Directions. There are many ways to get there; locate it on a map of D.C. east of the Anacostia River, directly opposite the National Arboretum. Perhaps the best route: exit the Capital Beltway (I-495) onto I-95 heading toward the City. At the fork in the road just before the D.C. line, bear left onto Kenilworth Ave. (I-295), then exit right at the Gardens' sign and continue to follow signs to the entrance.

Historical Profile. Civil War veteran and Federal employee Walter B. Shaw purchased 37 acres of marshland along the Anacostia River in Washington, D.C. in 1880. His hobby of dredging pools for native water lily species gradually expanded to a full time business, W.B. Shaw Lily Ponds, which visitors by the thousands frequented on Sunday mornings in the 1920s.

When the U.S. Army Corps of Engineers threatened to take the land by condemnation to reclaim the marshes, the U.S. Interior Department purchased the property in 1938, renamed it Kenilworth Aquatic Gardens, and re-opened it to the public. Over the years, the Interior Department has maintained and refined a truly international and historical collection of aquatic plants.

Description. Across the 15 acres are nearly four dozen ponds with aquatic plants, especially water lilies and lotuses. The hardy lilies, each bloom lasting 3-4 days, peak in June and July. The tropical lilies, stored in the greenhouses all winter, peak in July and August, including the impressive *Victoria amazonia* with platter-like leaves up to six feet across.

Lotuses, considered sacred in eastern religions long before Christ, are featured in many of the ponds. By the visitor center is a special display of East Indian lotuses, descendants of 500-year old seeds found in 1951 in a dry Manchurian lakebed.

Mornings are the best time for viewing before night bloomers close and as day bloomers open. Other plants to be seen include cattails, yellow flag iris, buttonbush, rose mallow shrubs, water primrose and hyacinths. The habitat also supports turtles, snakes, frogs, insects, mosquito fish, muskrats and dozens of species of resident birds and migratory waterfowl.

Guided tours are variably scheduled, especially for summer weekends. Group tours by prearrangement. There is a water lily festival in late July. Call to determine the current set of educational programs. Several of the ponds are labeled. Wheelchairs will sink in after heavy rains saturate the ground.

Ownership	Pet on leash	Brochure
pub., Fed.	yes	yes
Size	**Weddings**	**Ed. programs**
15 acres	yes	yes
Rest rooms	**Sell plants**	**Spec. events**
yes	no	yes
Pay phone	**Membership**	**Labeling**
no	yes	some
Visitor center	**Gift shop**	**Volunteers**
yes	yes	yes
Fees	**Off street parking**	
no	yes	
Library for public	**Ext. photo limits**	
no	no	
Garden clubs active	**Food**	
no	picnicing	

Personal Impression. This is a specialty garden of the highest quality. It's difficult to believe it thrives right in the middle of urban sprawl.

(7) Tudor Place
1644 31st St., N.W. (entrance address)
1605 32nd St., N.W. (mailing address)
Washington, D.C. 20007
(202) 965-0400
Hours: the mansion (also serving as visitor center) has guided tours by appointment Tue.-Fri., year round, and hourly tours without appointment 10-3 Sat.; the grounds are open 10-4 Tue.-Sat. without reservation and are self-guided.

Overview. The administering Tudor Place Foundation attempts to preserve the cumulative expression of gardening interest by one family over 180 years, with particular attention to the original Federal period design of the early nineteenth century and to period pieces. Trees and shrubs dominate the remaining 5 acres of the estate, and blooms range from mid-March (daffodils) to magnificent fall foliage in Oct.-Nov., with roses peaking at the end of May. Formal, informal and natural landscapes are blended.

Directions. Tudor Place is located in Old Georgetown in Washington, D.C. Locate Wisconsin Ave. there on a map; 31st St. runs parallel to it. From Wisconsin Ave., take P, Q, or R Sts. over to 31st St. There is considerable road repair at this writing and one may have to zig-zag a bit to get to the entrance address above.

Historical Profile. Thomas Peter and wife Martha Custis, granddaughter of Martha Washington, purchased the current one-city-block in 1805 and completed the still-standing Neoclassical mansion in 1816. Visited by such luminaries as the Marquis de Lafayette, Robert E. Lee, Henry Clay and Daniel Webster, the Peter family retained ownership for 180 years until a descendant deeded the property to the Tudor Place Foundation in 1984. Grounds and mansion opened to the public in 1988. The cultivated grounds, occupying nearly all of the estate's current 5 acres, retain much of the original formal/informal garden designs as modified marginally over the 1.8 centuries of Peter family ownership, with many century-old specimens surviving.

Description. The overall vertical dominance of these somewhat hilly grounds begins with massive white oaks and tulip poplars; proceeds to widely dispersed cedars, dogwoods, hollies and fruit trees; descends to hydrangeas, rhododendrons, beauty berries, old roses and an abundance of boxwood; and settles onto lawns, formal and informal garden segments and a generous use of ivy groundcover.

A set of small gardens on the northwest corner of the property highlights the flower knot--a boxwood parterre with seasonally changing inner plantings. The other, predominantly green "rooms" feature an imposing deciduous canopy with a lush shrub undergrowth and spaced perennial borders.

The "bowling green" east of the Flower Knot and below it features a small central lawn bordered by a grape arbor, a bird fountain and a lily pool. The "dell" below it contains

Ownership	Pet on leash	Brochure
priv., N.P.	no	yes
Size	**Weddings**	**Ed. programs**
5 acres	yes	yes
Rest rooms	**Sell plants**	**Spec. events**
yes	occasionally	yes[1]
Pay phone	**Membership**	**Labeling**
no	yes	yes
Visitor center	**Gift shop**	**Volunteers**
yes	small	yes
Fees		**Off street parking**
donation for grounds		no
Library for public		**Ext. photo limits**
no		commercial
Garden clubs active		**Food**
yes		picnicing only

27

massive oaks and tulip poplars with natural undergrowth and some ivy ground-cover.

To the immediate west and southwest of the mansion are a rose arbor, tea house, thistle terrace and, most impressively, the ever-blooming China Rose, Old Blush, planted by Martha Custis Peter. Early nineteenth century Sago Palms move from the facade to within the mansion's 400 square foot conservatory for the winter.

The mansion's expansive south lawn is continuously bordered by an informal aggregation of trees and shrubs, with osmanthus in particular abundance. Overall, the grounds are mature, diversified and invitingly warm.

Docent tours of the mansion are scheduled regularly (see above). Special garden tours are offered Wednesdays in season at 9:30. Several school programs are offered--call for details. There is a Christmas green sale the second Saturday in December. There is a spring flower sale scheduled to coincide with the Georgetown Garden Tour of private gardens in late April/early May.

Personal Impression. The mid-Atlantic region is blessed with the nation's most impressive set of preserved or restored estates with historically significant gardens. Add Tudor Place to your list.

(8) The U.S. Botanic Garden
245 First St., N.W.
Washington, D.C. 20024
(202) 226-4082
Hours: the outdoor displays are available continuously, year round; the Conservatory opens 9-5 daily, year round.

Overview. The Garden's mission (paraphrased) is to: highlight the importance of plants to the well-being of human life and to the fragile ecosystems that support all life; together, the Garden's indoor and exterior displays further our appreciation of the aesthetic, cultural, economic, therapeutic and environmental value of plants worldwide. The 12 acres are dominated by the 38,000 sq. ft. glass conservatory that provides year round displays, exhibits and shows for the public. The exterior grounds, already containing considerable displays, are scheduled for major development for Congress' Bicentennial.

Directions. Simply go to the Mall side of the Capitol in downtown D.C. and the large, glass conservatory is clearly visible southwest of the Capitol building.

Historical Profile. The U.S. Botanical Garden, established by Congress in 1820, is alleged to be the oldest botanic garden in North America. Located on the Mall almost in the shadow of the Capitol, the current conservatory was completed in 1933 and the outdoor display gardens surrounding it have evolved over the years. The across-the-street Frederic Auguste Bartholdi Park began in

1933 and features all seasons displays. A new National Garden will occupy three acres west of the conservatory in the near future.

Ownership	Pet on leash	Brochure
pub., Fed.	no	several
Size	**Weddings**	**Ed. programs**
12 acres	no	yes
Rest rooms	**Sell plants**	**Spec. events**
yes	no	yes
Pay phone	**Membership**	**Labeling**
yes	no[1]	yes
Visitor center	**Gift shop**	**Volunteers**
yes	no	no
Fees		**Off street parking**
no		no
Library for public		**Ext. photo limits**
no		commercial[2]
Garden clubs active		**Food**
yes, shows		no

[1]Donations are currently being accepted for the planned National Garden.
[2]Tripods in the Conservatory are discouraged.

Description. The principal outdoor garden, the Frederic Auguste Bartholdi Park, is a triangular island bordered by Independence Ave., First St. and Washington Ave.--directly across from the glass conservatory. Named after its designer who also designed the Statue of Liberty, the Park features a set of peripheral theme gardens surrounding the centered Bartholdi Fountain that was originally exhibited at the 1876 Centennial Exposition in Philadelphia and moved to its current location shortly thereafter. Obtain a self-guiding tour brochure of the Park for composition details, which change frequently.

The highlight of the Garden is the conservatory which contains five environments in seven compartments over 38,000 sq. ft. The "... collections include economic plants, orchids, begonias, carnivorous plants, cacti and succulents, bromeliads, epiphytes, palms, plus cyads and ferns set in a Dinosaur Garden." The tallest component, the Palm House, is under complete renovation at this writing. The grounds immediately surrounding the conservatory feature a tasteful rose garden, a very large assortment of container plants, ornamental grasses and much more. Seasonal shows in and around the conservatory include the summer terrace show, the annual chrysanthemum show, the annual poinsettia show and the annual spring flower show.

The Garden is administered by Congress through the Library of Congress. To commemorate the Bicentennial of Congress, a National Garden will be built in 1995 on a three-acre site at the western tip of the current grounds. It will include an environmental learning center, a rose garden and water sculpture.

Lunchtime lectures are scheduled regularly throughout the year. A hot line for persons with gardening questions is available by phone or mail. Group tours are by prearrangement. An expanded educational program is scheduled for the future, as is a gift shop.

Personal Impression. Aside from some parking difficulties, my dozen or so trips to the Garden have consistently been rewarding experiences, in any season. The current renovations and the planned additions should make it even more so.

---

(9) The United States National Arboretum
3501 New York Avenue, N.E.
Washington, D.C. 20002
(202) 475-4815
Hours: the grounds are open daily, year round except Christmas, from 8 to 5 weekdays and from 10-5 weekends; the Information Center (visitor center) opens weekdays 8-4 and on weekends only for scheduled events; the National Bonsai Collection opens 10-3:30 daily; the gift shop opens from early March to late December 10-3 daily, except for major holidays.

Overview. The U.S. Department of Agriculture administers this immense, 444-acre facility in the Nation's Capital for the education of the public and the advancement of science. Highly diversified, formal through naturalized, predominantly outdoor displays will satisfy even the most discerning visitor all year long. Clearly the Region's premier arboretum; unquestionably a world-class operation.

Directions. Locate the U.S. Capitol on a map of D.C. From there, you would proceed north on North Capitol St., turning right onto New York Ave. Shortly after the major intersection with Bladensburg Rd., you encounter the marked entrance to the Arboretum on your right. Call (202) 637-7000 for information on public transportation.

Historical Profile. Congress authorized the Department of Agriculture to develop the Arboretum in 1927 and it actually opened to the public in 1948. Legislation in 1975 allowed the Arboretum to receive private support for its mission. Growth and refinement have been continuous over the past half-century and several major additions are scheduled for completion over the next decade.

Description. A short description simply cannot do justice to the multitude of attractions at this immense and dazzlingly diversified facility. The paved road alone through the 444 acres totals nine miles and the pathways from it total more. A recent listing of *new* plant additions runs into the hundreds.

Just the National Herb Garden, jointly sponsored with the National Herb Society of America and open to the public since 1980, occupies two densely planted acres near the visitor center and divides into three free-standing components. The 1250 sq. ft. Knot Garden in 16th century English style is so large that medicinal and industrial dwarf evergreens replace the traditional, smaller herbs.

The Historic Rose Garden, containing varieties used for medicine, perfume, food and pleasure, occupies 4000 sq. ft. And the Specialty Garden actually consists of 10 specialty gardens (e.g., the Dye Garden, the American Indian Garden, the Beverage Garden), each separated from the others by boxwood hedges. The Herb Garden by itself warrants a visit. The excellent self-guiding brochure's map shows the distribution of 44 current plant collections and gardens, of which the Herb garden is one, and three future attractions. By itself, the spring bloom of 70,000 azaleas may draw 20,000 visitors in a day. In short, this is a huge operation.

Ownership	Pet on leash	Brochure
pub., Fed.	yes	excellent
Size	Weddings	Ed. programs
444 acres	no	yes
Rest rooms	Sell plants	Spec. events
yes	occasionally	yes
Pay phone	Membership	Labeling
yes	yes	excellent
Visitor center	Gift shop	Volunteers
yes	yes	extensive
Fees		Off street parking
not for grounds		yes[1]
Library for public		Ext. photo limits
by appointment		none
Garden clubs active		Food
extensive		picnicing

[1]There are nearly a dozen parking areas distributed throughout the grounds.

The Arboretum identifies plant groupings of unusual interest in addition to the herbs and azaleas: "aquatic plantings; the National Bonsai Collection; the collection of Oriental plants in the Cryptomeria Valley of the Garden Club of America; the Gotelli Dwarf Conifer Collection; the dogwood plantings of the Woman's National Farm and Garden Association; Fern Valley, sponsored by the National Capital Area Federation of Garden Clubs and other organizations ...." There are many single-genus groupings of "hollies, crabapples, azaleas, magnolias, boxwoods, cherries, irises, daylilies, peonies, viburnum, rhododendron, and maple."

Just prior to this writing, a new tropical Bonsai greenhouse opened and in 1995 a Chinese Pavilion and International Pavilion are scheduled for completion.

This completely understated description should not detract from the conclusion that this facility truly is the United States National Arboretum.

Special Features. The recently renovated gift shop (with its own surrounding garden) contains an excellent assortment of tasteful merchandise for the horticulturally-minded. Group tours by prearrangement may be led by Arboretum staff, plant society docents or volunteers from the National Capitol Area Federation of Garden Clubs. A quality newsletter (call or write to be placed on the mailing list) itemizes a full complement of educational and recreational events--classes, plant sales, clinics, off-site tours, specialized on-site walks, flower shows, demonstrations, workshops, lectures, plant auctions and exhibits. Many of these events are sponsored collaboratively with area garden clubs and plant societies. A vast quantity of educational material is available. All in all, the Arboretum is a very lively place.

Personal Impression. If it's not there, you probably don't need to see it.

DELAWARE

Only the Homestead lies south of Wilmington, on the coast. The shortest distance from downtown Wilmington to the four gardens northwest of it would begin with Rockwood Museum, then Nemours Mansion and Gardens, then Hagley Museum and Library, and finally to Winterthur Museum, Garden and Library.

(10) Hagley Museum and Library

P.O. Box 3630
Wilmington, DE 19807
(302) 658-2400
Hours: The grounds and structures open 9:30-4:30 daily from March 15 through Dec.; they open weekends (same hours) Jan.-March 14 and at 1:30 on weekdays for guided tour (subject to change); closed Thanksgiving, Christmas and Dec. 31.

Overview. From the brochure: "Located along the Brandywine River on the site of the first du Pont black powder works, Hagley provides a unique glimpse into American life at home and at work in the nineteenth century. Set amid more than 230 acres of trees and flowering shrubs, Hagley offers a diversity of restorations, exhibits, and live demonstrations for visitors of all ages." Surviving mill structures, the first du Pont home in America and the restored French Renaissance-style garden reside on hilly, rocky, heavily wooded terrain and suggest a rugged sort of pioneering splendor. The industrial setting for house and garden is unique in the Region.

Directions. Hagley is located north of Wilmington. From I-95, take Rte. 202 north for 1.3 miles, then turn left onto Rte. 141 for 2.4 miles, then right into Hagley at the sign.

Historical Profile. Trained in France as a chemist with particular interest in gunpowder, disturbed by post-Revolutionary times there and the turbulent Napoleonic era, and enthralled with the American economic opportunities Thomas Jefferson portrayed to his father, E.I. du Pont emigrated to America. He purchased in 1802 the initial 65 acres along the Brandywine River that has grown to 320 acres at present. Along the River, he built his black gunpowder manufactory that keystoned the family's industrial empire, the still-standing

32

family mansion (known as Eleutherian Mills) which housed generations of du Ponts, and the formal French garden that has been restored. Ownership passed to the current foundation in 1952, the 150th anniversary of the estate's beginning, and opened humbly to the public in 1956. Restoration proceeded incrementally until 1981, at which time it was basically complete; the 2-acre French garden, which had disappeared in the 1890s, was restored in the 1970s to its original design.

Ownership	Pet on leash	Brochure
priv., NP	no	several
Size	Weddings	Ed. programs
230 acres	no	yes[1]
Rest rooms	Sell plants	Spec. events
yes	occasionally	yes[1]
Pay phone	Membership	Labeling
yes	yes	yes
Visitor center	Gift shop	Volunteers
yes	yes	yes
Fees		Off street parking
yes		yes
Library for public		Ext. photo limits
yes[1]		commercial
Garden clubs active		Food
yes		yes

[1]*Mainly related to the industrial complex.*

Description. The formal French garden features the "Renaissance style of beds and paths in geometric design, bordered by dwarf fruit trees in espalier forms." Slightly raised beds contain both vegetables and blooming annuals. There is also a worker's kitchen garden near the coffee shop and a classically-inspired, early 20th century Italianate garden built on industrial ruins; due to crumbling foundations, the Italianate garden has not been restored and faces an uncertain future. Trails run through the surrounding woodland and, in spring, a profusion of azaleas, rhododendrons, dogwoods and wildflowers set the entire property ablaze.

The principal attraction, of course, is the mill area which contains about 60 preserved or restored structures, many of which contain educational exhibits or various demonstrations about the early industry there. Many special events are held throughout the year. The estate mansion contains exquisite period furnishings. Food is available on-site. The industrial history library is unsurpassed in the Region. The gift shop has a large assortment of merchandise of historical and contemporary interest. All in all, leave enough time to enjoy it all--the mill area, the estate mansion, the formal garden and the grounds. The aggregation of attractions on one site is unique in the Region. Most aggregations of work/home/grounds are on agricultural plantations, not industrial sites.

Personal Impression. I keep thinking about the rugged terrain there and the tour guide's tales of periodic gunpowder explosions at the mill, within sight of the mansion, that destroyed both property and human life. Impressive as the house, garden and grounds are, America's first du Pont experienced a harsher dimension of daily living than is evident at later du Pont estates such as Winterthur, Longwood and Nemours. Perhaps the "softening" effect of a garden was more greatly *needed* there and then than for members of later generations who physically separated home from work.

---

(11) The Homestead

Rehobeth Art League, Inc.
12 Dodds Lane
Henlopen Acres
Rehobeth Beach, DE 19971
Hours: grounds are open daylight hours, year round; the house/visitor center opens May-October, 10-4 Mon.-Sat., 1-4 Sun.; call in advance to determine changes in dates and hours open.

Overview. The Homestead is a 20th century estate garden on property with an 18th century house. The garden is amazingly diversified for the size with peak bloom in spring. The Homestead is the oldest house in Rehobeth Beach and is in the National Register of Historic Places. The gardens flourish in the general climate of art appreciation as sponsored by the owning Rehobeth Art League.

Directions. It's a little tricky getting there. Locate Rehobeth Beach on the Delaware coast. Take the main street into town (Rehobeth Ave.), which ends

Ownership	Pet on leash	Brochure
priv., NP	yes	yes
Size	**Weddings**	**Ed. programs**
1-acre garden	yes	more planned
Rest rooms	**Sell plants**	**Spec. events**
yes	occasionally	some
Pay phone	**Membership**	**Labeling**
no	yes[1]	some
Visitor center	**Gift shop**	**Volunteers**
in house	small	extensive
Fees		**Off street parking**
no[2]		no
Library for public		**Ext. photo limits**
not gardening		no--give credit
Garden clubs active		**Food**
no		no

[1] In the Rehobeth Art League.
[2] Donations are accepted.

at the ocean. Turn left (north) one block before the ocean, First St., and zig-zag north until you pick up the signs to the Rehobeth Art League/Homestead in Henlopen Acres.

Historical Profile. The original house was built by Peter Marsh in 1743. Colonel W.S. Corkran acquired the property in 1930 and the current garden was developed by his wife, Louise Chambers Corkran, founder of the Rehobeth Art

34

League in 1938. The League assumed ownership in 1979. Original garden contours have been preserved and restoration continues, especially in the Crisscross Garden.

Description. One approaches the Homestead through a fine, verdant community with a mature growth of trees. The immediately distinguishing feature of the Homestead and the adjacent grounds and structures owned by the League is the abundance of boxwood and ivy groundcover. The five-part box garden contains the Crisscross Garden (groundcovers, lilies, bulbs), the Chain Garden (roses, sedum, rockery), the Tea Garden (slate patio, rosewood furniture, vinca, Judas tree, dogwood), the Crown Garden (foxglove, begonia, columbine, topiary, wisteria), and the Herb Garden (culinary, medicinal and industrial). Trees include southern magnolia, crape myrtle, princess tree, birch, white pine, oak, fig. There is a fine assortment of hydrangeas. Rhododendrons and azaleas add to the spring explosion of color, especially around Mother's Day. All of this is creatively distributed over about an acre. Group tours are by prearrangement.

Much of the Homestead structure has been restored to its original style with period furnishings. The thousand-member Rehobeth Art League has purchased structures adjacent to the Homestead including the Paynter Studio, the Corkran and Tubbs Galleries, the Chambers Studio and the recent Children's Studio. Special events scheduled throughout the year include the garden sculpture show in June; call for current information.

Personal Impression. Homestead is one more example of how volunteers can successfully supplement a limited budget with dedication to offer a vital addition to the cultural life of the community.

---

(12) Nemours Mansion and Gardens
P.O. Box 109
Wilmington, DE 19899
(302) 651-6912
Hours: open only May through November; Tue.-Sat. tours leave the Visitor Center by bus at 9, 10, 1, and 3. Reservations are recommended for individuals and required for groups.

Overview. Alfred I. du Pont created these expansive, elegant, formal French (Versailles-style) gardens with English-style borders for personal enjoyment, and are preserved as such under private foundation management. The estate mansion is magnificent, but the grounds are truly regal.

Directions. From I-95 north of Wilmington, take Exit 8 (Rte. 202) north for 1.3 miles, then turn left onto Rockland Rd. (Rte. 141); Nemours is less than one mile, on your left.

Historical Profile. From the brochure: "Nemours, the site of the du Pont ancestral home in north-central France, was chosen by Alfred I. du Pont as the name for his beautiful 300-acre country estate north of Wilmington, Delaware

.... The mansion, a fine example of a modified Louis XVI French château was ... built between 1909-1910 ... containing one hundred and two rooms ..." and "fine examples of antique furniture, rare rugs, tapestries and outstanding works of art."

Work began on the gardens c. 1910 and was largely completed by the mid-1930s. Following the death of Mrs. du Pont, the mansion and grounds were opened to the public in 1977 on a carefully supervised tour basis. The Alfred I. du Pont Institute, a highly regarded hospital, opened on one corner of the estate in 1984.

Ownership	Pet on leash	Brochure
priv., NP	no	excellent

Size	Weddings	Ed. programs
300 acres	no	no

Rest rooms	Sell plants	Spec. events
yes	no	call

Pay phone	Membership	Labeling
yes	no	some

Visitor center	Gift shop	Volunteers
yes	in hospital	yes

Fees	Off street parking
yes	yes

Library for public	Ext. photo limits
no	none

Garden clubs active	Food
no	in hospital

Description. The view looking northwest from the steps of the mansion for a full one-third mile is simply astounding, a view so reminiscent of royal, pre-Revolution France that one expects to encounter attendants in Three Musketeer garb at every turn. Straight as an arrow, there is an uninterrupted procession from the mansion of five distinct areas bordered on either side by lovely, expansive meadows.

First comes the Vista, a long allée lined with Japanese cryptomeria, pink-flowering horsechestnuts and pin oaks.

This terminates at the large, one-acre, 750,000 gallon Reflecting Pool which occasionally explodes from its serenity through its 157 jets. "Four Seasons" sculpture surrounds the pool.

Immediately beyond the Pool is the Maze Garden. Centered with bronze mythological statuary, hemlock and holly edges are geometrically arranged and lined with pin-oaks.

Next one encounters a colonnade with statuary in honor of two generations of du Ponts, its height and dazzling white coloration constantly commanding the visitor's attention from nearly any point on the grounds.

Finally, the Sunken Garden of pools and statuary of bronze and white marble terminate the splendor at the Temple of Love.

This one-third mile extravaganza of orchestrated water, plantings and sculpture serves as the cornerstone of what many consider the finest example of French-style formal gardens in America.

There is more. Stretching away from the side of the mansion are the Southern Gardens, a procession of a boxwood-edged parterre, an 8500 sq. ft. arrangement of annuals and perennials, and a natural woodlands.

There is a rock garden featuring bulbs, dwarf conifers and gnome figurines. Production greenhouses border two acres of cutting, trial and nursery gardens. The orchard contains apple, peach and pear trees. Containers exhibit citrus fruits, oleanders, loquats, ornamental figs and plums. The bus tour of the grounds stops last at the antique automobile collection.

Although the emphasis here is on the gardens at Nemours, the mansion is truly lavish and meticulously maintained; the guided tour through it takes well over an hour.

Personal Impression. The grand mansion and regal gardens provide a stunning, almost overwhelming insight into the lifestyles of the wealthiest Americans in the first half of this century.

---

(13) Rockwood Museum
610 Shipley Rd.
Wilmington, DE 19809
(302) 571-7776
Hours: the grounds and museum open 11-4 Tue.-Sat., year round; closed Mondays and major holidays.

Overview. From the brochure: "Rockwood, a nineteenth century country estate, is an outstanding example of Rural Gothic architecture and gardenesque landscape design ... the estate includes a manorhouse and conservatory, porter's lodge, gardener's cottage, carriage house, and outbuildings on 70 of the original 200 acres ... administered by the County's Department of Parks and Recreation."

Directions. From I-95 north of Wilmington, take Rte. 202 (Concord St.) south for about six lights, then turn left onto Washington St. for 1.7 miles, then left onto Shipley Rd.--the entrance is almost immediately on your left.

Historical Profile. "In 1851, merchant banker Joseph Shipley, great grandson of William Shipley, founder of Wilmington, commissioned English architect George Williams to design a manor house for his property ...." The estate remained in the family until 1972 and it was deeded to Newcastle County in 1974, opening to the public in 1976. House and grounds have been preserved and restored in nineteenth century style.

Description. Although the family made relatively few alterations to the house and grounds over its century of ownership, the County is preparing at this writing a master plan to refine its already significant preservation of the natural gardenesque style of the mid- and late nineteenth century.

The gardens include: the kitchen garden site which now contains boxwood hedges and yew shrubs, walled against intruding animals; alternating lawns and wooded areas containing a mixture of native and exotic specimens (e.g., weeping beech, European larch, cedar, hemlock, spruce, fir, Chinese maidenhair tree); the site of Joseph Shipley's pleasure garden; and a conservatory at the eastern tip of the house that harbors period flora in winter. Along much of the perimeter of the lawn is a *ha-ha* wall; popular in Victorian England, it keeps grazing cattle and other animals away from the lawn and garden without obstructing the view of the surrounding landscape. Rhododendrons are featured on the grounds and blooms peak in May.

The imposing mansion/museum "holds a remarkable collection of English, Continental, and American decorative arts reflective of the tastes of a succession of family members who lived at Rockwood."

Personal Impression. Rockwood summons up visions of the graceful lifestyle of the Victorian wealthy. The peaceful ambience of the grounds welcomes the contemplative visitor.

---

(14) Winterthur Museum, Garden and Library
Winterthur, DE 19735
(302) 888-4600
Hours: the garden and grounds open Tue.-Sat. at 9 and Sun. at 11, year round: the gardens remain open until dusk and the museum closes at 5; closed Mondays, Jan. 1, July 4, Thanksgiving and Dec. 24-25.

Overview. Henry Francis du Pont, the last du Pont owner of Winterthur, rivaled in garden philanthropy the other du Ponts who gave us Hagley, Nemours and Longwood, but he did so with an unsurpassed commitment to naturalistic landscaping. The 200-acre "seamless" garden is reputed to be the finest of its kind in the Region, if not the country, offering awed visitors a continuous procession of color on terrain seemingly little-disturbed by the hand of man. Equally unsurpassed is the museum complex of early American decorative arts which, with the garden, provides a double-barreled attraction of the highest quality.

Directions. Locate Wilmington on a map of Delaware. The major artery (I-95) passes north of Wilmington and Rte. 1 runs parallel to, and north of, I-95. Winterthur is on Rte. 52, which connects the two, slightly closer to Rte. 1 than to I-95.

Historical Profile. Originally purchased in the early nineteenth century by the first du Pont, E.I. du Pont, the current site was acquired from him by son-in-law James Biderman, who developed it and named it Winterthur after his family's Swiss ancestral town. Acquired by Colonel Henry A. du Pont, the estate gardens grew steadily under his tutelage and especially that of his son, Henry Francis du Pont, who inherited the estate in 1927 and took great personal interest in it.

Henry Francis' decorative arts collection had grown to such proportions by the end of World War II that he created and opened to the public in 1951 the Henry Francis du Pont Winterthur Museum, which is still the principal attraction there. The garden also opened to the public at that time and continued to benefit from Henry Francis' attention until his death in 1969; it still comprises c. 200 of the estate's nearly 1000 acres.

Ownership	Pet on leash	Brochure
priv., NP	no	yes
Size	**Weddings**	**Ed. programs**
200 acres[1]	no	yes
Rest rooms	**Sell plants**	**Spec. events**
yes	yes	yes
Pay phone	**Membership**	**Labeling**
yes	yes	yes
Visitor center	**Gift shop**	**Volunteers**
yes	excellent	yes
Fees		**Off street parking**
yes[2]		yes
Library for public		**Ext. photo limits**
yes[3]		no
Garden clubs active		**Food**
no		excellent

[1] These are part of nearly 1000 acres on the estate.
[2] There is a basic admission charge with add-ons for guided tours, tram rides, etc.
[3] The principal focus is on decorative arts.

For details re: the history of the garden, see C. Gordon Tyrrell's introductory chapter in: Harold Bruce; *Winterthur in Bloom*; New York, Chanticleer Press, 1986 - 196 pp. Also a volume by Denise Magnani is due in 1995 for the Year of the Garden celebration.

Description. In my correspondence with Winterthur, the garden (note the singular) was described as "seamless," one continuous and highly naturalized garden that minimizes the visible hand of man. Yet distinct areas are evident from the names of sequentially planted sections; the Peony Garden, the Azalea Woods, the Corylopsis-Mucronulatum Walk, the Hellebore Walk, the Chaenomeles Walk, the Sycamore Area, Oak Hill.

One of the more completely naturalized areas is the Quarry. From Harold Bruce: "Great outcroppings of rock, in whose crevices grow ferns, mosses, and flowering plants, project from the sheer walls of a deep basin through which several spring-fed streams meander." Oaks, beeches and redbuds are undergrown with a great profusion of cyclamen, primulas, cinnamon ferns, mountain andromeda, marsh marigolds, dwarf bearded irises, wintergreen, late blooming satsuki azaleas and much more.

At the other extreme is the Pool Garden, a little world unto itself in which walls, gates, straight paths and the rectangular pool expose the hand of man uncharacteristically for the garden as a whole. The densely planted beds and borders include daylilies, begonias, snapdragons, chamomile, foxgloves, pansies, yuccas and many container plantings. The Pool Garden is a cheerful, colorful, inviting little summertime Eden in a naturalized world.

Between the Quarry and the Pool Garden in degree of naturalization is the Sundial Garden, an informal area with a hint of formality to it. The centered sundial is immediately surrounded by four beds of dwarf honeysuckles which, in turn, is encircled by four beds of mixed spireas, flowering almonds and quinces. The elegant pinetum backdrops it and cherries, crabapples, lilacs and magnolias complete its enclosure.

Aside from the distinct areas, however, the sheer diversification of species for all seasons may be the principal attraction for many visitors. And the major collections include native American azaleas, peonies, daylilies, conifers and davidia involucrata.

Whatever your interests, be sure to leave enough time--200 acres is a sizeable tract of land! I particularly recommend taking the tram tour first to get an overview of the garden, which may help you prioritize your on-foot viewing. A more detailed self-guiding tour brochure is in preparation at this writing. Call for a calendar of regularly scheduled lectures, seminars and workshops.

Also leave time for the museum complex, which seems to be in a continuous state of expansion. It features an unrivaled collection of early American decorative arts (1640-1860). The on-site reference library, specializing mainly in decorative arts, holds over a half million volumes. The food selection is excellent. The gift shop is first class. And Winterthur also owns houses in historic Odessa and a gift shop in Alexandria, VA.

Personal Impression. "Quality" describes every aspect of Winterthur. This is the place to visit if you want to see naturalistic landscaping at its finest.

MARYLAND

Only Brookside Gardens, McCrillis Gardens and Gallery, and Lilypons Water Gardens lie northwest of Washington, D.C.

In south-central Maryland, Sotterley is the southernmost garden, London Town Publik House and Gardens is north of it and, further north in Annapolis, one finds the William Paca House and Garden and the Helen Avalynne Tawes Garden.

In Baltimore City, there is the Baltimore City Conservatory, Sherwood Gardens and Cylburn Arboretum. The Hampton National Historic Site and Ladew Topiary Gardens lie north of the City.

(15) Baltimore City Conservatory

4915 Greenspring Ave.
Baltimore, MD 21209
(410) 396-0180
Hours: the Conservatory opens 10-4 daily, year round; the unrestricted grounds are open daylight hours, year round.

Ownership	Pet on leash	Brochure
priv., city	prefer not	yes

Size	Weddings	Ed. programs
1	yes	yes

Rest rooms	Sell plants	Spec. events
yes	periodically	yes

Pay phone	Membership	Labeling
yes	2	yes

Visitor center	Gift shop	Volunteers
yes	no	yes

Fees	Off street parking
none yet	limited

Library for public	Ext. photo limits
no	none[3]

Garden clubs active	Food
no	no

[1]*The Conservatory is currently expanding to over 10,000 sq. ft.; the formal garden to the side occupies one acre.*
[2]*No society, but donations are accepted; send care of Larry Smith.*
[3]*Please do not block pathways with tripods.*

Overview. This central-Baltimore City conservatory features a tall, center building with permanent tropical exhibits supplemented by a smaller greenhouse and a one-acre formal display garden outside. There are seasonal shows, spring/summer exterior blooms and continuous interior exhibits. The facility resides within the large recreational complex, Druid Hill Park, which includes a modern zoo. Many expansions are underway at this writing and will complement the mission of expanding the cultural dimension of Baltimore City life.

Directions. You can get there from many different points of origin. Locate on a map Reisterstown Rd. which runs NW/SE through Baltimore. Toward the center of the City, locate Druid Hill Park which lies east of Reisterstown Rd. Gwynns Falls Parkway intersects Reisterstown Rd. and takes one to within sight of the Conservatory a half-block away, inside the Park.

Historical Profile. The main conservatory building was completed in 1888 in elegant Victorian style and, over the years, three small greenhouses were added to the rear and a one-acre display garden to the side. The Conservatory is unique among municipal gardens and conservatories in that, while most city-owned and managed operqations cut back during the recession of the early 1900s, most of the small greenhouses were torn out and are being replaced with modern structures at this writing. Consequently, the Conservatory's history is in the future.

Description. The commanding, 90-foot tall, principal Conservatory building (2500 sq. ft.) allows full vertical growth of lush tropicals such as palms, rubber trees and banana trees all year. Underway at this writing is a major addition of conservatory space that will eventually expand the total area under glass to over 10,000 sq. ft. This, in turn, will allow expansion of educational programs and a currently-small apprenticeship program. Call to determine progress in this exciting addition.

The one-acre formal garden to the side features bulbs (especially tulips) in the spring and annuals/perennials into the fall. The flat contour of the terrain permits full wheelchair access. There is a small, tasteful sage collection and a crape myrtle collection. Group tours are by prearrangement. There is a spring flower show at Eastertime, a mums show in November and a poinsettia show in December/January.

The principal additional attraction in Druid Hill Park is the zoo, a modern facility that charges a modest entrance fee.

Personal Impression. It is rewarding to see a City forge ahead with its horticulture program when so many others are stalled or in retreat.

---

(16) Brookside Gardens
1500 Glenallan Ave.
Wheaton, MD 20902
(301) 949-8231
Hours: the grounds are open 9 a.m. to sunset daily; the visitor center opens from 9 to 5 daily; the conservatory opens 10-5 Mon.-Fri. and 10-4 Sat.-Sun.; hours are subject to periodic change; closed Christmas.

Overview. This large, modern, highly diversified garden set and conservatory occupy 50 acres within the enormous Wheaton Regional Park north of Washington, D.C. They are offered by Montgomery County, MD, and the Maryland-National Capital Park and Planning Commission for the enjoyment and education of County residents and visitors. The all-seasons gardens share Wheaton Regional Park with a large assortment of recreational and educational programs. It is a "one stop" garden in that it contains an impressive sampling of indoor/outdoor, formal and informal/natural components.

Directions. From I-495 (the Capital Beltway) north of Washington, take the Georgia Ave. exit away from the City (north) for 3.1 miles, then turn right onto Randolph Rd. for 2 blocks, then right onto Glenallan Ave. for a short distance to the entrance on your right.

Historical Profile. Wheaton Regional Park was conceptualized in the early 1960s, planned in the mid-1960s and opened in the late 1960s. The gardens received their first plantings in 1967 and were approximately half-completed by the 1969 opening to the public. Most additions were completed in the

1970s. Current planning projects a new visitor/educational facility, additional parking and expanded office/auditorium space for the mid-1990s.

Ownership	Pet on leash	Brochure
public, co.	no	excellent
Size	**Weddings**	**Ed. programs**
50 acres	1	many
Rest rooms	**Sell plants**	**Spec. events**
yes	no	5 indoor displays
Pay phone	**Membership**	**Labeling**
yes	2	excellent
Visitor center	**Gift shop**	**Volunteers**
yes	no	yes

Fees	Off street parking
none for grounds	yes³
Library for public	**Ext. photo limits**
yes⁴	call re: commercial
Garden clubs active	**Food**
yes, financial support	no, no picnicking

¹Weddings without receptions are permitted subject to the usual restrictions; call.
²No society; call to determine how cash gifts may be made.
³Call or ask on-site for current overflow parking information. There are 180,000 visitors each year who frequently overtax the off-street parking capacity.
⁴Separate hours are maintained for the 2000-volume library and are subject to change.

Description. The long structure by the parking lot houses the office, the library and a two-compartment conservatory of (combined) 8,800 sq. ft. The conservatory features permanent tropical displays and five highly-regarded seasonal displays that run virtually continuously throughout the year. Visit anytime. Call to determine current features.

The outdoor gardens are distributed throughout the 50 acres, the ones closest to the conservatory being more formal. These include a perennial garden (spring through fall), a yew garden (including a seasonal procession of bulbs, annuals, mums), a rose garden (both modern and old) with pergola, a rock garden with everchanging annuals, a trial garden with rotating educational/thematic plantings, a round garden (featuring plum trees and flowering groundcovers), a fragrance garden with fountain and a wedding gazebo. The gently sloping terrain shows these carefully maintained gardens to their best advantage.

The more informally landscaped and more natural areas include an azalea/rhododendron garden (over 400 varieties throughout a 7-acre woodland), a butterfly garden, an aquatic garden, a winter garden, a viburnum garden (over 40 varieties), and an award-winning gude garden (9 acres of sculpted ponds and mature specimen trees, and a Japanese tea house).

Overall, this is a "you-gotta-see" garden that deserves many happy returns.

The larger Wheaton Regional Park is also of interest, containing a nature center, an ice skating rink, riding stables, tennis courts, a campground, an athletic complex and a new action adventure playground.

Special Features. Educational programs are so numerous that the staff produces twice-a-year listings of tours, lectures, field trips, etc. Much free literature on plant care is available. A separate brochure for persons in wheelchairs is provided. A call-in-your-questions program is offered to the public. Group tours by prearrangement. Self-guided tours are by brochure or borrowed cassette.

Subjective Impression. This is one of the mid-Atlantic states' first class, all-seasons gardens with a degree of diversification and commitment to excellence that should gratify all.

---

(17) Cylburn Arboretum

4915 Greenspring Avenue
Baltimore, MD 21209
(410) 396-0180
Hours: the grounds are open 6 a.m.-9 p.m., year round; museums and library open 1-2 Thursday; museum and library hours subject to change.

Overview. Cylburn Arboretum occupies 176 acres in north-central Baltimore City. It offers a spectrum of features from nearly a dozen predominantly formal, specialty and demonstration gardens to native woodlands with criss-crossing wildflower trails. It serves as the hub of horticultural activities in the City and uniquely blends the management efforts of municipal departments and voluntary organizations.

Directions. From the northern part of the Baltimore Beltway (I-695), take I-83 (the Jones Falls Expressway) south for about 4 miles into the City. Exit onto Northern Parkway heading west and almost immediately turn left onto Cylburn Avenue and proceed to stop sign; turn left onto Greenspring Ave. and left immediately into the Arboretum.

Historical Profile.

Ownership	Pet on leash	Brochure
public[1]	yes	yes
Size	**Weddings**	**Ed. programs**
176 acres	yes	yes
Rest rooms	**Sell plants**	**Spec. events**
yes	occasionally	yes
Pay phone	**Membership**	**Labeling**
yes	yes	yes
Visitor center	**Gift shop**	**Volunteers**
yes	no	yes
Fees	**Off street parking**	
no	yes	
Library for public	**Ext. photo limits**	
yes	none	
Garden clubs active	**Food**	
yes	no	

[1]*Collaboratively maintained by Baltimore City and the Cylburn Arboretum Association, Inc.*

Jesse Tyson, wealthy Baltimore businessman, completed construction of Cylburn Mansion in 1888 and his widow lived in it continuously until her death in 1942, whereupon Baltimore City purchased it for a park. A citizens group, incorporated as the Cylburn Wildflower Preserve and Garden Center, successfully petitioned the Board of Recreation and Parks in 1954 to convert Cylburn into a center for environmental education and horticulture. The citizens group also participated in the design, development and maintenance of the trails and gardens. In 1982, Cylburn Park officially became Cylburn Arboretum and the citizen's association subsequently became the Cylburn Arboretum Association, Inc.

Description. The estate house sits well back from Greenspring Ave. on the flat portion of the property, surrounded by an attractive set of theme and demonstration gardens: the All American Selection Display Garden; the Bird Garden; the City Garden (small demonstrations); the Garden of the Senses (elevated; braille labeling); the Herb Garden; the Perennial Beds; the Probst Garden (small pool, ferns, groundcovers); the Heritage Rose Garden (old roses); the Shady Garden. Four trails (c. three miles) through the natively wooded, sloped portion of the property expose the visitor to a profusion of wildflowers and azaleas in spring. Collections include tree peonies, daylilies, magnolias, ornamental maples, Maryland oaks, viburnums and chestnuts.

The estate house serves as an all-purpose building. In addition to staff and volunteer offices, it contains a growing horticulture library (available to the public for on-site use), a nature museum, an herbarium, a bird museum and meeting rooms. School children benefit from continuing educational programs and adults benefit from frequently scheduled open houses, lectures, demonstrations, etc. Plants are usually sold the Saturday before Mother's Day and in mid-September.

Personal Impression. I have visited Cylburn for over twenty years and have always enjoyed intangible qualities that somehow make the visitor feel right at home. It's a family place.

(18) Hampton National Historic Site
535 Hampton Lane
Towson, Maryland 21204
(410) 962-0688
Hours: the grounds are open 9-5 daily, year round; the mansion opens 9-4 daily, year round; the gift shop opens 11-4 Mon.-Sat. and 11:30-3 Sun.; the Tearoom opens 11:30-3 Tue.-Sun.; closed Thanksgiving, Christmas and New Year's Day.

Overview. On this 67-acre site the U.S. Park Service is restoring and preserving the cumulative expression of gardening interest by six generations of the same family over 200 years. Both formal and informal garden sections surround the 33-room mansion, "one of the largest and most ornate Georgian houses in America."

Directions. The historic site is north of Baltimore City, just outside the Beltway (I-695). Leave the Beltway at Exit 27B and take an *immediate* right onto Hampton Lane for half a mile to the entrance on your right.

Historical Profile. Originally purchased in 1745 by the Ridgely family which retained ownership for 200 years, the mansion "Hampton Hall" was constructed between 1783 and 1790 and the formal gardens were developed in the early 1800s; 24,000 acres at its height, the Ridgely enterprise encompassed an ironworks, a dairy and a merchandising operation. The National Park Service assumed the property in 1948. Garden maintenance was performed by the Society for the Preservation of Maryland Antiquities until 1976, when the park service assumed that responsibility.

Ownership	Pet on leash	Brochure
pub., Fed.	yes	yes
Size	**Weddings**	**Ed. programs**
67 acres	yes	yes
Rest rooms	**Sell plants**	**Spec. events**
yes	no	yes
Pay phone	**Membership**	**Labeling**
no	yes	some
Visitor center	**Gift shop**	**Volunteers**
yes	yes	yes
Fees		**Off street parking**
no		yes
Library for public		**Ext. photo limits**
no		commercial
Garden clubs active		**Food**
yes[1]		yes

[1]*Many sections of the grounds (e.g., the herb garden) are maintained by local garden clubs.*

Description. The mansion sits on the high ground of 67 gently rolling acres with spacious lawns and well-spaced, immense trees that include five State champions. The verdant grounds north of the mansion are naturally landscaped, interweaving native oaks, beeches, maples and poplars with exotics such as copper beech, larch and Norway spruce. The formal garden features six very large, boxwood-edged parterres and lies south of the mansion at the base of a steep slope that, from the top, offers an impressive panoramic view of the grounds. The densely planted cutting garden lies southeast of the mansion and a very tasteful, well-maintained, well-labeled herb garden is near it. Beds, borders and interesting groundcover are scattered throughout.

Bulbs, lilacs, dogwoods, saucer magnolias, redbuds and more greet the spring colorfully. Roses and perennials carry bloom to the fall. Hollies and evergreens brighten the winter.

Group tours are by prearrangement. Small group tours of the mansion proceed regularly. The brochure summarizes the site as a whole: "Hampton's special combination of grand and distinctive architecture, impressive formal gardens and landscaped grounds, representative dependencies and significant decorative arts collection echo the social and economic mores of one family, realizing the American dream."

Personal Impression. Hampton is one of the few sites in the Region to have been continuously owned by many generations of the same family during the transition of U.S. gardening taste from geometrically formal to natural. I find it interesting to see preserved elements of both at one site that is made possible by the large size of the property and the administrative decision to favor neither style over the other.

---

(19) The Helen Avalynne Tawes Garden
Maryland Department of Natural Resources
Tawes State Office Bldg.
Annapolis, MD 21401
(410) 974-3717
Hours: grounds open during daylight hours daily, year round; the visitor center in the adjacent Tawes State Office Bldg. opens 8-5 Mon.-Fri.; the gift shop in it opens 11-3, Mon.-Fri., and the cafeteria in it opens 7:30-3 Mon.-Fri. The office building closes for all State holidays.

Overview. This unique, 5-acre, State-managed operation offers the public a sampler garden of the various environments and habitats of Maryland from the Appalachian Mountains to the Atlantic Ocean. The overall landscape is mainly naturalistic.

Ownership	Pet on leash	Brochure
pub., state	no	excellent

Size	Weddings	Ed. programs
5 acres	no	yes

Rest rooms	Sell plants	Spec. events
yes	in spring	yes

Pay phone	Membership	Labeling
yes	no	yes

Visitor center	Gift shop	Volunteers
yes	yes	yes

Fees	Off street parking
no	yes

Library for public	Ext. photo limits
no	none

Garden clubs active	Food
no	yes

Directions. Locate Annapolis on a Maryland map, south of Baltimore and east of Washington, D.C. From Rte. 50/301, take Rte. 70 east for almost one mile, then turn right onto Taylor Ave. The Tawes Office Bldg. (and garden) is immediately on your left and off-street parking at the Naval Academy's stadium is on your right.

Historical Profile. J. Millard Tawes, after whose wife the garden was named, was a two-term Maryland governor and the State's first Secretary of Natural

Resources. After the construction in the early 1970s of the Tawes State Office Bldg. which still houses the Dep't of Natural Resources, a committee completed a plan for the garden next to the building; development began c. 1972 and it was dedicated in 1977. The maturation of the garden continues to the present.

Description. A serpentine path takes the visitor through or past eight distinct areas. (1) A large, brick "touch and taste" planter at the entrance offers plants of various textures, tastes and fragrances. (2) You pass a pond inhabited by frogs, turtles, catfish, bass, bluegills and an occasional mallard--over 40 species of birds and waterfowl have been identified in the garden. (3) The "plant mural" displays bee- and butterfly-attracting annuals and perennials. (4) A stream flows through a simulated lowland forest with native trees, shrubs, ferns and wildflowers. (5) A stand of evergreens. (6) The view from a boardwalk first encompasses pines and bayberries, then sand dunes, finally water--Maryland's Eastern Shore. (7) A sloping forest representative of Western Maryland, which also demonstrates forest succession. (8) The Xeroscape, featuring drought-resistant plants.

The bloom season begins with azaleas and wildflowers in spring, especially early May, and continues to fall; blooms, however, are not the principal feature. Many plants are labeled. Group tours by prearrangement. Be sure to obtain from the visitor center an excellent self-guiding tour brochure. Educational programs focus mainly on children and include off-site tours. Some plants are sold in spring.

Personal Impression. This highly imaginative and unique garden does a skillful job of sampling the natural resources of Maryland with a particular emphasis on things botanical and aquatic. There is nothing quite like it in the Region.

---

(20) Ladew Topiary Gardens

3535 Jarrettsville Pike
Monkton, Maryland 21111
(410) 557-9570
Hours: open mid-April to Oct. 31, 10-4 Tue.-Fri., 12-5 Sat.-Sun.; closed Mondays and Nov. to mid-April.

Overview. From the brochure: "Mr. Ladew (1886-1976) was awarded the Distinguished Service Medal by the Garden Club of America in 1971 for his 'interest in developing and maintaining the most outstanding topiary garden in America, without professional help.'" Although the exquisite topiary components of the garden are unsurpassed in the Region, the 22-acre site is fully diversified in design and material, making it one of the premier gardens in the mid-Atlantic states. Both formal and informal components bloom continuously throughout the open season.

Directions. Monkton, MD is due north (and slightly east) of Baltimore.

From I-695 (the Baltimore Beltway), take Rte. 146 (Jarrettsville Pike) north for 10-15 minutes; the marked entrance is on your right. (If you intersect Rte. 23, you have passed it.)

Historical Profile.

Harvey S. Ladew, businessman and heir, purchased this farm in 1929 partly in support of his fox-hunting hobby. His hunting trips to England exposed him to formal topiary gardens which he began emulating here. Cultivated areas expanded, diversified and matured continuously until his death in 1972, at which time ownership and maintenance passed to the non-profit foundation he had established to continue his work.

Description.

Topiary gardening, the art of training and trimming trees and shrubs into ornamental shapes, appears here as a multitude of massive walls, geometric shapes, animal figures and even a life-size mounted horseman following his hounds on the chase. This highly labor-intensive form of gardening clearly is the specialty of the Gardens and ranks at the top of Region gardens containing topiaries.

Ownership	Pet on leash	Brochure
priv., NP	no	excellent
Size	**Weddings**	**Ed. programs**
22 acres	no	yes
Rest rooms	**Sell plants**	**Spec. events**
yes	occasionally	yes
Pay phone	**Membership**	**Labeling**
no	yes	good
Visitor center	**Gift shop**	**Volunteers**
yes	yes	yes[1]
Fees	**Off street parking**	
yes	yes	
Library for public	**Ext. photo limits**	
no	commercial	
Garden clubs active	**Food**	
no	light fare	

[1] *Over 100 volunteers keep the site maintained and the fees modest.*

Yet the two dozen distinct garden areas with attractions other than topiaries would qualify Ladew as a premier garden by themselves. These include: the white garden (e.g., oxydendrum, hydrangea, roses, hosta, aruncus); the pink garden (e.g.;, crab apples, dogwood, bleeding heart, giant sedum); the formal rose garden (an ample selection underplanted with pansies and lined with espaliered pears and apples); the water lily garden (water lilies in the central pond, water irises in four arc pools); the topiary sculpture garden (lyrebirds, Churchill's top hat, a unicorn, sea horses); the wild garden (ferns and wildflowers native to the area); the swan hedge ("swans swimming atop its topiary waves of yew"), and much more—call for the detailed garden guide.

Most of the garden areas run parallel to Jarrettsville Pike and surround the Great Bowl, a large oval pool encircled by a lawn spacious enough to accommodate summer concert events. The immense number of genera and species on site will tax, perhaps overtax even sophisticated plant taxonomists.

Non-botanical attractions include an iron and glass fountain, ornate concrete furniture, statuary, a colonnaded Temple of Venus, a stream and the Tivoli Tea House. The grounds as a whole are very well maintained.

Special Features. The drive to Ladew through the pleasant, gently rolling countryside provides a bonus for the entering and departing visitor. Group tours are by prearrangement. Lectures (esp. Thursday mornings), workshops, concerts, arts and crafts shows and other events are scheduled regularly throughout the year. The site is on the National Register of Historic Places. The interestingly furnished manor house contains an abundance of fox-hunting memorabilia and the Oval Library, described in the book "100 Most Beautiful Rooms in America." In the barn one finds Mr. Ladew's personal studio and a carriage collection. The gift shop warrants your attention.

Personal Impression. Just go. A verbal description alone does injustice to the plethora of visual and aesthetic stimuli awaiting the visitor. And leave enough time to enjoy it fully.

---

(21) Lilypons Water Gardens

6800 Lilypons Rd.
P.O. Box 10
Buckeystown, MD 21717-0010
(301) 874-5133 or 1-800-723-7667
Hours: open March-October, 9:30-5:30 seven days a week except Easter; Nov.-Feb., 9:30-4:30, closed Sundays, Thanksgiving and Christmas week. Telephone operators for orders are available nearly around the clock.

Overview. This family-owned, 300-acre aquatic garden northwest of Washington, D.C., both displays aquatic plants and sells them and supporting items on site, by phone or by mail order. (Call the 800 number above for a free catalog.) The organization's self-stated mission is to be America's best source of water gardening products and information.

Directions. Locate Frederick in central Maryland; Lilypons is about nine miles south of it along the Monocacy River. From I-270, take Rte. 80 west for 1.7 miles, then left onto Park Mills Rd. for 3.5 miles, then right onto Lilypons Rd. for half a mile to the entrance on your right.

Historical Profile. The owning family started the business in 1917 as a wholesale fish production operation. Throughout the 1920s and 1930s, aquatic plant sales grew steadily. When the Post Office requested a single-name title, the owners chose Lilypons after both the best-selling plant, the water lily, and also the celebrated opera performer of the times, Lily Pons. In 1978, the family formally changed emphasis to plants and adopted the current name.

Description. This truly off-the-beaten-track aquatic garden occupies 300 acres of display pools, production ponds and a visitor center/sales building. The features are water lilies, lotuses, marginal plants (e.g., irises, reeds, cattails),

Ownership	Pet on leash	Brochure
priv., comm.	yes	catalogue

Size	Weddings	Ed. programs
300 acres	yes	yes

Rest rooms	Sell plants	Spec. events
yes	yes	yes

Pay phone	Membership	Labeling
no	no	some

Visitor center	Gift shop	Volunteers
yes	yes	no

Fees	Off street parking
none to enter	yes

Library for public	Ext. photo limits
no	none

Garden clubs active	Food
no	mostly weekends

ornamental fish, books and various types of equipment. There are c. two dozen display pools and c. 170 production ponds, with extensive labeling. Morning viewing is best because it straddles night-bloomers and day-bloomers. Visit Memorial Day through Labor Day for best viewing.

Group tours by pre-arrangement. Lectures and demonstrations are scheduled regularly, especially on weekends; call to determine dates and times. There is an elaborate Koi (Japanese carp) Festival the weekend after Labor Day and a Lotus Blossom Festival in July. Sturdy shoes are recommended. Customers may call back free for clarification of plant or fish care.

Subjective Impression. This is a fascinating, unique, large specialty garden with the extra benefit of being able to take home a sample of what you see at reasonable cost.

---

(22) London Town Publik House and Gardens
839 Londontown Rd.
Edgewater, MD 21037
(410) 222-1919
Hours: the grounds, visitor center and Publik House are open March through Dec., 10-4 Tue.-Sat., 12-4 Sun.; closed Mondays, major holidays and for inclement weather.

Overview. The Publik House, an 18th century structure with an unusually varied use-history, has been restored to its colonial appearance by Anne Arundel County and serves as a historical museum. Nine of the 23 acres are devoted to predominantly informal/naturalized gardens along a continuous path through native woodlands. One finds an unbroken succession of blooms and special events throughout the open season.

Directions. The gardens are located southwest of Annapolis, MD, which is on the Chesapeake Bay. From Rte. 50/301, which runs east/west north of Annapolis, take Rte. 2 south; soon after passing over the South River, turn left onto Rte. 253 (Mayo Rd.) for over a mile, then left onto Londontown Rd. which ends at the Gardens. "A public pier for park users is located opposite Buoy 15 on the South River approximately six miles from the Chesapeake Bay."

Historical Profile. London Town, a 17th century trading town located in a tobacco growing region of Maryland, served briefly as the county seat in Anne Arundel County.

Completed in the mid-1760s, the Publik House on the present 23 acre site served as an inn into the 1790s, served as a residence for Maryland Governor John Hoskins Stone, was purchased by Anne Arundel County in 1829 and served first as an almshouse and later as a residence for indigents until 1965. Restored to its colonial appearance and furnished in 18th century tavern style, the House was designated a National Historic Landmark in 1970 and opened to the public in 1973. Nine of the 23 acres contain modern gardens for the cultural enrichment of the County.

Ownership	Pet on leash	Brochure
pub., co.	no	very good
Size	**Weddings**	**Ed. programs**
9 of 23 acres	yes	yes
Rest rooms	**Sell plants**	**Spec. events**
yes	occasionally	yes
Pay phone	**Membership**	**Labeling**
no	yes	yes
Visitor center	**Gift shop**	**Volunteers**
yes	yes	extensive
Fees		**Off street parking**
yes		yes
Library for public		**Ext. photo limits**
no		no
Garden clubs active		**Food**
many		no

Description. Bordered on two sides by the South River and Almshouse Creek and with a stream (with waterfall) in the center, the hilly terrain and its informal, garden-laced woodlands are blessed with a stronger "aquatic ambience" than other gardens in the Region. A circuitous pathway takes the visitor past distinct areas such as the herb garden, the winter garden, a marsh garden bordering a salt marsh and a section planted with 18th century crops. Mostly, however, one travels a continuous trail through the densely wooded and steeply sloped site with nearly continuous, mostly naturalized groupings of viburnums, camellias, azaleas, rhododendrons, Japanese irises, daffodils, hollies and more. Most introduced plants are indigenous to the eastern United States, and native wildflowers abound throughout. The collections of rhododendrons, azaleas, tree peonies and cold-hardy camellias are particularly impressive. Strategically located along the trail are places to sit, a meditation area and two delightful overlook terraces. Steps and the hilly terrain, however, make wheelchair access to some parts difficult.

The Publik House, of course, is the principal attraction for many. On site one also finds a separate visitor center, a tobacco barn, a production greenhouse, a bath house and a pier. Guided tours by prearrangement. A full calendar of events throughout the year features the Annual Daffodil Show in early April and Horticulture Day (tours, lectures, plant auctions) in early October. A volunteer organization, the London Town Publik House Assembly, additionally operates a gift shop, sponsors educational programs for school groups, conducts tours of the museum and gardens, and produces special events throughout the year.

Personal Impression. This program demonstrates once again that the local public sector and private volunteers can culturally enrich the community in ways neither could do so well alone. In spite of the high degree of community use, this is a comtemplative garden well worth your visitation and support.

---

(23) McCrillis Gardens and Gallery

6910 Greentree Rd.
Bethesda, MD 20817
(301) 365-5728--recorded information
     365-1657--information on the Gallery
     365-6509--additional information from Brookside Gardens
Hours: grounds are open 10-sunset daily, year round; the Gallery opens 12-4 except Mondays and Christmas.

Overview. This modern estate garden northwest of Washington, D.C., is maintained as a premier, 5-acre, informally landscaped, spring-blooming *shade garden* in the tradition of its original owner and developer.

Directions. From I-495 (the Capital Beltway) northwest of Washington, take Exit 36 (Old Georgetown Rd.) toward the City for 1.2 miles, then turn right onto Greentree Rd. for 1.8 miles. The entrance is on your left.

Historical Profile. William McCrillis, Assistant to the Secretary of the Interior under Presidents Roosevelt, Truman and Eisenhower, purchased this 5-acre property for his residence c. 1941, and immediately began collecting a wide assortment of azaleas and rhododendrons, and a more limited collection of rare shrubs and trees. Presented by McCrillis to Montgomery County in 1978, the grounds opened to the public in 1980 and have since been continuously maintained and improved by the Brookside Gardens' staff.

Description. The property as a whole lies under a dense canopy in a tasteful D.C. suburb and features azaleas and rhododendrons. There are over 750 varieties of azaleas, including a large collection of Satsuki azaleas from Japan. Scattered about are many rare or unusual trees and shrubs, including Japanese umbrella pine, dawn-redwood, littleleaf boxwood, kousa dogwood, bigleaf magnolia, Korean stewartia, longstalk holly, Japanese andromeda and Serbia spruce--to name a few. An assortment of bulbs, ground-covers and shade-loving perennials add color and texture.

The gallery occupies the first floor of the residence and features regularly changing exhibits of local artists as well as periodically scheduled special events.

S u b j e c t i v e Impression. The informal design and meandering paths under the canopy make the grounds a thoroughly relaxing and meditative experience at any time, and an awesome one in spring, especially during peak bloom in early May. McCrillis' designation as a shade garden makes it unique.

Ownership	Pet on leash	Brochure
pub., co.	no	yes
Size	**Weddings**	**Ed. programs**
5 acres	yes[1]	[2]
Rest rooms	**Sell plants**	**Spec. events**
in residence	no	yes
Pay phone	**Membership**	**Labeling**
no	[3]	some
Visitor center	**Gift shop**	**Volunteers**
residence	no	yes
Fees		**Off street parking**
no		no[4]
Library for public		**Ext. photo limits**
[5]		no[6]
Garden clubs active		**Food**
no		no

[1]Receptions are also possible on site.
[2]Occasional weekend tours.
[3]No society membership; call to determine how to make cash donations.
[4]Street parking; off-street parking is available across the street late adternoons & weekends.
[5]Some shade garden books may be reviewed on-site.
[6]Check out most recent policy on commercial photography.

(24) Sherwood Gardens

c/o Stratford Green, Inc.
P.O. Box 4677
Baltimore, MD 21212
(410) 366-2572
Hours: daylight, year round.

Overview. Described in the brochure as "one of the most famous tulip gardens in North America," this 7-acre, community-operated Gardens enriches the community especially in spring and also through the summer and into the fall.

Directions. From the Beltway (I-695) due north of Baltimore, proceed south into the City on Charles St. Soon after you pass the clearly visible Loyola College on your left, bear left at the fork onto St. Paul St. for 2 blocks, then left onto Stratford Rd. for a block. The gardens are on your right.

Historical Profile. Originally a spring-fed lake that dried up in 1924, the core of the current site was purchased by businessman John Sherwood and con-

Ownership	Pet on leash	Brochure
private, NP	discouraged	yes
Size	**Weddings**	**Ed. programs**
7 acres	no	no
Rest rooms	**Sell plants**	**Spec. events**
no	no	yes
Pay phone	**Membership**	**Labeling**
no	yes[1]	no
Visitor center	**Gift shop**	**Volunteers**
no	no	yes

Fees	Off street parking
no	no
Library for public	**Ext. photo limits**
no	none
Garden clubs active	**Food**
no	no

[1]*Not in society; in Stratford Green.*

verted to a garden in 1927. Generously open to the public in Sherwood's lifetime, the site was purchased after his 1965 death and expanded to seven acres by the Guilford Association and its Stratford Green subsidiary. The site, occupying over half of a large city block, is maintained with the assistance of the City of Baltimore.

Description. As the management of Sherwood Gardens told me, "Let's be clear about one thing--this is a *tulip* garden." About 80,000 bulbs overwhelm the site in late April/early May to the delight of community residents and more distant travellers alike. Equally delightful for some is the annual tulip dig on the Saturday of Memorial Day weekend when energetic visitors may retrieve the bulbs for personal use.

There is more. In peak azalea season the surrounding, mature community comes ablaze with a drive-thru attraction in its own right. And on the Gardens' site abound dogwoods, wisterias, magnolias, boxwoods and beds of summer annuals under an adopt-a-bed program for community residents. Remember, though, this is a *tulip* garden.

Personal Impression. Probably more so than any competitor, the tulip symbolizes the transition from winter indoor-living to the aesthetic appreciation of the outdoor season's advent. It's difficult not to be appreciative of Sherwood Gardens.

(25) Sotterley
P.O. Box 67
Hollywood, MD 20636
(301) 373-2280
Hours: grounds are open daylight hours year round; the visitor center and

mansion are open (1) June 1-Oct. 31, 11-4 Tue.-Sun. and (2) April, May, Nov. and early Dec. by appointment.

Overview. This 70-acre historical estate in southern Maryland contains an elegant early 18th century mansion, an early American working farm maintained for public education and cultural enrichment, and a preserved early 20th century garden complex. Extensive restorations and improvements to all the features of the property are underway at this writing.

Directions. Locate on a map of southern Maryland the Patuxent River and Leonardtown--due south of Baltimore and between the Potomac River and the Chespeake Bay. From the intersections of Routes 235 and 245 near Leonardtown, proceed northeast on Rte. 245 for 3.0 miles; the marked entrance is on your right. (You can also get there by boat on the Patuxent River.)

Ownership	Pet on leash	Brochure
priv., NP	yes	yes
Size	**Weddings**	**Ed. programs**
70 acres	yes	yes
Rest rooms	**Sell plants**	**Spec. events**
yes	occasionally	yes
Pay phone	**Membership**	**Labeling**
no	yes	some
Visitor center	**Gift shop**	**Volunteers**
yes	yes	yes

Fees	Off street parking
¹	yes
Library for public	**Ext. photo limits**
no	no
Garden clubs active	**Food**
financial aid	call to arrange

¹*Donations are accepted for the garden; there is a modest fee to tour the mansion.*

Historical Profile. Originally a 1650 manoral grant from Lord Baltimore, Sotterley has been owned by a series of distinguished citizens over the centuries, including a Maryland governor and an organizer of the medical corps of the Confederacy. The grounds, still a working farm, once harbored a significant eighteenth century port of entry on the Patuxent River and a girls' academy. The still-standing mansion, reputed to have been an architectural inspiration for George Washington's Mount Vernon, was constructed c. 1717 and contains an excuisitely carved drawing room (ranked as one of the "100 most beautiful rooms in America" by Helen Comstock). Purchased in 1910 and restored by the Satterlee family, Sotterley was ultimately deeded to the Sotterley Mansion Foundation in 1961 to open the site to the public. The Satterlee family partially restored and partially redesigned the garden area after 1910, and it is mainly preserved as such now.

Description. The formal garden next to the mansion features distinct areas for the rose garden, the herb garden, the vegetable garden and perennial beds. Plant selection includes tulips, jonquils, daffodils, peonies, dogwoods, Judas trees, pyracantha, columbines, irises and more. An ante-bellum orchard is located closer to the entrance. Massive hardwoods dot the landscape. Large meadows provide a feeling of openness, especially on the slope down to the river. Group tours by prearrangement.

The mansion, as described above, is the most distinctive single attraction, but far from the only one. Other structures on the property include a guest cottage, a smokehouse, a customhouse, a custom warehouse, a display-only outside nec-essary, the only surviving slave quarters in the area, gatehouses and numerous farm exhibits. Overnight accommodations may be arranged in advance in the guest cottage as may meals for groups. There is an extensive set of educational programs for children and special events are scheduled throughout the year--call for up-to-date details. This is a lively, family-oriented place.

Personal Impression. Take the whole family for an adventure back into history. There's something for everybody.

---

(26) William Paca House and Garden
1 Martin St.
Annapolis, MD 21401
(410) 267-6656
Hours: the grounds open 10-5 Mon.-Sat. and 12-5 Sun., year round: the mansion is open for the same hours, but is closed some Mondays; the grounds close an hour earlier Nov.-April. Closed Thanksgiving and Christmas.

Overview. Considered the finest garden in the area in the 17th century, this two-acre set of gardens has been restored to some of its original features and to plant material and designs of the period. It creatively blends formal and informal designs with attention to all-seasons plantings.

Directions. Locate Annapolis on a Maryland map and then get to State Circle currounding the seen-from-a-distance State House in the old historic dis-trict adjacent to the U.S. Naval Academy; exit the circle onto East St. and shortly exit left onto Prince George St. (one block) and park immediately near the entrance.

Historical Profile. William Paca, a Maryland signer of the Declaration of Independence and Revolutionary period governor, built his mansion in 1765 and his garden between 1765 and 1772. Although the gardens were considered the class of the times, they fared poorly from the mid-1800s to the 1960s, being serially covered by an earth-fill, hotel, parking lot and bus depot. To save the mansion and grounds from major development in 1965, Historic Annapolis pur-chased the mansion and the State of Maryland bought the garden site, which is managed for it by Historic Annapolis. Given that most traces of the gardens had been obliterated, the restoration was principally to the style and material of the Revolutionary period. The gardens opened to the public in 1973.

Description. The 2-acre, rectangular gardens gently slope down from the rear of the mansion toward the U.S. Naval Academy, proceeding from highly formal to informal.

Immediately behind the mansion, one encounters a magnificent set of four squarish parterre gardens: the boxwood parterre (with cyclamens, vinca, hellebores, cedar, topiary); the flower parterre (seasonal bloomers, creeping thyme, wax myrtle, hemlock); the rose parterre (old roses); and the holly parterre. Beside the flower parterre are a small kitchen garden (with a significant assortment of herbs) and a small physick garden. Scattered around and through the formal parterres is an assortment of southern magnolias, oaks, white pines, a tulip poplar, fruit trees, yews and more.

Ownership	Pet on leash	Brochure
public [1]	no	excellent
Size	**Weddings**	**Ed. programs**
2 acres	yes	some
Rest rooms	**Sell plants**	**Spec. events**
yes	occasionally	some
Pay phone	**Membership**	**Labeling**
no	yes	some
Visitor center	**Gift shop**	**Volunteers**
yes	yes	yes
Fees		**Off street parking**
yes		no
Library for public		**Ext. photo limits**
small, by app't.		commercial
Garden clubs active		**Food**
[2]		no

[1]The grounds are owned by the State of Maryland and managed by Historic Annapolis.
[2]Some clubs meet there.

The more distant, more informal half of the garden contains a veritable explosion of indigenous species--wildflowers, shrubs, trees (e.g., sourwood, persimmon, fothergilla, witch hazel, pawpaw)--surrounding a bridged pond and flanked by a bath house, pavilion and spring house.

It is difficult to imagine a greater degree of plant diversification and garden design on a property this size. Moreover, the grounds are well-kept and the gardeners, helpful.

Group tours by prearrangement. Plants are occasionally sold. The history-rich mansion is well-worth touring; it also offers conference and lodging facilities.

Personal Impression. The gardens are just beautiful any time of the year. I was particularly impressed with the four parterre gardens.

Chapter 3
New Jersey

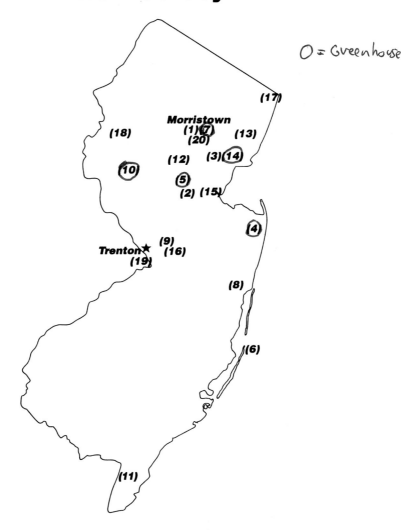

O = Greenhouse

(17)

Morristown
(1)(7)
(20)   (13)

(18)

(12)   (3)(14)

(10)

(5)
(2) (15)

(4)

(9)
Trenton★ (16)
(19)

(8)

(6)

(11)

New Jersey has a most unusual constellation of gardens. It has more specialty gardens than the rest of the Region combined. Gardens specialize in annuals (Leaming's Run Gardens), oceanside plants (the Edith Duff Gwinn Garden), indoor cultural displays (Duke Gardens), herbs (Well-Sweep Herb Farm) and irises (Presby Memorial Iris Gardens).

More local governments own and manage gardens than in any other state: the Leonard J. Buck Garden, Colonial Park (Somerset County), Deep Cut Gardens (Monmouth County), Frelinghuysen Arboretum/Willowwood Arboretum/Bamboo Brook (Morris County), Hamilton Veterans Park, Hunterdon County Arboretum, and Sayen Gardens (Hamilton Township). State-owned facilities include Skylands and Rutgers Gardens, and local ownership that shares or delegates management to private associations includes the William Trent House, Reeves-Reed Arboretum, the Cora Hartshorn Arboretum and Presby Memorial Iris Gardens.

Privately owned and managed diversified (in contrast to specialized) gardens include Acorn Hall and Georgian Court College.

---

(1) Acorn Hall

68 Morris Ave.
Morristown , NJ 07960
(201) 267-3465
Hours: the grounds are open daylight hours, year round; the house is open 9-5, Monday through Friday, and occasionally on weekends.

Overview. This informally planted, late nineteenth century, period, estate garden on five acres of northern New Jersey land was created by the joint effort of a local historical society and a local garden club. The diversified plantings bloom April-October, with a spring peak.

Directions. Locate Morristown on a map of north-central New Jersey. Proceeding north on I-287, take the Morris Ave. exit (also for the National Historic Park); at the Morris Ave. fork, keep right and then take two immediate lefts to come back to Acorn Hall next to the motel. It's a little tricky. If you make a wrong turn, just get back to Morris Ave. and follow the house numbers to 68.

Historical Profile. Augustus Crane, a New York merchant and banker, purchased this five-acre Morristown property with a four-year-old Italianate mansion in 1857. He and his descendants lived there continuously for 114 years until his granddaughter donated the property in 1971 to the Morris County Historical Society, which headquarters itself in the estate house. As the Historical Society refurbished the house, the Town Home Garden Club of Morristown began creating a Victorian period garden on the badly neglected grounds, bringing it close to its present standards in the late 1980s.

Description. The three landscaped areas surrounding the house are uninterrupted except by a U-shaped driveway in front (innovative in the Victorian era) and a white picket fence in back which separates the upper garden (by the house) from the lower garden. There are open lawns in front and on either side of the picket fence. The plantings are intense and continuous along the periphery of the lawns and beneath a canopy of oaks, ashes, beeches, and an occasional horsechestnut or elm.

Ownership	Pet on leash	Brochure
private, NP[1]	no	yes
Size	**Weddings**	**Ed. programs**
5 acres[2]	yes	no
Rest rooms	**Sell plants**	**Spec. events**
in house	no	yes
Pay phone	**Membership**	**Labeling**
no	in garden club	expanding
Visitor center	**Gift shop**	**Volunteers**
yes	yes	extensive
Fees		**Off street parking**
no		yes
Library for public		**Ext. photo limits**
no		no
Garden clubs active		**Food**
yes		no

[1]*Owned by a historical society which shares management of the grounds with a garden club.*
[2]*Three acres are landscaped.*

The principal distinct garden area is an "herb wheel" far to the rear of the house. In the style of the period, most of the plantings are in continuous and integrated borders of annuals, perennials, bulbs and shrubs, with a preponderance of shrubs. A partial list; rhododendrons, wisteria, roses, peonies, hostas, hemlocks, lilacs, hydrangeas, trumpet vines, ferns, hyacinths, bleeding hearts and many more. A gazebo and a flagstone patio are nestled among the plantings. The sheer number of represented species is impressive.

Much of the garden material of the previous owners has been retained and supplementation has proceeded within the master plan developed by landscape architect Alice Kollar.

Personal Impression. Although this Victorian period garden is a delight unto itself, I find myself once again impressed with how far historical societies and garden clubs--in combination here--can take a property in spite of limited financial resources. Without volunteers, this sparkling little gem would not exist.

---

(2) Colonial Park
R.D. 1, Mettler's Rd. *Near Rutgers*
Somerset, NJ 08873
(201) 873-2459
Hours: the grounds are open daylight hours, year round.

61

Overview. The 467-acre Colonial Park, a Somerset County recreational complex, has set aside 144 acres for a formal, nationally recognized rose garden, a sensory and fragrance garden, an informal bridal garden and an arboretum. Although the garden may be enjoyed year round, thousands of roses provide the principal attraction beginning in early June.

Directions. Locate Somerville on a map of north-central New Jersey. From Rte. 206 south of it, take Rte. 514 east (toward New Brunswick) to the Colonial Park sign on your left at Mettler's Rd. The entrance is about a mile on your left.

Historical Profile. Colonial park has evolved from an 18th century Dutch farm to the 20th century Mettler estate to ownership by Somerset Co. in 1965. Rudolph W. van der Goot, Somerset County Park Commission's first horticulturist, spent seven years refining and expanding the Mettler gardens and grounds, the principal component of which was named after him in 1981.

Description. The horticultural pride and joy of Colonial Park is the very formal Rudolph W. van der Goot Rose Garden, an accredited garden of All America Rose Selections since 1973, containing over 4000 plants of 275 varieties and blooming nearly continuously from early June into October. The long, rectangular garden is actually three sequential gardens, the first and third featuring a squarish set of beds, the middle one exhibiting a more circular design.

First comes the Mettler Garden with miniature roses surrounding a centered pool and the geometrically arranged beds containing hybrid teas; to one side are old roses, some dating back as far as 1820.

Ownership	Pet on leash	Brochure
pub., co.	yes	yes
Size	**Weddings**	**Ed. programs**
467 acres[1]	[2]	some
Rest rooms	**Sell plants**	**Spec. events**
yes	no	one major
Pay phone	**Membership**	**Labeling**
yes	no	yes
Visitor center	**Gift shop**	**Volunteers**
no	no	some
Fees		**Off street parking**
no		yes
Library for public		**Ext. photo limits**
no		none except [2]
Garden clubs active		**Food**
no		picnicing

[1]144 acres of the total 467 acres are devoted to the arboretum & gardens.
[2]Permission required for wedding photos.

The Center Garden, bisected by long beds of polyantha roses, contains hybrid teas, grandifloras and floribundas radiating from the axis and they, in turn, are flanked by trellises with climbing roses.

Finally, the compact Dutch Garden, in the style of a formal rose garden in

Holland, features dwarf candytuft edgings and an impressive collection of heritage roses.

During peak bloom, the stunning color is exceeded only by the mesmerizing fragrance.

Proceed from the Rose Garden to the contiguous Fragrance and Sensory Garden for the physically impaired, containing raised beds (with braille labeling) of annuals, herbs and perennials of unusual fragrance or texture. There also is an informal Bridal Garden with a procession of spring bulbs (esp. daffodils), shrubs (esp. lilacs) and perennials. And there is an arboretum specializing in native central New Jersey trees.

There is a nature trail off Colonial Drive. Group tours by prearrangement. "Rose Days" is held the first weekend in June.

Personal Impression. Stated simply, this is a rose lover's paradise. They have some of just about everything in tasteful designs. A very informative brochure provides considerable information for the beginner.

---

(3) Cora Hartshorn Arboretum and Bird Sanctuary

324 Forest Drive South   *Watchung area*
Short Hills, NJ 07078
(201) 376-3587
Hours: grounds are open daylight hours, year round; the "Stone House" visitor center is closed in August, open Sep't.-July, 9-3 Mon. and Fri., 9-4:30 Tue./Wed./ Thurs., 9:30-11:30 Sat.

Overview. This 16-acre, natively wooded and planted property is intended to enhance awareness of the natural woodlands habitat of New Jersey. Seasonally adjusted trail guides identify both natural and introduced labeled species.

Directions. Locate Short Hills on a New Jersey map, west of New York City. From I-78, take the Morris-Essex Turnpike, then turn north on Forest Dr. to the Arboretum. It's a little tricky getting there, so don't delay asking locals for help if you need it.

Historical Profile. Cora Louise Hartshorn, artist and naturalist, bequeathed this property upon her death in 1958 to Millburn Township. The private Arboretum Association was founded in 1961 to assume for the Township the management of the Arboretum and the development of its programs.

Description. The 16-acre tract with wildflowers and mountain laurel in abundance comes close to being a naturally preserved area. Limited introductions include azaleas, rhododendrons, flowering trees and four types of trilium. Peak bloom is in spring.

The property might also be considered a nature center with activities heavily clustered in and around the "stone house" that Cora Hartshorn built in 1931 for artistic and naturalistic enjoyment by herself and her friends. There is a full set of educational workshops, lectures, programs and other activities for pre-schoolers through seniors with emphasis on the total biological environment. There are senior citizen luncheons and programs on Tuesdays. Three miles of labeled trails with printed guides introduce the visitor to the various natural and introduced species there. Group tours are by prearrangement.

Ownership	Pet on leash	Brochure
public[1]	yes	yes
Size	**Weddings**	**Ed. programs**
16 acres	no	many
Rest rooms	**Sell plants**	**Spec. events**
yes	no	yes
Pay phone	**Membership**	**Labeling**
no	yes	yes
Visitor center	**Gift shop**	**Volunteers**
yes	yes	extensive
Fees		**Off street parking**
not for grounds		--
Library for public		**Ext. photo limits**
yes		no
Garden clubs active		**Food**
yes		no

Personal Impression. Although my guide to gardens focuses primarily on cultivated gardens, I also

[1] *Although the property is owned by Milburn Township, it is primarily managed by the Arboretum Association.*

thoroughly enjoy seeing introduced species in a predominantly natural setting such as one finds here. It is also rewarding to find such a broad spectrum of educational programs for local citizens and interested visitors.

(4) Deep Cut Gardens
Monmouth County Park System
Newman Springs Rd. (mailing address)
Lincroft, NJ 07738
352 Red Hill Rd. (location)
(908) 671-6050
Hours: the grounds are open 8 to dusk, year round; the Horticulture Center opens 8-4, year round.

Eyebright area

Overview. The Monmouth County Park System has created one of the Region's premier publicly owned and operated set of formal and informal gardens on the expanded (53 acres) Wihtol estate. Explicitly dedicated to the home gardener and equally diversified in garden design and educational programs, the site is a joy to visit any time of the year.

Directions. The Gardens are located in east-central New Jersey, due south of Staten Island. Take Exit 114 from the Garden State Parkway heading east for about 1.5 miles on Red Hill Road. The entrance is on your right.

Historical Profile. Originally a farm when Lord Cornwallis retreated from the Battle of Monmouth along Red Hill Rd., the property underwent numerous changes of ownership until Mrs. Marjorie Wihtol willed 20 acres of her property to the County Park System upon her death in 1977. The County subsequently purchased an additional 20 acres from her estate and opened the park to the public in 1978. In 1990, 13 more acres were added. Although a mature garden now, additions and refinements are still being planned.

Ownership	Pet on leash	Brochure
pub., co.	no	excellent
Size	**Weddings**	**Ed. programs**
53 acres	yes	yes
Rest rooms	**Sell plants**	**Spec. events**
yes	yes	yes
Pay phone	**Membership**	**Labeling**
no	yes	yes
Visitor center	**Gift shop**	**Volunteers**
yes	yes	many
Fees		**Off street parking**
no		yes
Library for public		**Ext. photo limits**
yes		no
Garden clubs active		**Food**
some		no

Description. The Horticulture Center near the parking lot contains the library, classroom, gift shop and office, and it is surrounded by an intriguing set of attractions. These include: a Butterfly and Hummingbird Garden (attracting annuals, perennials and shrubs); the Lily Pond (tropical and hardy waterlilies, bog plants, Koi fish); the Display Greenhouse (3 compartments--27x27--with orchids, succulents and various house plants); a Shade Garden; an Azalea and Rhododendron Walk; and the Rockery (3 cascading pools; ericaceous specialties) which has survived from the private estate.

Looking northeast from the Horticulture Center, one overlooks the future site of a perennial parterre to a vine-covered pergola, then a large, open meadow, then native woodlands. To the left is an orchard featuring dwarf fruit and nut trees. To the right is a stream-fed pond stocked with Koi, a meadow walk (naturalized wildflowers), a dried flower production field, a production greenhouse and a vegetable garden.

Tidy beds and borders are found throughout the property. From daffodils in spring to witch hazel and hollies in winter, there is always something at peak. Crabapples, cherries, dogwoods, magnolias and more contribute to the springtime flamboyance.

The Elvin McDonald Horticultural Library at the Center, the Gift Shop and a

seasonal newsletter are first class. Educational programs are offered year round-
-call for up-to-date information. Arbor Day at the end of April is a principal
event. Guided tours by prearrangement. This is one of the few gardens in the
Region to offer a horticultural hot line for County residents.

Personal Impression. From the moment you enter the parking lot, you
know this is a special place. It combines showcase quality with high public use.
I found it difficult to leave.

---

(5) Duke Gardens Foundation, Inc.

P.O. Box 2030,
Somerville, NJ 08876   *near Hutcheson*
(908) 722-3700
Hours: open noon-4 daily, Onct. 1-May 31; closed June-Sept., Thanksgiving,
Christmas and New Year's Day.

Reservations are required for individuals and groups.

Overview. From the brochure: "PERFECTION UNDER GLASS .... The precision of a sculptured French parterre garden, the lushness of a tropical jungle, the arid stark beauty of the American desert, the stylized naturalism of Japan. A never-never land that recreates the world's horticulture in a series of exquisite gardens, each caught at the peak of perfection, all under an acre of glass."

A one-hour guided tour takes the visitor through 11 dazzling display rooms representative of various countries, areas or cultures, an unparalleled adventure into visual harmony and beauty. Breathtaking!

Ownership	Pet on leash	Brochure
private	no	yes
Size	**Weddings**	**Ed. programs**
1 acre¹	no	no
Rest rooms	**Sell plants**	**Spec. events**
yes	no	no
Pay phone	**Membership**	**Labeling**
yes	no	no
Visitor center	**Gift shop**	**Volunteers**
yes	no	no
Fees		**Off street parking**
yes		yes
Library for public		**Ext. photo limits**
no		no cameras
Garden clubs active		**Food**
no		no

¹All under glass.

Directions. Locate Somerville in north-central New Jersey; take Rte. 206 due south from the Somerville Circle for about 1 mile to the entrance on your right.

Historical Profile. This is a most unusual blend of private estate and public view garden. Members of the Duke family still live on the site but want to share their indoor gardens with the public on a scale that is limited to protect their privacy. A managing Foundation was created in 1959 for this purpose and the conservatory opened to the public in 1964.

Description and Personal Impression. There are 11 distinct gardens under one acre of glass, each representing different cultures, areas or countries. There is an Italian Garden, Orchid Garden, French Garden, English Garden, Chinese Garden, Japanese Garden, Indo-Persian Garden, Semi-tropical Garden, Arizona Desert and much more. It is the most visually stunning, thematically diversified conservatory in the Region, possibly in the country.

The Foundation asked me to help them prevent a rush of visitors beyond their capacity that would compromise the privacy of the still-resident Duke family. Advance reservations *must* be made to control the number of visitors that a continuous procession of tour guides can lead through the rooms comfortably in about an hour. This is a garden at someone's home, not a recreational area, so only serious connoisseurs of ornamental botany and cultural horticulture should occupy the limited number of spaces. If that is you, you cannot be disappointed.

Cameras are prohibited and high-heel shoes are dangerous for obvious reasons.

---

(6) Edith Duff Gwinn Garden

c/o Barnegat Light Historical Society *Near Island Beach*
Fifth St. and Central Ave.
P.O. Box 386
Barnegat Light, NJ 08006
(609) 494-8578
Hours: the grounds open daylight hours, year round; the Museum/visitor center opens 2-5 daily in July and August and 2-5 weekends in June and September.

Overview. On the tip of a low-lying, wind-swept barrier island, one unexpectedly finds a maritime museum surrounded by a small garden specializing in native and introduced species that survive and thrive under adverse conditions next to the ocean.

Directions. Barnegat Light is located on the northern tip of Long Beach Island, a long barrier island north of Atlantic City. From the Garden State Parkway which runs parallel to the ocean, take Exit 63 to Route 72 east for 6.5 miles, then turn left (north) at the Barnegat Light sign for 8.5 miles; the garden and museum are on a corner to your left, one block from the ocean.

Historical Profile. Barnegat Light, home of the second oldest (but now decommissioned) lighthouse on the northeastern seaboard, now hosts the Barnegat Light Museum with exhibits related to the lighthouse, the history of the town, the fishing industry, and the northern portion of Long Beach Island, a barrier island. The 1904-1951 one-room schoolhouse, deeded to the town by the Board of Education, now houses the Museum and the surrounding garden which

67

began in the late 1950s. The site is jointly managed by the Garden Club of Long Beach Island and the Barnegat Light Historical Society.

Description. On a one-acre corner lot and surrounding the Museum, the Garden features trees, shrubs, flowering annuals and herbs that survive a block from the ocean on a barrier island. A circuitous path takes one through a densely planted garden with scattered bird baths, boulders, a sundial and Oriental statuary.

Some of the introduced herbs that have survived the ocean wind and salt spray are rosemary, lovage, lavender, lemon balm, pot marigold, sweet woodruff, sweet marjoram, oregano, sage, thyme, chives, basil, coriander, rue and tansy.

Ownership	Pet on leash	Brochure
public[1]	yes	yes
Size	**Weddings**	**Ed. programs**
c. 1 acre	yes	some
Rest rooms	**Sell plants**	**Spec. events**
no	no	no
Pay phone	**Membership**	**Labeling**
no	yes	no
Visitor center	**Gift shop**	**Volunteers**
yes	yes	yes
Fees		**Off street parking**
no		no
Library for public		**Ext. photo limits**
no		no
Garden clubs active		**Food**
yes		no

[1]*Private management.*

Personal Impression. I also live by the ocean and can appreciate from personal failures how difficult it is to grow anything in high winds and salt spray beyond the native, low-lying bayberry, conifers and various grasses and wildflowers. This garden has experienced more success under such conditions than mine.

(7) The Frelinghuysen Arboretum
53 East Hanover Ave.
Morristown, NJ 07960
(201) 326-7600
Hours: the grounds are open daylight hours, year round; the visitor center opens 9-4:30 Mon.-Sat. and 12-4:30 Sun.; the gift shop opens 10-4 daily; closed for major holidays.

Overview. The George Griswold Frelinghuysen Arboretum is one of the finest county-owned and managed gardens in the Region. It is an all-seasons garden, fully diversified in plant material and design, and has special attractions for the physically impaired. It offers a complete set of educational opportunities and provides one of the best sets of brochures in the Region. It is visually stunning and meticulously groomed. All 127 acres are worth seeing.

Directions. From I-287 north, take Exit 32A to Morris Ave. (Rte. 24) for half a mile to the light (there's a Friendly Restaurant); turn left and follow signs (Library & Arboretum) for 1.8 miles.

Historical Profile. Patent attorney George G. Frelinghuysen built his Colonial Revival-style mansion in the 1890s on property he named Whippany Farm. His surviving daughter, Mathilda, carefully planned the conversion of the estate to a public arboretum, bequeathing the property to Morris County. Although the original rose garden has survived, the more formal gardens on the site have been gradually added over the past two decades.

Ownership	Pet on leash	Brochure
pub., co.	no	many
Size	**Weddings**	**Ed. programs**
127 acres	yes	many
Rest rooms	**Sell plants**	**Spec. events**
yes	no	yes
Pay phone	**Membership**	**Labeling**
yes	yes	good
Visitor center	**Gift shop**	**Volunteers**
yes	yes	yes[1]
Fees		**Off street parking**
no		yes
Library for public		**Ext. photo limits**
excellent		commercial
Garden clubs active		**Food**
yes		no

[1]*Volunteers fill 13 different roles.*

Description. The most varied set of attractions lies near the parking area and includes the spacious Haggerty Education Center (with adjoining Carriage House) and a separate gift shop. Between and around these structures are the Mary Linder Perrenial Garden, the entrance terrace, the Beth Fisher Winter Garden (the separate brochure for it itemizes 28 types of trees, shrubs, perennials and bulbs), the Watnong Rock Garden (the separate brochure itemizes 37 shrubs and 18 perennials), the Klipstein Blue Garden (28 perennials and 14 shrubs), the Vera Scherer Garden (raised beds, hanging baskets and other features the physically impaired cam reach), and the Katherine Porter Branching Out Garden (for the children's gardening program).

Distributed throughout the larger property are the Rose Garden (surviving from private ownership days), the Bald Cypress Swamp, the Glossary Garden (for educational programs), the Margaret O. Neil Knot Garden and the Elmer O. Lamp Shade Garden. The Pikaart Garden features two cranes wading in a pond surrounded by 18 perennials and 7 shrubs.

The two principal trails through the property are designated red and blue, each with its own brochure. The red trail offers 28 stations, reasonable wheelchair access and takes roughly an hour to complete comfortably. The longer blue trail offers 61 stations. Both trails feature trees and shrubs. There are several smaller trails and paths, including the Braille Nature Trail.

An impressive array of educational programs and special events proceeds year round--call for an up-to-date list. Group tours by pre-arrangement. The first floor of the Frelinghuysen mansion, which headquarters the Morris County Park Commission, is open to visitors during business hours.

Personal Impression. I particularly appreciated two aspects of the Arboretum. First, it's a friendly place--just about everything there is named after somebody. Secondly and more importantly, it quite simply is a first-class, thoroughly enjoyable garden to visit. The site as a whole blends quantity with quality impressively, and it's viewable every week of the year.

---

(8) Georgian Court College: the S. Mary Grace Burns Arboretum

900 Lakewood Ave.   S.E. of Mom at shore
Lakewood, NJ 08701
(201) 364-2200
Hours: the grounds open 9-4 daily; closed for major holidays; call to assure entrance.

Overview. The exotic trees and formal gardens of the Arboretum are distributed throughout this lovely liberal arts college's campus, sharing the spotlight with spectacular statuary and artwork. The college administration is maintaining the historical integrity of this early 20th century estate's grounds. Blooms are continuous from spring daffodils in April to fall splendor.

Directions. Locate Lakewood in east-central New Jersey. From Rte. 9 heading north, look for the College after the intersection with Rte. 88.

Historical Profile. Originally the estate of George Gould who purchased it in 1896, the grounds were purchased at auction by the Roman Catholic Sisters of Mercy in 1924 and converted to the present liberal arts college on 151 acres. The gardens and statuary, which were largely introduced before 1915, have been retained and enhanced, providing the college with a completely unique atmosphere. The Arboretum is named after Sister Mary Grace Burns, the first chairperson of the Biology Department.

Description. Three Gould-era gardens survive to this day. The formal elliptical parterre contains four sections, each with four boxwood-edged beds, and a bronze sundial. The Japanese Garden, designed by Takeo Shioto, includes a tea house purchased at the 1900 Anglo-Japanese Exhibition in London. The Italian Garden, which extends a quarter mile down to the lake, is known principally for the artwork in and near it. This includes a massive Apollo (designed by sculptor

Ownership	Pet on leash	Brochure
priv., relig.	no	yes
Size	**Weddings**	**Ed. programs**
151 acres	no	no
Rest rooms	**Sell plants**	**Spec. events**
yes	no	no
Pay phone	**Membership**	**Labeling**
yes	no	yes
Visitor center	**Gift shop**	**Volunteers**
no	no	no

Fees	Off street parking
no	yes
Library for public	**Ext. photo limits**
no	no
Garden clubs active	**Food**
no	no

Massey Rhind) astride a bronze nautilus shell chariot; a wrought iron eagle perched on a dragon; and a 20-foot high 17th century marble dolphin fountain. A rock garden was added later.

The international collection of trees distributed throughout the campus includes black oak, ginkgo, Atlas blue cedar (Algeria and Morocco), white mulberry (China), Norway spruce, moss cypress (Japan), European beech, Himalayan pine, and *many* more.

Since secutiry is maintained at the College, visitors are requested to call in advance to the Office of Public Relations or the Office of Special Events. This is more to facilitate your entrance through the gate than to hinder it.

Personal Impression. Stated simply, I've never seen a campus like it. Beautiful. Stately. Artful. Completely unique.

---

(9) Hamilton Veterans Park

2206 Kuser Rd.
Township of Hamilton, NJ 08690   *Toward Trenton*
(609) 581-4124
Hours: the grounds are open daylight hours, year round.

Overview. Hamilton's Department of Parks and Recreation offers this 330-acre recreational complex to the public with a variety of formal and natural gardens distributed throughout. The spacious size and variety of attractions make it an ideal place for a family outing.

Directions. Locate Hamilton due east of Trenton. From I-295, take Exit 63 heading east on Rte. 33 for 2.2 miles, turning right on Whitehouse Rd. for 0.7 miles; turn left onto Klockner Rd. and proceed a half-block to the entrance on your right.

Historical Profile. Hamilton Township built this complex on undeveloped land in 1980 and has continuously refined it to this time.

Description. The Park's 330 acres occupy most of an enormous square that would contain many city blocks of usual size and shares the square with some housing development and a hospital. There are entrances to the Park on all four sides; the most formal garden is accessed from Klockner Rd.; Park Administration is accessed from Kuser Rd. on the opposite side.

The formal area consists of circular, shrub-planted beds around a concentric fountain and separating rings of parking spaces. There are many open lawns, well-spaced trees and scattered, seasonally-changing beds. About two miles of nature trails wind through the centrally wooded property. There are some bog gardens by the lake.

Ownership	Pet on leash	Brochure
pub., town	yes	no
Size	**Weddings**	**Ed. programs**
330 acres	yes	no
Rest rooms	**Sell plants**	**Spec. events**
yes	no	no
Pay phone	**Membership**	**Labeling**
yes	no	some
Visitor center	**Gift shop**	**Volunteers**
no	no	yes
Fees		**Off street parking**
no		yes
Library for public		**Ext. photo limits**
no		none
Garden clubs active		**Food**
no		picnicing

Recreational opportunities include tennis courts, soccer fields, playgrounds, ballfields, a bike trail, and much more, even an Indian museum.

From tulips and wildflowers and flowering cherries in spring, through annuals and crape myrtles in summer, to fall splendor, there is continuous color. And wheelchair access is excellent.

Personal Impression. I particularly enjoyed the cleanliness and openness of the Park, and how well-groomed it was. That type of commitment to excellence is frequently missing in public parks.

(10) Hunterdon County Arboretum
1020 Highway 31
Lebanon, NJ 08833   West - North tow Wash. Crossing
(908) 782-1158
Hours: the grounds are open daylight hours, year round; the visitor center opens 8-4:30 Mon.-Fri., year round.

Overview. The Hunterdon County Park System manages 14 parks and nature preserves with over 3000 acres! Only the Hunterdon County Arboretum contains informal display gardens and a partially display greenhouse on 73 densely wooded acres.

Directions. Locate I-78 which runs east/west in the northern third of New Jersey. Locate Rte. 31 which intersects I-78 in the western part of the state. Take Rte. 31 south from the intersection for 4 miles to the entrance on your left.

Historical Profile. Originally a commercial nursery, the site was purchased by Hunterdon County in the mid-1970s. Display gardens were introduced in the early 1980s and are still in process of refinement and expansion.

Ownership	Pet on leash	Brochure
pub., co.	yes	no

Size	Weddings	Ed. programs
73 acres	yes	yes

Rest rooms	Sell plants	Spec. events
yes	no	no

Pay phone	Membership	Labeling
yes	no	some

Visitor center	Gift shop	Volunteers
yes	no	yes

Fees	Off street parking
no	yes

Library for public	Ext. photo limits
no	no

Garden clubs active	Food
yes	no

Description. The Arboretum is a long, rectangular property stretching away from Route 31. The visitor center near the road contains a one-compartment, 1500 sq. ft., production and display greenhouse with a sub-tropical environment. Around the visitor center and penetrating into the larger property is a tasteful variety of beds and borders (blooms from spring daffodils to fall perennials), ornamental grasses and a new hummingbird and butterfly garden.

The remainder of the property is quite unique. Surviving from the private nursery days are whole, large clusters of white pine, maple, honey locust, pin oak, grey birch, weeping cherry and much more, with a self-naturalizing undergrowth. Crisscrossing trails wind through the Arboretum; the longest trail loop is 1.5 miles.

The County's seasonal newsletter contains a significant list of weekly activities, some of which are horticulturally related and held at the Arboretum. Call for an up-to-date list. Group tours by prearrangement.

Personal Impression. I shared my early morning walk in fog through the Arboretum with half a dozen curious deer. It was one of the more poignant communions with nature I've experienced. This is a restful place.

(11) Leaming's Run Gardens

1845 Route 9 North
Swainton, Cape May County, NJ 08210
(609) 465-5871
Hours: the gardens open May 15 to Oct. 20, 9:30-5 daily; the Cooperage (gift shop) opens May 15 to Christmas, 10-5 daily.

Overview. This is one of the most uniquely specialized gardens in the Region--it features summer annuals. Considered the largest annual garden in the U.S.A., selected as one of the top 20 gardens in the East by Great Gardens of America, featured in Architectural Digest and various other magazines and newspapers, Leaming's Run Gardens proves that, if you build a better specialty, the world will beat a path to your door. Blooms are spectacular and continuous during the open season, and hummingbirds arrive in quantitiy in August.

Directions. Locate Cape May County on the southern coast of New Jersey. From the Garden State Parkway, take Exit 13 to Rte. 9, proceeding north on it for a mile to the Gardens' entrance on your left.

Historical Profile. Created within 30 acres of pine forest, the gardens opened to the public in 1977 and have been in a continuous process of refinement to this time.

Description. Under a tall, stately pine canopy, a one-mile path winds around and through 25 annually planted, distinct gardens; the crisscrossing paths allow the tired visitor to exit in less than a mile, and rest spots are provided along the way.

During my trip, several of the gardens grouped annuals by color or color combinations-- a yellow garden, a blue and white garden, a blue and red garden, an orange garden. Others featured a species--a hibiscus garden, a celosia garden, shades of rose. And there were tasteful blends-- the houseplant garden, the corner garden, the everlasting garden, the bridal garden and "Down Jersey." Most of the gardens took the form of informal borders along the path; as a set, they are remi-

Ownership	Pet on leash	Brochure
private	no	yes
Size	**Weddings**	**Ed. programs**
30 acres	--	no
Rest rooms	**Sell plants**	**Spec. events**
yes	occasionally	1
Pay phone	**Membership**	**Labeling**
no	no	no
Visitor center	**Gift shop**	**Volunteers**
no	yes	no

Fees	Off street parking
yes	yes
Library for public	**Ext. photo limits**
no	no
Garden clubs active	**Food**
no	no

1*Hummingbird tours in August. Call for information.*

niscent of a museum hallway with masterpieces-to-view on either side. The intriguing aspect of the garden is that you may see something quite different than I did; the annuals (and some perennials treated as annuals) are dug out every winter and replanted from seed. There is no guarantee that sections will not change significantly from time to time.

There is running water, a gazebo and a profusion of ferns under the pine canopy, but clearly the blooming annuals command one's attention. The place is charming; it is enchanting; it is ... entirely unique! And August provides a bonus for the visitor when countless hummingbirds arrive to savor the annuals in their own fashion; the Audubon Society conducts special tours at that time.

Also on site are the 1706 Thomas Leaming house, a small sampling of a 17th century farm (period animals, tobacco, cotton and herbs outside a one-room log cabin), and the Cooperage (a gift shop specializing in dried flowers and creations with them).

Personal Impression. To be completely candid about it, I wasn't sure I wanted to go out of my way to view an annual garden. Somehow I thought it might just be an open field next to a mall with alternating beds of zinnias and marigolds--something like the average homeowner puts in the back yard. Indeed, many gardens in the Region use annuals only as a pleasant little filler between the brilliance of spring and the arboreal splendors of fall. To the contrary, this informal garden has all the taste and charm and class and design sophistication that more traditional gardens have *plus* the distinction of being entirely original. It is very definitely worth going out of your way to view.

---

(12) The Leonard J. Buck Garden
11 Layton Rd. North of Hutcheson
Far Hills, NJ 07931
(908) 234-2677
Hours: the grounds open 10-4 Mon.-Sat., year round, and 12-4 winter Sundays & 12-5 summer Sundays; holiday closings vary--call to determine.

Overview. The Somerset County Park Commission offers this unique, naturalized rock garden in north-central New Jersey. From the Commission's Fact Sheet: "The Leonard J. Buck Garden is one of the premier rock gardens in the eastern United States. Begun in the late 1930's, the garden has reached a breathtaking point of maturity. It consists of a series of alpine and woodland gardens situated in a 33-acre wooded stream valley."

Directions. Generally orient yourself to the area by locating on a map the intersection of I-78 and I-287. North of it on I-287, take Exit 18 to Rte. 202-206, staying on 202 when the two roads split. Turn right just before the tracks at the Far Hills station and proceed 1.0 mile to the sign for the garden.

Historical Profile. Leonard J. Buck, a mining engineer who became intrigued with the basalt rock outcroppings on his property and the relationship

75

of their mineral composition to the native plants, began collaborating in the 1930s with landscape architect Zenon Schreiber on a preservative, naturalistic landscape that accented outcroppings, native species and introduced exotics. The 33-acre property was donated by Helen Buck, his wife, to the Somerset County Park Commission in 1976. It immediately opened to the public by appointment only; it opened daily in 1985 upon completion of the visitor center.

Description. From the Fact Sheet: "One of the greatest delights in visiting the Leonard J. Buck Garden is discovering its variety of plants. Tucked among the rocks are rare and exotic garden plants. The wooded trails connecting the outcroppings are lined with beautiful wild flowers that have flourished and multiplied through the years. Throughout the gardens grow various ferns. At the base of the valley walls, azaleas and rhododendrons produce a colorful display in May and early June. The Buck Garden's peak bloom is in spring, when favorite wildflowers, diminutive alpines, and delicate azaleas all compete for attention, but there is something interesting in bloom almost every week of the year."

Ownership	Pet on leash	Brochure
public	no	several
Size	**Weddings**	**Ed. programs**
33 acres	no	yes
Rest rooms	**Sell plants**	**Spec. events**
yes	yes[1]	yes
Pay phone	**Membership**	**Labeling**
yes	no[2]	yes
Visitor center	**Gift shop**	**Volunteers**
yes	no	yes
Fees		**Off street parking**
donation		yes
Library for public		**Ext. photo limits**
no		no
Garden clubs active		**Food**
yes		no

[1] Usually the third Saturday in April.
[2] Although there is no membership in this publicly owned facility, one may join the Watnong Chapter of the American Rock Garden Society.

More than 150 heathers have been planted in the raised demonstration beds next to the parking lot, especially calluna and erica. The overall design calls for an even blend of woody and herbaceous plants, both highly diversified and specialized.

A very good selection of literature on the Garden is available at the visitor center, including plant lists and a unique walking tour guide to the rock scenery on the property. Guided tours may be arranged for a modest fee. The very nature of the terrain makes wheelchair access difficult.

Personal Impression. It took me some time to appreciate the scale of this Garden. Whereas most places take rocks to the garden for a rock garden, here they brought the garden to the rocks. The entire 33-acre property is the rock garden!

(13) Presby Memorial Iris Gardens

474 Upper Mountain Ave.
Upper Montclair, NJ 07043   (Haboken)
(201) 783-5974
Hours: daylight hours, year round

Overview. Owned by the township of Montclair and managed by the Citizens Committee of the Presby Memorial Iris Gardens, this highly specialized, semi-formal garden may be the premier iris garden in the country. Peak bloom is in mid-May.

Directions. Locate on a map of northeast New Jersey the intersection of Routes 3 and 46 south of Patterson. From Rte. 46, turn left (south) onto Valley Rd., then right onto Normal Ave. and finally left onto Upper Mountain Ave. to the Gardens.

Historical Profile. The iris, an adaptable northern hemisphere wildflower from the arctic to the tropics from time immemorial, has enjoyed a prominent role in recorded history in both wild and cultivated forms. Drawing its name from the Greek goddess of the rainbow, many believe the Biblical mention of "lilies of the field" actually refers to irises. The tomb of Pharaoh Thotmes III included iris carvings 3500 years ago. Mohammedan soldiers carried its roots (rhizomes) into battle to plant on the graves of their fallen comrades. French heraldry featured the fleur de lis, an iris. The rhizomes were used in Elizabethan England to remove freckles and in China as a facial beauty application.

In the United States, Frank H. Presby of Montclair founded the American Iris Society, and the Presby Memorial Iris Gardens were

Ownership	Pet on leash	Brochure
public[1]	yes	yes
Size	**Weddings**	**Ed. programs**
c. 5 acres	--	yes
Rest rooms	**Sell plants**	**Spec. events**
no	occasionally	yes
Pay phone	**Membership**	**Labeling**
no	yes	excellent
Visitor center	**Gift shop**	**Volunteers**
no	no	many
Fees		**Off street parking**
no		no
Library for public		**Ext. photo limits**
no		no
Garden clubs active		**Food**
no		no

[1]*Management is private.*

77

established in 1927 in his honor. To this day, the Gardens specialize solely in irises.

Description. Impressively, the garden displays over 6,000 iris varieties (c. 50,000 plants), some dating as far back as the 15th century. Over two dozen beds form a rainbow curve on a slope in Montclair's Mountainside Park. Starting at the north end, several hundred antique varieties are displayed in chronological order with excellent labeling. The other beds contain Siberian, Louisiana, Japanese, remontants, spuria, tall-bearded, wild, dwarf, median and more.

Although peak bloom occurs in mid-May, the range of blooms starting in April is described in the brochure as continuing intermittently into the fall.

Docented tours proceed from late May into early June: "The annual Open House, set for a Saturday at the end of May, attracts visitors with special garden tours, and displays and festivities at the adjoining Walther House, headquarters for the Citizen's Committee." Special group tours by prearrangement.

Personal Impression. The individual iris bloom has been my favorite since childhood. The sheer quantity of blooms here defies imagination.

---

(14) Reeves-Reed Arboretum

165 Hobart Ave.
Summit, NJ 07901 *Near Jersey City*
(908) 273-8787
Hours: the grounds are open daylight hours, year round; the Wisner House opens 9-3, Mon./Tue./Thurs.; closed Thanksgiving, Christmas, Jan. 1, Labor Day, Memorial Day and July 4.

Overview. Combining horticultural with other cultural activities, the Reeves-Reed Arboretum may be unsurpassed in diversification in the mid-Atlantic region. In addition to the principal feature, a two-habitat arboretum, it offers a spring daffodil explosion, a small greenhouse, several distinct garden areas, a varied educational program, concerts, outdoor art classes, travel lectures, a reference library, poetry readings, bird seed sales and more. Caution: visiting the Arboretum may be habit-forming.

Directions. Locate Summit on a New Jersey map due west of Newark. Exit I-78 onto Route 24 heading northeast; exit onto Hobart Avenue heading southwest to the Arboretum.

Historical Profile. Contoured into steep slopes and kettles (bowls, depressions) by the retreating Wisconsin glacier 10,000 years ago, the property was farmed in colonial times and was converted to a residential estate by John Wisner in 1889; his house still stands. Mrs. Wisner planted the first daffodils and these expanded plantings are still a major April attraction. In 1916 the Reeves family purchased the property, hired landscape architect Calvert Vaux to develop an overall design for the property, and introduced the still-present rose garden. The Reed family purchased the property in 1968, adding the herb garden and woodland trails. Private funds purchased the property in 1974 for a public arboretum and garden.

Ownership	Pet on leash	Brochure
[1]	no	yes
Size	**Weddings**	**Ed. programs**
12.5 acres	yes	yes
Rest rooms	**Sell plants**	**Spec. events**
yes	occasionally	yes
Pay phone	**Membership**	**Labeling**
no	yes	some
Visitor center	**Gift shop**	**Volunteers**
yes	planned	yes
Fees		**Off street parking**
no		yes
Library for public		**Ext. photo limits**
yes		no
Garden clubs active		**Food**
yes		no

[1]*Municipally owned; independently managed by non-profit organization.*

Description. The brochure describes the glacier-gauged terrain: "The Reeves-Reed's numerous native trees are typical of an eastern deciduous forest. Two distinct habitats are represented. The low, wetland woods feature red maple, swamp white oak, skunk cabbage and jack-in-the-pulpit. The dry, upland areas are carpeted with mayapple and shaded by stands of white oak, maple-leaved viburnum and shagbark and mockernut hickories." Scattered introductions include magnolia, sourwood, Franklinia, princess tree and cutleaf maple.

The kettle sloping from the house contains a meadow peppered with a century's plantings of daffodils. The rose garden has survived since 1925. The herb garden, perennial borders, ferns, ground-cover and the azalea garden add to the "rooms" of the more formal part of the property. Hollies and tropical plants (including orchids) in the greenhouse extend and enrich the viewing period. Trails wind through the forest. All told, there are 12.5 acres of hardwood forest, open fields, lawns and formal garden rooms. The self-guiding tour brochure identifies individual species very nicely.

As stated above, the Arboretum offers a full calendar of events in horticulture, art, music, nature and crafts. The calendar available at this writing offers a particularly fine selection of tours as far away as Pittsburgh. Call for an up-to-date listing. Without exaggeration, there appears to be something of interest for virtually all ages (especially children) and tastes. The Arboretum is quite lively. Blooms are continuous April-October.

Personal Impression. Of all the dimensions of Reeves-Reed worth appreciating, I find the historical dimension most fascinating. Geologically, we can understand how glaciers contoured the land thousands of years ago.

Ecologically, we can understand how different arboreal habitats evolved over those contours. Culturally, we can understand how families serially and indelibly modified the flora and floral designs of the property up to the creation of the Arboretum. Organizationally, we can trace the evolution of the current diversified programs and attractions of the Arboretum. All in all, this is a very interesting place. And understandable.

(15) Rutgers Gardens

Care of: Friends of the Rutgers Gardens
Cook College Office of Continuing Education
New Brunswick, NJ 08903
(908) 932-9317 or 8451
Hours: the grounds are open daylight hours, year round.

Overview. Rutgers University, with the assistance of a large volunteer corps, maintains a set of gardens as a public and green industries education center. On 50 acres separate from the main campus, the featured attractions include display (esp. annuals) gardens, collections (esp. a world class holly collection) and various demonstration gardens and projects. A 64-acre virgin forest lies adjacent to the cultivated areas.

Ownership	Pet on leash	Brochure
pub., univ.	yes	yes
Size	**Weddings**	**Ed. programs**
50 acres[1]	yes	yes
Rest rooms	**Sell plants**	**Spec. events**
--	occasionally	yes
Pay phone	**Membership**	**Labeling**
no	yes	some
Visitor center	**Gift shop**	**Volunteers**
no	no	many
Fees		**Off street parking**
no		yes
Library for public		**Ext. photo limits**
no		no
Garden clubs active		**Food**
yes		no

[1]The adjacent Helyar Forest adds another 64 acres.

Directions. Locate on a map New Brunswick in north-central New Jersey and Rte. 1 running parallel to the New Jersey Turnpike. Exit Rte. 1 onto Ryders Lane, turning left almost immediately into the Gardens.

Historical Profile. Originally a farm near, but not contiguous to, the Rutgers campus, the Rutgers Gardens began in 1921 with an emphasis on shrubs. It has expanded its diversification gradually over the years with plans to continue to do so into the future.

Description. The Helyar Forest, one of the last stands of virgin forest in central New Jersey, occupies 64 acres next to the Rutgers Gardens and includes about two miles of trails.

The Gardens occupy 50 acres just off Ryders Lane. The original 1920s shrub garden still survives. The Donald B. Lacey Annual Display Garden has profited from an infusion of volunteer energy in recent years and is the featured attraction at the Annual Open House in late July. The collection of American and Japanese hollies is world class, providing a major attraction in winter. Other attractions include: an azalea and rhododendron display (over 500 varieties); an evergreen garden; a hedge and vine display; a terrace garden (drought-tolerant plants); a turf plant demonstration; and more.

Through university courses, continuing education and on-site experiences, Rutgers offers educational opportunities to persons of all ages and education levels. Research focuses on plant genetics, horticultural techniques and forest ecology; new dogwood hybrids are a recent contribution. There is a flower fair in May and a fall foliage festival. Group tours by prearrangement.

Personal Impression. I enjoyed Rutgers even more when I got home and read a back issue of the Newsletter, Friends of the Rutgers Gardens. Dr. Bruce Hamilton, Coordinator of the Gardens, thanked in writing the army of volunteers who came forward to compensate for the recession-induced budget cuts of 1990, saving entire sections from deterioration, if not ruination. The mid-Atlantic region's tally-sheet of volunteer accomplishments and triumphs continues to grow.

---

(16) Sayen Gardens

155 Hughes Drive
Hamilton Township, NJ 08690
Near Trenton
(609) 890-3874
Hours: the grounds are open daylight hours, year round.

Overview. This relatively new, 30-acre estate garden is still in process of development. Hamilton Township purchased it in 1985 from the Sayen family and opened it to the public in 1988. The informal landscaping at this stage of development accents spring bulbs and shrubs, and native species.

Directions. Locate Hamilton due east of Trenton. From I-295, take Exit 63 heading east on Rte. 33 for 2.2 miles, turning left on Whitehorse Rd. for a block to the stop sign; turn right onto Nottingham Way and immediately left onto Mercer St. for three blocks; turn left onto Hughes Dr. and the entrance is immediately on your left.

Description. Springtime dominates the horticultural year at Sayen Gardens when 80,000 daffodils explode into bloom. And the recently introduced Mother's Day Azalea Festival drew 8,000 people in its first year. Rhododendrons are also particularly plentiful.

At other times, however, boulders command the visitor's attention. From the parking lot to a large, shrub-planted mound in front of the Sayen house, enormous boulders are informally distributed about. It seems diminutive to refer to it as a "rock" garden.

The disposition of the remaining acres (a substantial pine canopy with mainly indigenous wildflower and shrub undergrowth, with trail) and the Sagen house remains uncertain. A substantial rose garden is in planning. Many are leaning toward restoring the Sayen house to an earlier period. But final decisions have yet to be made.

Ownership	Pet on leash	Brochure
pub., town	discouraged	no
Size	**Weddings**	**Ed. programs**
30 acres	yes	yes
Rest rooms	**Sell plants**	**Spec. events**
no	in future	yes
Pay phone	**Membership**	**Labeling**
no	yes	some
Visitor center	**Gift shop**	**Volunteers**
no	no	yes
Fees		**Off street parking**
no		yes
Library for public		**Ext. photo limits**
no		none
Garden clubs active		**Food**
yes		no

In the meantime, spring is spectacular.

Personal Impression. I personally enjoy seeing a garden in process of development. Things are off to a first rate start, but much more can be done with this large property, and I find it exciting to return periodically to see the progress.

---

(17) Skylands
The New Jersey State Botanical Garden   No. Bergen Co.
Ringwood State Park
Ringwood, NJ 07456
(201) 962-7527
Hours: grounds open year round, daylight hours; call for hours of the visitor center, gift shop and manor house.

Overview. Officially designated the New Jersey State Botanical Garden, Skylands (an appropriate name for the elevation) occupies 96 acres in the larger Ringwood State Park in the northernmost part of New Jersey. It is restoring, maintaining and enhancing an early 20th century estate and gardens with an impressive diversity of plant material and garden design. It is an all-seasons operation.

Directions. Locate Ringwood just below New Jersey's border with New York State. Take Rte. 511 one mile north of Ringwood to the entrance to Ringwood State Park and follow signs to Skylands, which is in it.

Historical Profile. Originally a set of pioneer farmsteads high in the Ramapo Mountains near the border with New York State, they were purchased by Francis Stetson (a New York attorney) for his "Skylands Farms," and he retained Samuel Parsons, Jr. to design the estate.

Clarence Lewis, an investment banker, purchased Skylands in 1922. He replaced the Stetson house with the current Tudor mansion with granite quarried on site and engaged the firm of Vitale and Geiffert to convert the grounds into a botanical showplace. He collected plants worldwide for 30 years, employing over 60 gardeners in peak season.

Shelton College owned the property briefly, selling the 1117 acres to the State of New Jersey in 1966, which opened them immediately to the public.

In March of 1983, Governor Kean designated the central 96 acres surrounding the manor house as the State's official botanical garden, and it has subsequently been placed on the State and National Registers of Historic Places. Efforts to restore and preserve Lewis' gardens are still in process.

Description. Maple Avenue cuts the property into two large tracts with the more formal gardens immediately on either side. Immediately on the west side are the Tudor mansion, a magnolia walk, an azalea garden, a summer (daylily) garden, a tree peony garden, a lilac garden and an octagonal (rock) garden with pool; there also are a winter garden, a pinetum and open lawns. On the immediate eastern side of Maple Ave. are an annual garden, a perennial garden and an awesome, half-mile Crab Apple Vista (two straight parallel rows). Also on the east side are less formal areas including a barberry collection, a carriage shop with visitor center and gift shop, statuary, a horsechestnut collection, Swan Pond and meadow, a dry garden, cactus rock, a bog garden, a wildflower garden, a heather

Ownership	Pet on leash	Brochure
pub., state	no	excellent
Size	**Weddings**	**Ed. programs**
96 acres	yes	yes
Rest rooms	**Sell plants**	**Spec. events**
yes	occasionally	yes
Pay phone	**Membership**	**Labeling**
yes	yes	yes
Visitor center	**Gift shop**	**Volunteers**
yes	yes	yes
Fees		**Off street parking**
not for grounds		yes
Library for public		**Ext. photo limits**
yes		no
Garden clubs active		**Food**
yes		no

83

garden, a pergola and a rhododendron display garden. An international assortment of trees (e.g., Japanese umbrella pine, Algerian fir, Chinese toon tree) is scattered throughout the property.

Overall, the genus/species/variety diversification is spectacular as is the diversity of design and habitat.

The (non-profit) Skylands Association sponsors walks and programs throughout the year--call for an up-to-date list. There are Open Houses on Mother's Day and in the Thanksgiving/Christmas season. Miles of trails run through the larger Park.

Personal Impression. I had a feeling of unreality and incongruity about finding such a large and gorgeous set of gardens at such a high altitude seemingly in the middle of nowhere--something like, how did *this* ... get *here?* It was an exuberant feeling, however, that enhanced my appreciation of a truly first-rate garden complex. Don't debate with yourself, just go.

---

(18) Well-Sweep Herb Farm

317 Mt. Bethel Rd.
Port Murray, NJ 07865   *Tow, Del. water Gap*
(908) 852-5390
Hours: open 9:30-5 Tue.-Sat., year round; open Mon. 1-5, year round; closed Sundays and for all major holidays.

Overview. This family-owned, commercial herb farm has both production and display beds, selling herbs both on-site and through a mail-order catalogue. It has been gradually diversifying displays beyond herbs and has developed a significant educational program.

Directions. Find on a map of northwestern New Jersey the intersection of Rtes. 57 and 31. Take Rte. 57 northeast toward Hackettstown, turning left at Port Murray Rd., then left again onto Mt. Bethel Rd. and the farm. Don't be afraid to stop for more detailed information.

Historical Capsule. The owning family purchased 4.5 of the current 120 acres in 1967 for their herb farm. Growth has been progressive over the years. The display area for the public opened in 1970.

Description. Although this is a commercial farm that maintains its existence through sales, it also offers educational displays and events. The blooming season proceeds from mid-May to the end of October. The display herb garden peaks in July and August.

The terrain slopes down from the road. Near the road one finds a traditional knot with dwarf crimson barberry, dwarf hyssop and lavender. Further down are flowering perennials and a new area for ornamental grasses. In between are dozens of beds of oregano, lavender, rosemary, sage, basil, thyme and *much*

Ownership	Pet on leash	Brochure
priv., com.	no	catalogue
Size	**Weddings**	**Ed. programs**
120 acres	only photos	yes
Rest rooms	**Sell plants**	**Spec. events**
yes	thousands	yes
Pay phone	**Membership**	**Labeling**
no	no	excellent
Visitor center	**Gift shop**	**Volunteers**
yes	yes	no

Fees	Off street parking
only special events	yes
Library for public	**Ext. photo limits**
no	none
Garden clubs active	**Food**
no	picnicing

more. The greenhouses are mostly production. Labeling, as one would expect in a commercial establishment, is excellent.

There is a $2.00 annual catalogue that identifies in 68 pages hundreds of plants grown there by sun requirements, hardiness, uses (e.g., cooking, ornamental, fragrance, etc.), flower color and price. Both common names and botanical names are given.

Although there is no general admission fee, guided tours for groups (by pre-arrangement) do require a modest fee. Also there may be a fee for some of the regularly scheduled lectures and workshops during the growing season. The principal major events include the Midsummer Herb Festival (July), the Open Houses (June and September) and the Annual Christmas Shop (from early November to just before Christmas); the annual catalogue gives the exact dates and features for that year.

Personal Impression. I enjoy specialty gardens like this because the personnel provide me with more informative answers to my questions. Also, herbs are fascinating and the gift shop there offers a fine selection of books on them. Also, this is one of the few gardens in the Region with a traditional knot; I'll return there just to see that.

(19) William Trent House

15 Market St.
Trenton, NJ 08611
(609) 989-3027
Hours: the grounds, house and gift shop open 10-2 daily, year round; closed for all major holidays.

Overview. The Garden Club of Trenton has created an elegantly simple, early 18th century period garden on three acres owned by the City of Trenton and featuring William Trent's house. Herbs, boxwood and mature trees dominate the landscape.

85

Directions. Locate Trenton on a New Jersey map on the western border of the State, northeast of Philadelphia. From Rte. 29 in downtown Trenton, take the Market St. exit and the Trent House is immediately on your right.

Historical Profile. William Trent's incredibly diversified life is really a tale of two cities. Emigrating from Scotland to Philadelphia about 1682, he became a successful businessman there, a politician and State Supreme Court Justice. In 1714 he purchased land across the river which later became part of Trenton, NJ and constructed the still-standing house in 1719. He became a colonel in the militia, a successful politician and a NJ Chief Justice. Only an early death in 1724 curtailed his long list of accomplishments.

The last private owner of the current grounds, Edward Ansley Stokes, deeded the property to the City of Trenton in 1929 on condition that it be restored and preserved as a historic site. Restoration was completed in 1936 and period refurnishings (Queen Anne and William and Mary) have been continuously refined to the present. The Garden Club of Trenton, aided by plans drawn by landscape architect Isabella Pendleton Bowen, created in the 1930s an early 18th century period garden and grounds with as much attention to the original design and composition as surviving information permitted; public viewing began in 1939.

Ownership	Pet on leash	Brochure
pub., city	discouraged	yes
Size	**Weddings**	**Ed. programs**
3 acres	yes	no
Rest rooms	**Sell plants**	**Spec. events**
yes	occasionally	no
Pay phone	**Membership**	**Labeling**
no	yes	yes
Visitor center	**Gift shop**	**Volunteers**
yes	yes	yes
Fees		**Off street parking**
not for grounds		no
Library for public		**Ext. photo limits**
no		no
Garden clubs active		**Food**
yes		no

Description. The *piece de resistance* of the grounds is the herb garden, surrounding a centered sun dial and surrounded by boxwood. Medicinal, ornamental and culinary beds are featured. There is a pear tree allee, wisteria vines, large boxwood trees, hawthornes, crabapples, cherries, magnolias, ivy groundcover and more. The Garden Club of Trenton has been recognized by the Garden Club of New Jersey for decades of devoted maintenance. And rightfully so because the grounds are so tastefully kept. The principal plant sale is held on Mother's Day.

The house has been completely restored and has been very carefully furnished with period pieces, mainly Queen Anne-style. Although no fee is charged for the grounds, there is a modest fee for touring the house.

86

Personal Description. This is a contemplative oasis in the middle of a major city. The trees and brick/wrought iron fencing not only provide a surprisingly effective soundbreak, but also contribute to a sense of privacy.

---

(20) Willowwood Arboretum and Bamboo Brook Outdoor Education Center

c/o Morris County Park Commission
P.O. Box 1295
Morristown, NJ 07962-1295
(908) 234-0992
Hours: the grounds are open daylight hours, year round; on-site structures open irregularly.

Overview. The Morris County Park Commission owns and manages these two contiguous properties in rural Morris County. Both properties were horticulturally developed from farms in the early 20th century and feature arboreal diversity and innovative landscaping. Together the two properties occupy 309 rolling acres of alternating meadows and woodlands.

Ownership	Pet on leash	Brochure
pub., co.	no	yes
Size	**Weddings**	**Ed. programs**
309 acres	yes	yes
Rest rooms	**Sell plants**	**Spec. events**
yes	in spring	no
Pay phone	**Membership**	**Labeling**
no	yes	yes
Visitor center	**Gift shop**	**Volunteers**
no[1]	no	yes
Fees		**Off street parking**
donations		yes
Library for public		**Ext. photo limits**
reference only		no
Garden clubs active		**Food**
no		no

[1]*The structures on site open irregularly.*

Directions. Locate I-78 going east-west in the northern third of New Jersey. Exit onto Rte. 206, proceeding north about five miles to Pottersville Rd. (Rte. 512); in about half a mile, take a right onto Lisk Hill Rd., then a quick right onto Union Grove Rd., then a quick left onto Longview Rd. to the sites. There are signs along the way.

Historical Profile. Both of these contiguous properties were farmed from colonial times until new owners in the early 20th century modified them into rural, nature-loving estates. The Tubbs brothers purchased Willowwood in 1908 and primarily added trees for 50 years including a large collection of willows after which the Arboretum is named. Under the proprietorship of Rutgers University

87

from 1967 to 1980, the property was finally acquired by the Morris County Park Commission in 1980.

Bamboo Brook was purchased by Martha and William Hutcheson in 1911. Martha, an MIT-trained landscape architect, transformed the property into a casual country estate. Morris County acquired the property from her daughter in 1972. Thus, both properties were privately developed at the same time and passed to public trusteeship at roughly the same time.

Description. Although there are flowering plants and shrubs around the 1783 house, the principal attraction in Willowwood's 131 acres is the set of trees with extensive trails winding through them. There are collections of northern hemisphere willows, oaks, maples, magnolias, hollies, cherries, lilacs and various conifers, with an extensive fern undergrowth and a spring wildflower explosion. The diversity in all "has about 3,500 kinds of native and exotic plants ...." The excellent tour guide draws one's attention to features such as a hedge maple, a hydrangea vine growing on the barn, the Japanese varnish tree, turkey oak, sassafras, snowbell, Korean stewartia and the cottage garden, the most formal attraction on the property.

Bamboo Hook's 178 acres feature more open meadows than Willowwood with a carefully landscaped area around the main residence of about 5 acres. It is reminiscent of Italian gardens in that plantings are subordinated to the overall design, sculpture and various architectural features. There is a wisteria arbor, a rose and clematis arbor, a ha-ha ditch (it contains grazing animals without obstructing the view), pools, a stream, a patio (innovative in the early 20th century) and lawns, all orchestrated carefully. Farm structures occupy a section to the side. Highlights in the excellent trail guide include English yew, buckeyes, Kentucky coffee tree, an allee of northern white cedar with a tunnel effect, eastern red cedar and shrubs. The floral content of Martha's garden will be restored in the future.

Educational programs are offered throughout the year by the Morris County Park Commission and/or the Friends of the Frelinghuysen Arboretum--call for an up-to-date listing.

Personal Impression. Although there are some formal sections on these properties, the overall atmosphere is casual, informal, natural. Interestingly, the surviving farm structures on the properties remind me of rural New England which I love to visit. It's a calm place, and relaxing.

Chapter 4
North Carolina

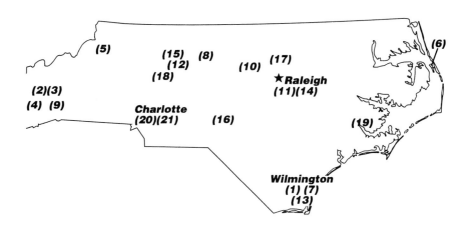

(1) Airlie Gardens
(2) Biltmore Estate
(3) The Botanical Gardens at Asheville
(4) Campus Arboretum of Haywood Community College
(5) Daniel Boone Native Gardens
(6) Elizabethan Gardens
(7) Greenfield Park
(8) Greensboro Beautiful
(9) North Carolina Arboretum
(10) North Carolina Botanical Garden
(11) North Carolina State University Arboretum

(12) Old Salem Gardens
(13) Orton Plantation Gardens
(14) Raleigh Municipal Rose Garden
(15) Reynolda Gardens
(16) Sandhills Horticultural Gardens
(17) Sarah P. Duke Gardens
(18) Tanglewood Park
(19) Tryon Palace
(20) UNC at Charlotte Botanical Gardens
(21) Wing Haven Gardens

Most of the gardens in the mid-Atlantic region lie in the eastern half of the Region, with North Carolina as the exception. North Carolina has the most evenly distributed set of gardens of any state. The dominance of colleges and universities over NC gardens (and their even distribution across the State) helps to explain why, since 9 of the 21 gardens are college-based or college-affiliated--more than the rest of the region combined.

The content of the gardens also differs from the rest of the Region slightly because North Carolina is both a mid-Atlantic state and a southeastern state in terms of native flora. Visitors are more likely here to encounter features such as live oaks and camellias, and many collections are explicitly of southeastern specimens.

These differences enhance the uniquely diverse set of mid-Atlantic gardens as a whole and enrich the viewing opportunities of the public.

---

(1) Airlie Gardens

P.O. Box 210
Wilmington. NC 28402
(919) 763-4646
Hours: the grounds are opem 8-6, March 1-Oct. 3.

Overview. Although this privately owned garden is not a "specialty" garden in the narrow sense of the term, the extraordinarily fine collections of azaleas and camellias seem to dominate the other fine attractions there. After their bloom, the 50-acre property becomes a deep green, lush, naturalized garden with a pleasing blend of arboreal splendor, aquatic scenery and graceful waterfowl--a sort of quiet dreamland.

Directions. Locate Wilmington in southeastern North Carolina. Airlie is due east of the center of Wilmington just off Rte. 76 that terminates at Wrightsville Beach.

Historical Profile. The gardens are pre-Civil War in design. From the brochure: "Airlie Gardens was once the estate of Pembroke Jones, a wealthy nineteenth-century rice magnate. The grounds overlook picturesque Money Island on Wrightsville Sound, where Captain Kidd reputedly buried his treasure.

"Airlie is now owned by the sons of the late W. Albert Corbett, reknowned planter and industrialist of Wilmington, NC. They share the famous gardens with the public, charging a small admission fee which defrays only a small part of maintenance costs."

The estate residence is not open to the public since the family still resides on-site.

Description. This is one of the Region's few drive-through gardens,

Ownership	Pet on leash	Brochure
private	yes	yes

Size	Weddings	Ed. programs
50 acres	yes	no

Rest rooms	Sell plants	Spec. events
yes	no	yes[1]

Pay phone	Membership	Labeling
no	no	no

Visitor center	Gift shop	Volunteers
no	no	no

Fees	Off street parking
yes	yes

Library for public	Ext. photo limits
no	none

Garden clubs active	Food
no	no

[1]*The annual Azalea Festival is a major event for the entire region.*

although visitors are free to stop and walk the many trails. Shortly after entering through a massive hand-forged gate embroidered with leaves and flowers, the visitor drives beneath a thick canopy of mixed evergreens and hardwoods with a seemingly never-ending undergrowth of azaleas that explode into springtime color.

Shortly thereafter you drive by a large, spring-fed lake (with a reflecting pool to one side) on which you will frequently see swans gracefully gliding along. Then one passes by a rural 1835 Episcopal Chapel that was restored in the mid-1970s. One also passes the Spring Garden (a pool-centered area that comes closest to a formal segment of Airlie) and an impressive concentration of camellias.

Throughout the property one encounters massive, moss-draped live oaks, an arbor, an historic stone pergola and never-ending serenity.

The bloom period ranges from early March to mid-June, with a mid-April peak. The annual Azalea Festival is generally held the weekend before Easter. (Local motels are generally filled by visitors long in advance.)

Personal Impression. The visitor leaves Airlie Gardens in a pleasant stupor induced by total immersion within the verdant, large forest and gardens. The drive-through nature of the grounds is a definite plus for persons with ambulation problems.

(2) Biltmore Estate

One North Park Square
Asheville, NC 28801
(800) 543-2961
Hours: open daily, year round, except Thanksgiving, Christmas and New Year's

Day; the ticket office opens 9-5 and the exterior gardens, 9-dusk; the conservatory opens 9-5:30.

Overview. Originally 125,000 acres, the current Biltmore Estate occupies 8,000 acres in western North Carolina and is more aptly described as a mega-estate than simply as an estate. It includes the Biltmore House (still the largest private home in America), a winery, the grounds/gardens, several restaurants, several gift shops, statuary and a long list of special events, and much more. The entrance fee covers a two-day visit, which many may need. The garden set includes both formal and informal, indoor and outdoor sections with impressive diversity of design and material, plus the enormous scale. Of necessity, it is one of the few drive-through grounds in the Region.

Directions. Locate Asheville in western North Carolina. Take Exit 50 from I-40; proceed north for less than a mile to the entrance on your left.

Historical Profile. George Vanderbilt purchased this enormous property in western North Carolina in the 1880s with intentions to develop a 255-room mansion, gardens, a working farm and a village. He commissioned architect Richard Morris Hunt to model the mansion after chateaux in France's Loire Valley; and he commissioned landscape architect Frederick Law Olmstead to design the grounds.

To appreciate the magnitude of Olmstead's challenge, consider that it is now a three-mile drive from the entrance to the mansion and a five-mile drive from the mansion to the winery, and the current estate is only six percent of the original size. He managed the challenge by confining most of the introduced gardens to the areas near the mansion and by sponsoring an extensive forest preservation initiative. Olmstead began this task at age 66 and it was the terminal project of an illustrious career. His work here was somewhat more formal around the mansion than in the naturalistic gardens he had built his reputation on.

The Vanderbilt family still owns the estate. Various portions of it have been sold or deeded to the government for forest conservation, but the family has recently undertaken some major restoration.

Description. The "flagship" of the garden-set near the mansion is the 4-acre English Walled Garden in the tradition of the old English private garden, considered by many to be the finest of its type in America. Walled for warmth, a windshield, privacy and protection from grazing and other animals, it contains a large number of seasonally rotated beds, a premier rose garden, a tasteful periphery, a relatively new/restored butterfly garden and a conservatory. In square pattern beds, 50,000 tulips emerge in spring followed by summer budding plants (e.g., zinnias, cannas), ending with fall mums. The rose garden, featuring All-America Rose Selections, contains a blend of more fragrant heritage roses and longer blooming hybrids--3000 plants. Along the periphery within the wall are espaliered fruit trees and perennial borders. The butterfly garden contains many of Olmstead's favorites (phlox, tickseed, asters) as supplemented with flowers with known color/petal shape/fragrance attractions. The 3-compartment, 8,000 sq. ft. Conservatory contains palms, ferns, succulents,

Ownership	Pet on leash	Brochure
private	yes[1]	yes

Size	Weddings	Ed. programs
8,000 acres	yes	yes

Rest rooms	Sell plants	Spec. events
yes	very good	yes

Pay phone	Membership	Labeling
yes	no	some

Visitor center	Gift shop	Volunteers
yes	very good	no

Fees	Off street parking
yes	yes

Library for public	Ext. photo limits
no	commercial[2]

Garden clubs active	Food
no	very good

[1]*Only in designated areas.*
[2]*Also use common sense re: blocking pathways, putting tripod legs in beds, etc.*

tropicals, sub-tropicals and plants rotated at the mansion.

Closer to the mansion is the formal Library Terrace covered with old wisteria and trumpet creeper vines, overlooking a boxwood-edged pool, and decorated with statuary, a tea house and jardinieres. Also formal, the Italian Garden features a 16th century design that subordinates the importance of plantings to the design; it contains three very large pools with ancient lotuses, water lilies and other aquatic plants, and some statuary.

The Ramble Garden finally provides the type of informal garden Olmstead loved, a winding pathway bordered by flowering shrubs and trees. Also informal is the Azalea Garden which may include the largest collection of native azaleas in the country. The remaining grounds are highly naturalized in Olmstead's style and retain as much as possible native wildflowers, shrubs and sections of native forest. Much current restoration focuses on the Spring Garden. Lovers of ornamental grasses will not be disappointed in the fall.

The paragraphs above merely highlight some principal features on an immense estate in which the gardens are but one attraction. It took an army of workers five years to complete the mansion, which is lavishly furnished beyond words. The winery is smaller, but also unique. The food is excellent and the shops feature quality merchandise. Although the entrance fee is relatively high for the Region, the scale of attractions is unsurpassed and the fee covers a two-day visit.

Visit anytime. Although the "official" blooming season is early April through October, hollies and conifers and the Conservatory and more make the colder months appealing. Don't hesitate to call for information, clarification or brochures; the staff seem very eager to help. The principal horticultural event of the year is the Festival of Flowers, which proceeds from early April to early May coincident with the spring bloom explosion; it also features music, children's activities, and annually changing special attractions. The pre-Christmas season is replete with festivities.

Personal Impression. I spent an entire day there and did not see it all. The quality, of course, is extraordinary, but the quantity of quality is awesome.

---

(3) The Botanical Gardens at Asheville

151 W.T. Weaver Boulevard
Asheville, NC 28804
(704) 252-5190
Hours: grounds open year round, daylight hours.

Overview. This publicly owned, privately managed garden provides a repository of over 800 species of native plants of North Carolina and the southern Appalachian region for the enjoyment of the general public. The entirely informal and natural garden areas feature a spring bloom from early April to mid-June over its 10 acres.

Directions. Locate Asheville in western North Carolina and I-240 running through it. From I-240, take Merriman Ave. north for 1.2 miles, then left onto W.T. Weaver Blvd. for half a mile to the entrance on your right.

Historical Profile. Representatives of various Asheville garden clubs organized in 1960 to initiate the present gardens on land owned by the University of North Carolina at Asheville. Work began the following year on a design by landscape architect Doan Ogden and opened to the public shortly thereafter.

Description. Possibly the *piece de resistance* of the Gardens is the Creighton Wildflower Trail which explodes into bloom in spring. Azaleas, rhododendrons and dogwoods add to a truly spectacular spring show. The alternating meadows and heavily wooded ridges, however, present a restful ambience any time of the year.

Ownership	Pet on leash	Brochure
public[1]	no	yes
Size	**Weddings**	**Ed. programs**
10 acres	yes	yes
Rest rooms	**Sell plants**	**Spec. events**
yes	in season	yes
Pay phone	**Membership**	**Labeling**
no	yes	yes
Visitor center	**Gift shop**	**Volunteers**
yes	excellent	many
Fees	**Off street parking**	
no	yes	
Library for public	**Ext. photo limits**	
on-site	no	
Garden clubs active	**Food**	
many	no	

[1]*Private management.*

The Botany Center (visitor center) houses an on-site-use library and excellent

94

gift shop. Near it, the Garden for the Blind is due for 1994 renovation. Other distinct areas include a sycamore concentration, a rock garden, an azalea grouping, a Sunshine (tree-lined meadow) Garden and the Hayes (pioneer cabin) Cabin. The principal attraction, however, is the uniform distribution of native material. Planted areas are dense.

During prime season, docented tours are scheduled regularly, usually on Sundays--call for schedule. The annual Day in the Gardens anchors a constellation of events, usually in early May. Group tours by prearrangement.

Personal Impression. Sometimes the story behind the garden rivals the garden in interest. Here, the story revolves around the collection of native plantings for the Gardens. When Asheville developers spread to an undeveloped area, a small--actually, large--army of volunteers took to the hills and dug out massive quantities of native botanicals for transplant, with the approval of the developers. "They worked furiously like dogs," a local official told me. I heard this story on Christmas eve, which seems appropriate.

---

(4) Campus Arboretum of Haywood Community College

Freedlander Drive
Clyde, NC 28721
(704) 627-2821
Hours: the campus opens 8 a.m.-11 p.m. Mon.-Fri. and 8-4 Sat., year round; closed Sundays and major holidays.

Overview. Many colleges have placed an arboretum somewhere on campus; Haywood Community College, however, has innovatively placed the campus in its arboretum. From masses of tulips and daffodils in spring to massive trees in fall splendor, the entire 80-acre campus is a visual delight for all to behold. It is the westernmost garden complex both in North Carolina and in the mid-Atlantic region.

Directions. Locate Asheville in western North Carolina. Proceeding west from it on I-40 toward Clyde, take Exit 27 onto Routes 19 and 23 and follow signs to the nearby campus.

Historical Profile. The College opened as Haywood Technical College in 1965 and acquired the core of the current 80-acre campus in 1970. Reknowned landscape architect Doan Ogden was retained to develop a master landscape plan for the campus, which had been a Southern Appalachian Highlands farm. Ogden designed the campus around a preserved section of native forest near the center of the property. The Arboretum was officially recognized by the Board in 1977. The largest single addition in a continuous procession of refinements came in 1984 in the form of a major rhododendron garden, also designed by Ogden. The additions have been campus-wide rather than concentrated in a designated area, thereby making "campus" and "arboretum" virtually synonymous.

Description. Score after score of introduced trees (complementary to the preserved native trees) literally dot the entire campus. A very small sample: Japanese maple, ginkgo, Alaska cedar, pignut hickory, southern magnolia, dawn redwood, black oak, Norway spruce, pond cypress, Chinese elm. It's an arborphile's delight.

The acclaimed rhododendron garden, near the center of the campus, contains so many varieties (principally along a series of S-shaped curves) that the Director of the Campus Arboretum publishes a separate listing. The additional features therein include a garden shelter "topped with a weathervane forged into the shape of a

Ownership	Pet on leash	Brochure
pub., co.	yes	yes
Size	Weddings	Ed. programs
80 acres	yes	yes
Rest rooms	Sell plants	Spec. events
yes	rarely	no
Pay phone	Membership	Labeling
yes	no	some
Visitor center	Gift shop	Volunteers
no	no	no
Fees	Off street parking	
no	yes	
Library for public	Ext. photo limits	
no	no	
Garden clubs active	Food	
no	college cafeteria	

rhododendron leaf," a tunnel through a long pleached walk of laburnum trees, an outdoor circular classroom surrounded by columnar boxwoods, a trail that was bent to circumvent (and save) a century-old shortleaf pine, a wind break of white pines and two rock walls flanking the entrance, nicknamed "Work" and "Patience," which every gardener understands.

By design, garden areas dot the campus: the Freedlander Dahlia Garden; the Class of '74 Rose Garden; a grand allee of Willow Oaks; a woodland area with nature trails; and an Oriental Garden. Specialty gardens managed by the horticulture students include: the Carson Terrace Gardens; a dwarf conifer collection; vegetable gardens; a perennial garden; a fruit tree orchard; a greenhouse conservatory; and a plant nursery.

Appropriately, a quaint millpond and grist mill greet the visitor at the entrance, a reminder of what had been there first.

Personal Impression. There are some places I like instantly. This is one of them. I think it provides a benchmark of quality for all campuses of moderate size.

(5) The Daniel Boone Native Gardens
c/o Lila Peterson

96

Box 2885
Boone, NC 28607
(704) 264-6390
Hours: open daily 10-6, May through Sept.; open weekends in October; may remain open till 8 p.m. in summer when the adjacent theater, Horn in the West, is in production.

Overview. Named after the famous pioneer and explorer, the Daniel Boone Native Gardens specialize in native North Carolina plants for education and preservation. Although the property is owned by the town, the informal gardens were developed, and are maintained, by the Garden Club of North Carolina.

Ownership	Pet on leash	Brochure
public, town[1]	yes	yes

Size ○	Weddings	Ed. programs
c. 6 acres	yes	yes

Rest rooms	Sell plants	Spec. events
yes	occasionally	yes

Pay phone	Membership	Labeling
no	yes	yes

Visitor center	Gift shop	Volunteers
yes	yes	no

Fees	Off street parking
yes, modest	yes

Library for public	Ext. photo limits
no	no

Garden clubs active	Food
yes	no

[1]*Private management.*

Directions. Locate Boone in western North Carolina, slightly west of the Blue Ridge Parkway, just off Rtes. 421, 321 and 105 extension. Once in the vicinity, follow signs to the adjacent "The Horn in the West," a summertime historical drama; the most direct entrances are from Rte. 421 or Rte. 105 extension.

Historical Profile. With leadership from the Garden Club of North Carolina and a design by landscape architect Doan Ogden, the c. 6-acre garden opened in 1966 and has grown incrementally to the present time.

Description. The self-guiding tour brochure takes one through the gatehouse (also visitor center and gift shop) to a grassed allee and an ample open lawn with a dogwood and sumac border; then past an arbor supporting honeysuckle, trumpet creeper and clematis; then down to the sunken garden with large rockery and pool; then to the wishing well, past the birch thicket and to the fern garden and natural spring; then past the reflecting pool to the meditation garden and a spacious meadow, frequently used for weddings. The most recent addition has been the bog garden in 1992, which has significantly expanded the variety of on-site species.

Also on site are native azaleas, rhododendrons, wildflowers, a statue of St. Francis, a sampling of perennials, a Squire Boone cabin, and wrought-iron gates made by Daniel Boone IV (a direct descendant) and donated by the Southern Appalachian Historical Association.

The design is delightfully casual and inviting. Group tours by prearrangement. Wheelchair access is better for the lower gardens than the upper.

Personal Impression. This charming garden is a jewel in the rough in the mammoth, rugged Appalachians. Daniel Boone must be resting peacefully.

---

(6) Elizabethan Gardens

P.O. Box 1150
Manteo, NC 27954
(919) 473-3234
Hours: the grounds open from 9 to dusk, year round; until 8 p.m. in summer months.

Overview. Located on Roanoke Island near the site of Sir Walter Raleigh's Lost Colony, the Elizabethan Gardens commemorate the first English colonists to settle in the New World in 1584-1587. It borders the Roanoke Sound (a body of water separated from the ocean by the Outer Banks) and historic Fort Raleigh National Park, which contains the settlement site of the Colony and an outdoor theatre. The predominantly formal design of the garden and some of the plant material are appropriate for the settlement period of Queen Elizabeth I. Thirty years of continuous maturation has provided the viewing public with a 10-acre garden of significant diversification in design and material. It is an all-seasons garden of incredible beauty and impeccable taste.

Directions. Locate on a map of coastal No0rth Carolina the Outer Banks, a long barrier island separating the ocean from various "sounds." Locate Roanoke Island off the Roanoke Sound, north of historic Cape Hatteras and south of historic Kitty Hawk, the site of the Wright brothers' first flight. Coming from the mainland on Rte. 64, you will encounter the entrance to Fort Raleigh and the Elizabethan Gardens on your left shortly after crossing the bridge.

Historical Profile. At its 1951 annual meeting, the Garden Club of North Carolina acted favorably on a proposal to begin a commemorative garden on the site described above. New York landscape architects Innocenti and Webel designed it as an Elizabethan pleasure garden. Development began on June 2, 1953, the date Elizabeth II was crowned in England. The gardens formally opened on August 18, 1960, the 373rd anniversary of the birth of Virginia Dare--the first child born in America to English parents. Growth and refinement have continued to this time.

Description. Planning and developing the garden began with the Sunken Garden due to the unexpected gift of statuary from the Whitney estate in Georgia. This "...fantastic gift of an ancient Italian fountain and pool with balustrade, wellhead, sundial, birdbaths, stone steps and benches, dating back beyond the time of Queen Elizabeth I, came to Roanoke Island and the Garden

Club of North Carolina." The fountain centers the sunken, four-section parterre, each section containing yaupon holly borders enclosing seasonal flowers and a single crape myrtle, the entire sunken area being surrounded by a magnificent, tall hedge. It truly exemplifies gardening as an artform.

Ownership	Pet on leash	Brochure
private, NP	no	excellent
Size	**Weddings**	**Ed. programs**
10 acres	yes	yes
Rest rooms	**Sell plants**	**Spec. events**
yes	excellent	no
Pay phone	**Membership**	**Labeling**
no	yes	yes
Visitor center	**Gift shop**	**Volunteers**
yes	yes	yes
Fees	**Off street parking**	
yes, modest	yes	
Library for public	**Ext. photo limits**	
no	commercial	
Garden clubs active	**Food**	
yes	no	

One enters the Gardens through the Gate House made of century-old, warmly colored, handmade brick. It is antiquely furnished and serves as a visitor center and gift shop. From there, one is immediately greeted by the herb garden and a charming white marble fountain. Many of the herbs are from the Elizabethan period and, uniquely, many of the labels provide the uses of the herbs as well as their names. Flowering beds and a perennial/shrub border complete the enclosure of the Gate House.

A short walk from the herb garden takes you to the Queen's Rose Garden. The tall brick wall surrounding the several dozen plants creates a sense of privacy and a meditative ambience. Another short walk takes you to the "youth triangle" featuring a delightful "bashful girl" statue. Then one encounters the principal axis of the Gardens, a straight procession of Virginia Dare statue, Mount and Well Head, Sunken Garden and "Hornbeam Walk." On the Roanoke Sound side of the Sunken Garden are a tastefully bordered "Overlook Terrace" and period gazebo.

Incredibly, this describes about half the gardens, the more formal half. The ingenious design prevents a feeling of overcrowding by locating the Great (open) Lawn slightly off the center of the property with trees on the periphery including some immense, stately live oaks draped with Spanish moss. There's a relatively informal, new woodland and wildlife garden in the far corner of the property. And finally there are the paths that integrate the components; under a mixed canopy, they are lined with azaleas, rhododendrons, camellias, exquisite hydrangeas and much more.

All on ten acres and all without a crowded feeling!

The moderating effect of the adjacent Roanoke Sound and the nearby ocean make winter viewing particularly pleasant. I have rated the plants for sale in season no lower than third for the entire mid-Atlantic region. The adjacent attractions at Fort Raleigh National Park make a full day's enjoyment possible, and there is an evening, summertime play about the Lost Colony.

Personal Impression. One may dwell on the pervasive attention to history there or on the extraordinary diversification of garden design and plant material, but I go frequently to the Elizabethan Gardens simply because they are beautiful. The staff and volunteers maintain the grounds marvelously. Easily one of the top ten gardens in the Region for public viewing.

(7) Greenfield Park

P.O. Box 1810
City of Wilmington Dept. of Parks
Wilmington, NC 28402
(919) 341-7855
Hours: the grounds are open daylight hours, year round.

Overview. This 180-acre recreational and cultural complex in southeastern North Carolina has widely dispersed many informal botanical attractions throughout its ample grounds. The long bloom season supports the overall public recreation of the Park.

Directions. Locate Wilmington near the southeast NC coast. Rte. 421 runs through town; proceed southeast on it into town and you cannot miss it on your left.

Historical Profile. Originally known as Greenfields Plantation under the early 1700s ownership of Dr. Samuel Green, the property passed to the McIlhenny family who completed two grain mills by the pond now called Greenfield Lake. Ownership and use changed frequently until 1925 when the City of Wilmington purchased it. To provide work for the unemployed in the Great Depression of the 1930s, the citizens of Wilmington raised about $110,000 over two winters to employ 1500

Ownership	Pet on leash	Brochure
public, town	yes	no
Size	**Weddings**	**Ed. programs**
180 acres	yes	no
Rest rooms	**Sell plants**	**Spec. events**
yes	no	yes
Pay phone	**Membership**	**Labeling**
yes	yes	no
Visitor center	**Gift shop**	**Volunteers**
no	no	many

Fees	Off street parking
no	yes
Library for public	**Ext. photo limits**
no	no
Garden clubs active	**Food**
yes	in season

people for the construction of a scenic, 5-mile perimeter road around the park; originally known as Community Drive, it is now more commonly known as Lake Shore Drive. Also in the 1930s, the first production greenhouse was constructed for bedding plant propagation and rose cultivation--civic associations still maintain the rose garden. City staff, civic associations and an active volunteer corps still collaborate on the maintenance of the grounds and gardens.

Description. From a local newspaper article: "Greenfield Gardens and Drive now have an estimated number of plants and trees far in excess of a million. Azaleas, some of them immense, are possibly the largest and most beautiful attraction in the park. Thousands of different trees are spread along the shore. These constitute an impressive sight for the visitor. Cypress trees are adorned with graceful hanging Spanish moss. Literally hundreds grow in the lake, thus affording a perfect background for flowering trees and shrubs along the road.

"In addition to the natural features that include a nature trail and fragrance garden, the lake offers seasonal canoe and paddleboat rentals, play areas, an amphitheater, picnic areas, two tennis courts, two picnic shelters, concessions and restroom facilities ... a far cry from the plantation and mill pond days in the lake's rich history."

There is a continuous procession of color from tulips to azaleas and dogwoods to roses and summer annuals to late summer crape myrtles to fall foliage. In addition to the rose garden, the seasonal beds and the widely dispersed azaleas and crape myrtles, there is a fragrance garden by the amphitheater. When you plan your trip, remember that Wilmington is the southernmost city in the Region; that and its proximity to the ocean provide a spring bloom well in advance of the rest of the Region.

Personal Impression. It is difficult to consider the community involvement in the development and maintenance of Greenfield Park without concluding that this is a park Of the People, By the People and For the People.

(8) Greensboro Beautiful
Parks & Recreation Department
P.O. Box 3136
Greensboro, NC 27402-3136
(910) 373-2558
Hours: the grounds of the three sites are open daylight hours, year round.

Overview. Charming, wild and stately. Those are the three descriptors of the three major sites of Greensboro Beautiful in central North Carolina--the Bicentennial Garden, the Bog Garden and the Arboretum. The non-profit Greensboro Beautiful, Inc. collaborates with the City of Greensboro "to promote, enhance, and maintain our community's visual and environmental quality." As a set, the three gardens offer all-seasons enjoyment with diversified flora in designs covering the spectrum from formal to natural.

Directions. I-85 and I-40 enter Greensboro from the east together, then fork inside the City; stay with I-40, exiting at 217B onto High Point Rd. for just over a mile; turn left onto Patterson St. (Rte. 6) for less than a mile, then right onto Holden Rd. for 2.5 miles whereupon you can see the Bicentennial Garden on your right; turn right onto Cornwallis Dr. for a block, ignoring the small parking area off it; turn right onto Hobbs St. and park immediately on your right. This is the Bicentennial Garden's parking lot and the Bog Garden is just across the street.

To reach the Arboretum, turn right from the parking lot onto Hobbs St. for 1.4 miles to West Market St.; turn left onto it for 0.4 miles to the Arboretum on your right.

Historical Profile. Greensboro Beautiful, Inc., a non-profit organization of volunteers and an affiliate of the (national) Keep America Beautiful, Inc., has instituted over 100 environmental protection and beautification projects in Greensboro since its inception in 1968. These include a unique public/private partnership with Greensboro Parks and Recreation Department in the creation of the Bicentennial Garden (1976), the Bog Garden (1991) and the Greensboro Arboretum (1991), which are described here.

Ownership	Pet on leash	Brochure
public[1]	discouraged	yes
Size	**Weddings**	**Ed. programs**
see text	yes	planned
Rest rooms	**Sell plants**	**Spec. events**
in Arboretum	no	Arbor Day
Pay phone	**Membership**	**Labeling**
no	yes	yes
Visitor center	**Gift shop**	**Volunteers**
no	no	an army
Fees		**Off street parking**
no		yes
Library for public		**Ext. photo limits**
no		no
Garden clubs active		**Food**
many		no

[1]*Planning and management are a joint public/private responsibility.*

Description. The Bicentennial Garden features flowering plants in 7.5 acres; the Bog Garden features natural, native plants in a 7-acre swampy habitat; the Arboretum features woody plants over 17 acres.

As part of the 1976 Bicentennial Celebration, Greensboro Beautiful converted a city-owned flood plain into a public formal garden featuring "...flowering and deciduous shrubs, and bulb and annual beds containing mass and design plantings, which bring color to the garden throughout the year." Distinct areas include a rose garden, a wildflower trail, a fragrance garden, a camellia/azalea area and two rock gardens. "Charming" is the descriptor I wrote in my notes during my first visit there, and I underlined it during the second.

The Bog Garden takes the visitor right into the wild bog and over the fringe of the lake on a half-mile elevated wooden walkway. There is extensive labeling of "trees, shrubs, ferns, bamboo, wildflowers, and many other plants and wildlife inigenous to a bog." Mallards and hungry catfish commanded the attention of visitors on my last visit.

The stately Arboretum lies below, and partially on, a steep slope in the larger Lindley Park, a recreational complex. The heavily wooded slope and the open plain at its base provide a wide selection of terrains for various collections, including: seasonal bloomers; conifers; ground cover; sun-loving plants; compact trees; cold-hardy plants; moisture-loving plants; vines; and shade plants. Special areas include a hosta garden, a wildflower trail, a rhododendron garden and a very large butterfly garden with fountain.

Group tours are by prearrangement and a new educational program is in preparation.

Personal Impression. Each of these three gardens is significant unto itself, well-maintained and absolutely beautiful. I decided to write them up together because their unique, common feature is their joint public/private sponsorship. More so than anywhere else in the Region, Greensboro offers medium-sized cities a role model for public/private collaboration with nearly three decades of accomplishments that any city *can* emulate, and all probably *should*.

---

(9) The North Carolina Arboretum

P.O. Box 6617
Asheville, NC 28816
(704) 665-2492
Hours: the grounds and visitor center open 8:30-4 Mon. through Fri., year round; weekend hours are being considered for the future.

Overview. This is a brand new, still developing arboretum which organizationally is an interinstitutional facility of the University of North Carolina, located in the Bent Creek Research and Demonstration Forest of the Pisgah National Forest. The visitor center and several garden areas are open now with major expansions planned to begin in the spring of 1994.

Directions. Locate Asheville in the western part of the State and I-26 running southeast from it. Take Exit 2, Rte. 191--Brevard Rd., and continue south for two miles, then follow directional signs.

Historical Profile. This 424-acre tract of land was partially farmed early in this century as part of the Biltmore Estate. Passing to government ownership in the 1930s, it was given arboretum status by the State Legislature in 1986 and has been in the early stages of development since then.

Description. As of January 1, 1994, a master plan had been completed and several parts of it had been implemented, including: a major Visitor Education Center; a production greenhouse and maintenance area; a Plants of Promise Garden (featuring both new and too-long-overlooked plants); a perennial border near the greenhouse; a stretch with 50,000 recent plugs of wildflowers and native grasses; miles and miles of trails through native woodlands; and a wheelchair access garden. The bloom season for the combined informal and formal areas proceeds from March (crocuses and daffodils) into the fall.

Ownership	Pet on leash	Brochure
public, state	discouraged	yes
Size	**Weddings**	**Ed. programs**
424 acres	not yet	yes
Rest rooms	**Sell plants**	**Spec. events**
yes	no	no
Pay phone	**Membership**	**Labeling**
no	yes	yes
Visitor center	**Gift shop**	**Volunteers**
yes	planned	yes
Fees	**Off street parking**	
no	yes	
Library for public	**Ext. photo limits**	
not yet	no	
Garden clubs active	**Food**	
no	no	

A \$4.5M development initiative will begin shortly after this writing with a 1995 completion date and will include: a display garden area near the parking lot; a set of small demonstration gardens; and an outdoor event garden around a natural amphitheater.

Planned for the future are: a visitor orientation complex; a synoptic terrace garden; a demonstration greenhouse; the core gardens, carefully integrated into a woodland setting; water gardens; horticultural therapy; and an ethnobotanical interpretive center.

Some educational programs are up and running, and will expand. Group tours by prearrangement.

Personal Impression. This promises to evolve into a highly diversified garden area with particular attention to demonstration and education. I find it fascinating to watch the newcomer gardens make their dreams come true.

(10) North Carolina Botanical Garden

(UNC-Chapel Hill)
CB#3375 Totten Center
University of North Carolina
Chapel Hill, NC 27599-3375
(919) 962-0522

◀Indoors at Longwood
Gardens (PA)

▲ The Lewis Ginter Botanical Garden (VA)

▲ *Indoors at Brookside Gardens (MD)*

A lush border at Leaming's Run (NJ) ▼

▲ *Fall at Ladew Topiary Gardens (MD)*

Sandhills Community College (NC) ▼

◀ *Hershey Gardens (PA)*

▲ *A panorama at Nemours (DE)*

▲ Dumbarton Oaks (DC)

Spring at UNC-Charlotte (NC) ▼

▲ *Indoors at the Norfolk Botanical Garden (VA)*

The parterre at Tryon Palace (NC) ▼

◀ *Indoors at Phipps
Conservatory (PA)*

Agecroft Hall (VA) ▶

▲ *Handicapped-accessible at Frelinghuysen Arboretum (NJ)*

The Biltmore Estate (NC) ▼

Hours: "The Botanical Garden Display Collections are open Monday through Friday 8:00 a.m.-5:00 p.m. throughout the year except winter holidays, and 8:00 a.m.-5:00 p.m. on weekends from mid-March to mid-November. You are invited to walk the Garden trails and visit the Coker Arboretum and Mason Farm Biological Reserve during daylight hours throughout the year."

Overview. The University of North Carolina at Chapel Hill operates this multi-site botanical garden with great emphasis on natural habitat preservation, especially for plants native to the southeast. Most of the 600-acre Garden is slightly off the main campus except for the less natural, 5-acre Coker Arboretum, which is on it. The garden is open to visitors year round.

Ownership	Pet on leash	Brochure
pub., state coll.	no	yes
Size	**Weddings**	**Ed. programs**
600 acres	yes	yes
Rest rooms	**Sell plants**	**Spec. events**
yes	yes	yes
Pay phone	**Membership**	**Labeling**
no	yes	some
Visitor center	**Gift shop**	**Volunteers**
yes	yes	many
Fees		**Off street parking**
no		yes
Library for public		**Ext. photo limits**
in Totten Center		no
Garden clubs active		**Food**
yes		no

Directions. Heading west from Durham on I-40, exit south on Rte. 15/501 for 1.5 miles to the Y, bearing left for 2.7 miles; just after the intersection with Rte. 54, turn left into the Garden. (To get to the Coker Arboretum, return to the Y, this time bearing right; in about a mile--on Franklin St.--you encounter the Arboretum beside the Planetarium on your left.)

Historical Profile. The smaller Coker Arboretum was designed by botany professor William Coker in 1903. The larger area that revolves around Totten Center (a multi-purpose building that I will call a visitor center) opened to the public in 1966.

Description. This is a university-based facility that appropriately accords priority to its teaching and research functions. The public, however, is not only welcome, but actively supportive through the non-profit Botanical Garden Foundation, Inc.

From the brochure: "The Coker Arboretum, the William L. Hunt Arboretum, the Coker Pinetum, and the Mason Farm Biological Reserve are included in the Garden's nearly 600 acres .... The main visitor area located off Old Mason Farm Road features collections of native southeastern plants arranged by habitats and more than two miles of trails through piedmont woods. Around the Totten Center there are collections of native wildflowers, ferns, carnivorous and aquatic plants, an extensive herb garden, and a plant families garden that displays representatives of major botanical groups."

The Totten Center, the nerve center of the complex, contains necessaries, a gift shop, offices and vending machines. Just off it are the mainly production greenhouses that also house the excellent carnivorous plant collection. Group tours are by prearrangement. Call for an up-to-date list of significant activities.

The smaller and less natural Coker Arboretum features stately evergreens and deciduous trees extensively underplanted with tulips, daffodils, daylilies and summer annuals. The exquisite rose garden adjacent to both the Coker Arboretum and the Planetarium is not considered part of the Arboretum.

Personal Impression. There is a bit of wild seclusion to the main section of the Garden which one does not find in less natural places. Hopefully your great-grandchildren will find it just as it is now, which is UNC's intention.

---

(11) North Carolina State University Arboretum
Department of Horticultural Science
Box 7609
Raleigh, NC 27695-7609
(919) 515-3132
Hours: the grounds open 8 to 8, 365 days a year.

Overview. North Carolina State University offers this beautiful *pot pourri* of garden styles, garden designs, plant species and collections to a fortunate public. "The primary function of the collection is to serve as a research facility to evaluate and display the widest possible range of exotic species and superior cultivars of landscape plants. Today about 5,000 species and cultivars of annuals, perennials, bulbs, vines, groundcovers, shrubs and trees are on display." Truly a premier garden, visit it any time of the year.

Directions. Locate Raleigh in central NC. From I-40 northwest of the City, take Hillsborough St. southeast to the City line. Shortly over the line, the Arboretum is on your right, across the street from the fairgrounds, on Beryl Rd. which runs parallel to Hillsborough.

Historical Profile. "Conceived in 1976 and formally dedicated in September 1980, the NCSU Arboretum grew out of a need to strengthen the Department of Horticultural Science's program in ornamentals and landscape design. Since 1978 over 5,000 different plants from around the world have been planted." The Department attributes the Arboretum's rapid growth (in the context of limited University support) to private donations and to volunteer efforts by private citizens and students.

Description. Whereas many of North Carolina's university and university-affiliated gardens specialize in native plant preservation, NCSU Arboretum emphasizes the introduction of new plants from around the country and the world, many of which are discontinued after their acceptance by sister institutions and the green industries as a whole.

Ownership	Pet on leash	Brochure
pub., univ.	no	yes
Size	**Weddings**	**Ed. programs**
8 acres	yes	many
Rest rooms	**Sell plants**	**Spec. events**
yes	no	many
Pay phone	**Membership**	**Labeling**
no	yes	yes
Visitor center	**Gift shop**	**Volunteers**
yes	no	yes
Fees	**Off street parking**	
no	yes	
Library for public	**Ext. photo limits**	
no	commercial	
Garden clubs active	**Food**	
no	no	

Some special features of the Arboretum include: the White Garden (a popular spot for weddings); the Japanese Garden (a meditative place); the Perennial Border (thousands of plants in a 300-foot long strip); the Shade House (1500 species); Dwarf Loblolly Pines; a Magnolia Collection (over 100 species); a Juniper Collection (a world reference collection). Additionally, there are a French parterre and numerous specialty gardens such as a wildflower garden, a townhouse garden, an edible garden, a water garden and a reading garden. One also finds annual trial beds, ornamental grasses, a hosta collection, a fern collection, a rose garden and *much* more.

Incredibly, all of this is distributed over 8 predominantly flat acres. This is accomplished without a feeling of overcrowding by segregating the trees from the annual displays, the perennial borders and the specialty (model) gardens. To the contrary, there is a feeling of openness to the grounds.

Group tours are by prearrangement. Call for an up-to-date listing of the frequently scheduled educational programs and special events.

Personal Impression. My gleeful reaction to the Arboretum was that I had fortuitously stumbled onto a fantastic garden playground. There is no overall design for the Arboretum with a unifying theme, there is just plenty of everything, one thing after another, each item and each area being a fascination unto itself. Everything is beautiful and well-kept and, at least during my visit, everyone there was in high spirits. This is a happy, playful place in addition to being an innovative, diversified, pioneering garden.

(12) Old Salem, Inc.
Box F, Salem Station
Winston-Salem, NC 27108

1-800-331-7018 outside NC
(910) 721-7300 inside NC
Hours: the gardens and commons open daylight hours, year round; structures, shops and restaurants also open year round except Thanksgiving, Dec. 24 and 25, and Sundays and Mondays in January.

Overview. Old Salem, near the current downtown area of Winston-Salem, is a restored late 18th and early 19th century community. Although the restoration principally features the structures of the period, general landscape restoration includes the re-creation of primarily kitchen gardens with plant material of the times and the Piedmont area of North Carolina. The community is administered by a non-profit foundation.

Directions. Locate Winston-Salem in north-central NC; I-40 cuts right through it. In the downtown area, exit I-40 at the signs to Old Salem and follow the signs to it nearby.

Ownership	Pet on leash	Brochure
private, NP	yes	yes
Size	**Weddings**	**Ed. programs**
1	yes	some
Rest rooms	**Sell plants**	**Spec. events**
yes	some	yes
Pay phone	**Membership**	**Labeling**
yes	yes	yes
Visitor center	**Gift shop**	**Volunteers**
yes	yes	yes
Fees		**Off street parking**
not for grounds		yes
Library for public		**Ext. photo limits**
no		no
Garden clubs active		**Food**
many		yes

[1]Gardens are distributed throughout the town.

Historical Profile. The Moravians, a religious group from Pennsylvania, settled Old Salem in 1766; after a century of deterioration, structural and landscape restoration began in 1972 and refinements continue to the present.

Description. Old Salem occupies about a dozen city blocks and features period houses, inns, churches & other structures that exhibit domestic lifestyles, foodstuffs, crafts and other dimensions of daily life. A modern visitor center, museum, parking area, gift shops and cafes cater to the inquisitive and famished visitor.

Be sure to obtain the "Old Salem Gardens" brochure which changes seasonally. It lists 18 garden stops throughout the district, most of which are private residence gardens. Most of these feature kitchen gardens, some with perennial borders and some with assorted fruit trees. The garden periods with period-appropriate plants range from 1759 (the Triebel garden) to 1847 (the Cape Fear Bank garden). There are also several small orchards.

Frontier life required green gardens, but native dogwoods, perennials and fruit trees did offer intermittent color throughout the season.

Perhaps the most important annual event is October's Restoring Southern Gardens Conference, cosponsored with the Southern Garden Historical Society. Also, group tours are by prearrangement.

Personal Impression. Since I include a historical profile on each garden in this guidebook, I obviously am a history buff and love places like Old Salem. If you have never tried enjoying the understanding of lifestyles in other times and places, this is a good place to start. At that time and place, gardening was associated more with survival than with aesthetics, but the latter was certainly not ignored. I think you'll like it.

---

(13) Orton Plantation Gardens

RFD 1
Winnabow, NC 28479
(919) 371-6851
Hours: the Plantation is open March through November, 8-6 daily in spring and summer, 8-5 in autumn.

Overview. A gem in the wild. The Orton Plantation near the southeastern NC coast offers an impressive set of formal and informal gardens on 20 of the estate's 30 acres. Wildlife and birdlife abound on the former rice plantation that prides itself on its enormous live oaks and overall landscaping. It's a fine, history-rich garden of the South in the mid-Atlantic region.

Directions. From downtown Wilmington in southeastern NC, cross the river to Rte. 133, which you take south to the signs for Orton Plantation.

Historical Profile. The originally small Orton House was built c. 1735, adding a second story and columns in 1840 and wings in 1910. Modest gardens began around 1910 and were enlarged to their present size in the mid-1930s. At its height, it was one of the leading rice plantations of the lower Cape Fear. The Sprunt family has continuously owned and managed the gardens from their 1910 inception.

Description. As you drive into the Plantation between two rows of enormous, moss-laden live oaks, the visitor knows there is something very special ahead, something out of the Deep South. You know that it is located in the southeasternmost corner of the mid-Atlantic region in a climate so atypical of the Region that rice plantations once flourished there. You know it is near the ocean in a desolate area along the river with the intimidating name, Cape Fear. Something different lies ahead, beyond the gnarled oaks.

A couple of hours later you realize that you have experienced a biological extravaganza so unexpected that you wonder whether you really saw what you just saw. Did you really see two monster alligators wander through the annuals?

Was that really a timid, multi-colored wood duck that zipped by just 10 feet ahead? Could unseen birds in unknown quantities really have made such a colossal din in the thick canopy overhead? Was that really a deer staring at you from behind a clump of azaleas and camellias? Where did all the butterflies come from so early in the season? What were all those unseen little things that scurried so noisily through the undergrowth? Was that really a tung oil tree?

Orton Plantation is a biological extravaganza unlike anything else in the Region. The publication, *The Story of Orton*, summarizes the biological diversity very nicely, albeit humbly: "Among the predominant species are camellias, azaleas, flowering peach, daphne, hydrangea, crape myrtle, dogwood and colorful annuals in spring and summer. Lawns and water gardens lend variety to the lush vegetation. The woodlands are devoted largely to pine forestry.

"Wildlife, including alligators, still abound, and the footprints of deer, raccoons, opossum and other wild animals can be seen each day following their nightly forays in search of food ....

Ownership	Pet on leash	Brochure
private	yes	excellent
Size	**Weddings**	**Ed. programs**
20 acres	yes	no
Rest rooms	**Sell plants**	**Spec. events**
yes	yes	no
Pay phone	**Membership**	**Labeling**
no	no	yes
Visitor center	**Gift shop**	**Volunteers**
yes	yes	no
Fees		**Off street parking**
yes		yes
Library for public		**Ext. photo limits**
no		none
Garden clubs active		**Food**
no		picnicing

"In recent years over 200 different species of birdlife have been identified in the area. Nesting of shorebirds occurs on nearby isolated beaches. Of great interest are heron, egret, ibis and brown pelican rookeries on the spoil islands of the Cape Fear River."

The gardens, of course, are tastefully distributed over 20 acres, formal beds dominated by annuals and perennials and informal path borders lined with azaleas and camellias in unknown numbers, and mixed pines and deciduous hardwoods creating a thick canopy over the upper paths. The architecture of the house (not open to the public) and the c. 1915 Luola's Chapel seems reminiscent of Tennessee Williams' deeper south. And there are ponds, lakes and lagoons in addition to the river.

Personal Impression. As you might expect, I visit a rather large number of gardens on a regular basis, and it is not often that something stuns me, but

Orton Plantation did. I'm not really sure I saw what I saw. It's a biological extravaganza.

---

(14) Raleigh Municipal Rose Garden

P.O. Box 5637
Raleigh, NC 27650
(919) 831-6840
Hours: the garden is open daylight hours, year round.

Overview. The City of Raleigh offers a first class rose garden to its citizens on 6.5 beautifully landscaped acres that the Garden shares with an outdoor amphitheatre and an indoor teaching theatre. Roses bloom from mid-May until frost. But it's more than a rose garden; the grounds also include an impressive sampling of a highly diversified set of blooming, ornamental and functional plantings. This property, virtually unknown outside Raleigh, is a real find.

Ownership	Pet on leash	Brochure
pub., city	yes	no
Size	**Weddings**	**Ed. programs**
6.5 acres	yes	no
Rest rooms	**Sell plants**	**Spec. events**
no	no	no
Pay phone	**Membership**	**Labeling**
no	no	yes
Visitor center	**Gift shop**	**Volunteers**
no	no	many
Fees		**Off street parking**
no		no
Library for public		**Ext. photo limits**
no		none
Garden clubs active		**Food**
yes		none

Directions. Find Raleigh on a central NC map and orient yourself to northwest Raleigh in the description of the NCSU Arboretum. Continue past the Arboretum on Hillsborough St. toward the center of town. Shortly after you come abreast of the NCSU campus on your right, turn left at Pogue St. to the 300 block. The Gaddy-Goodwin Teaching Theatre is on your left and the Garden is behind it.

Historical Capsule. Begun as a depression WPA project, the theatre was dedicated in 1940 and the gardens, 1951.

Description. There is a fairly large bowl behind the theatre that includes a 2000-seat amphitheatre on one side and the rose garden on the other, behind the stage. There are 60 beds with c. 1200 plants--the diversity of varieties (including All America Selections) would satisfy even the most demanding rosarian. Words cannot describe the cumulative fragrance on a humid, windless June evening. The Raleigh Rose Society contributes to the excellent condition of the beds.

But expect much more than a rose garden because the grounds contain a very large sampling of other plantings, including azaleas, forsythias, pyracantha, hollies, stately oaks, summer annuals, perennials for borders, a good selection of groundcovers, and a fountain and stone arbor under revitalization.

As much as anything, the tasteful layout and meticulous grooming create an inviting ambience, a sense of cozy seclusion.

Personal Impression. I found the Raleigh Municipal Rose Garden by mistake. I had made a wrong turn to the NCSU Arboretum and pulled onto Pogue St. to turn around. Before I could, I saw the Garden which, even at a distance, was irresistible. It's such a delightful, restful place. Why resist?

---

(15) Reynolda Gardens (of Wake Forest University)

100 Reynolda Village
Winston-Salem, NC 27106
(910) 759-5593
Hours: the grounds are open daylight hours, year round; the greenhouses open 10-4 Mon.-Fri., and seasonally on Saturdays, but close for major holidays.

Overview. Wake Forest University preserves this 126-acre garden in the context of the Thomas Sears design for the R.J. Reynolds family in the early 20th century. Four acres are formal and contain all-seasons attractions. Roses and nature trails highlight a diversified set of features.

Directions. Locate Winston-Salem in north-central NC. Exit Bus. I-40 onto Silas Creek Parkway (north) for 4.2 miles, then exit right onto Reynolda Rd. to the Gardens on your left.

Historical Profile. Reynolda Gardens, part of the original c. 1000-acre estate of R.J. Reynolds, were

Ownership	Pet on leash	Brochure
University	yes[1]	yes

Size	Weddings	Ed. programs
130 acres	yes	many

Rest rooms	Sell plants	Spec. events
yes	yes	yes

Pay phone	Membership	Labeling
?	yes	yes

Visitor center	Gift shop	Volunteers
yes	yes	yes

Fees	Off street parking
no	yes

Library for public	Ext. photo limits
no	commercial

Garden clubs active	Food
yes	yes[2]

[1]*But not in the formal gardens.*
[2]*Reynolda Village is across the parking area from the Gardens.*

112

designed in 1916 by Philadelphia architect Thomas Sears. The Mary Reynolds Babcock Foundation deeded 126 acres to Wake Forest University in 1958 for the "... maintenance of a garden having an aesthetic and educational value ...."

Description. The brochure summarizes the formal 4-acres succinctly: "The 130 acres of Reynolda Gardens contains 4 acres of formal gardens distinguished by Japanese cedars, Japanese weeping cherry trees, saucer magnolias, and English boxwood. Within the formal-garden area, labeled beds display annual and perennial flowers, vegetables, herbs, and the All-America Rose Garden, all of which demonstrate for visitors current gardening techniques and new plant varieties which are available to the home gardener."

Blooms proceed from mid-March through fall. Roses peak in June and July.

The three-compartment greenhouse serves both production and display with an emphasis on orchids, bromeliads and assorted tropicals.

The 126 informal and natural acres contain spring daffodils, dogwoods, wild-flowers, woodlands and log-lined nature trails.

Reynolda is a lively place with an impressive, ongoing series of educational and gardening-related events. Call for an up-to-date list.

Personal Impression. This is a much-frequented, casual garden that makes the visitor feel welcome from the outset. I was fortunate enough to visit while the roses were in bloom, which was a delightul experience. It's the type of garden that beckons you to return.

(16) Sandhills Horticultural Gardens
Landscape Gardening Dep't.
Sandhills Community College
2200 Airport Rd.
Pinehurst, NC 28374
(910) 695-3882
Hours: the gardens are open daylight hours, year round; Heutte Hall opens 8-5 Mon.-Fri.

Overview. The Landscape Gardening School at Sandhills Community College maintains 25 acres of mixed formal and informal/natural gardens in support of its training program. There is a world-class holly collection as well as an impressive set of thematic/specialty/demonstration gardens. Unobtrusive visitors are allowed to view the meticulously-kept grounds year round. It is a premier garden for all seasons.

Directions. Locate Sandhills in south-central NC, due east of Charlotte. Take Rte. 1 to Aberdeen; turn west onto Rte. 15/501 for 3.7 miles to the traffic circle; take first right off the circle (Rte. 21) for 1 block, then left onto Airport Rd. for 2.4 miles to the campus entrance.

Historical Profile. Sandhills Community College was chartered in 1963 and instituted the Landscape Gardening School in 1968; the Sandhills Horticultural Gardens began in 1978 with the Ebersole Holly Garden, has expanded continuously to the present and has plans for future expansion.

Description. The Ebersole Holly Garden is the historical keystone of the current Gardens. It is certified by the Holly Society of America and contains 28 species and 350 different cultivars--one of the largest collections in the country. The profusion of winter color attracts a significant number of visitors.

Ownership	Pet on leash	Brochure
pub., coll.	no	yes
Size	**Weddings**	**Ed. programs**
25 acres	yes	yes
Rest rooms	**Sell plants**	**Spec. events**
yes	no	yes
Pay phone	**Membership**	**Labeling**
no	yes	excellent
Visitor center	**Gift shop**	**Volunteers**
no	no	yes
Fees	**Off street parking**	
no	yes	
Library for public	**Ext. photo limits**	
only students	no	
Garden clubs active	**Food**	
no	coll. cafeteria	

Additional gardens include: the Rose Garden (modern roses displayed in promenade fashion); the Hillside Garden (a winding rock stream with bridges, pools and waterfalls); the Sir Walter Raleigh Garden (a highly formal, 1-acre complex with the Holly Maze, the Fountain Courtyard, the Sunken Garden, the Ceremonial Courtyard and the Herb Garden); the Conifer Garden; the Fruit and Vegetable Garden (fruit trees, berries, vegetables and vineyard); the Annual and Perennial Garden; and the recently-added Desmond Native Wetland Trail Garden (on a wooden boardwalk). Azaleas, rhododendrons and camellias will be featured in one of the future gardens. On-site greenhouses are mainly for production and student instruction.

In addition to this significant set of variably designed gardens, one is impressed with plant care. Especially individual conifers, hollies and flowering shrubs are displayed separately, rather than in contiguous clusters, and give every evidence of considerable individualized care--as if each plant is a precious work of art. The Gardens are unsurpassed in labor-intensity in the Region.

The training program, which uniquely requires an apprenticeship, has received national recognition. Yet, although the principal purpose of the Gardens is student instruction, the program integrates into the broader community through the Sandhills Horticultural Society which produces financial support, sponsorship of events and volunteers. (Call for dates of events.) There is no "visitor center," but visitors should sign in at Heutte Hall, which adjoins the gardens.

Personal Impression. I have met several graduates of the Sandhills program at gardens included in this guidebook. Without exception, they describe their training in superlatives. Visiting the gardens reveals why: there is a very evident commitment to excellence there.

---

(17) Sarah P. Duke Gardens
Duke University
Durham, NC 27706
(919) 684-3698
Hours: the gardens open daily 8 a.m. to dusk, year round.

Overview. Sarah P. Duke, wife of one of the University's founders, is memorialized in this 55-acre wonderland which is dedicated to gardening as an art form. Designed by landscape architect Ellen Shipman, the Terraces in a large bowl keystone the gardens which have grown to include formal and informal, landscaped and woodland gardens with over 1500 kinds of plants and four miles of allees, walks and pathways. Ornamental, native and Asiatic plants are featured.

Ownership	Pet on leash	Brochure
priv., univ.	yes	excellent
Size	**Weddings**	**Ed. programs**
55 acres	yes	no
Rest rooms	**Sell plants**	**Spec. events**
yes	occasionally	no[1]
Pay phone	**Membership**	**Labeling**
no	yes	yes
Visitor center	**Gift shop**	**Volunteers**
no	no	yes
Fees	**Off street parking**	
no	yes	
Library for public	**Ext. photo limits**	
no	[2]	
Garden clubs active	**Food**	
no	no	

[1]*Special events are generally not announced.*
[2]*Do not obstruct flow with tripods; give courtesy notice to the University if you publish a shot; obtain prior approval for a major, on-site photographic session.*

Directions. One may approach Duke's West Campus from any direction and enter the garden area from several sides. Your best bet is simply to drive to the campus (clearly identifiable in west-central Durham on road maps) and ask anyone for directions to the *main* entrance, which has off-street parking.

Historical Profile. The Terraces were a formal, romantic composition of the late 1930s and remain the most popular attraction in the Gardens. Growth has been continuous with the major Blomquist Garden of Native Plants added in the 1960s and the innovative Asiatic Arboretum initiated in 1985. Recently considerable attention has focused on

115

wheelchair access; the current brochure uniquely accents wheelchair-accessible routes in red.

Description. The overall landmass distinctly features the Terraces; two large, open meadows on either side of it; the large Blomquist Garden; the larger Asiatic Arboretum; and woodlands. Smaller features dot the landscape.

Start with the Terraces. Between the wisteria-covered pergola at the summit and the fishpond at the base is an amphitheatre-shaped bowl with steeply terraced rows of beds featuring tulips in spring, annuals in summer and mums in fall. The upward view from the far side of the fishpond is particularly stunning.

An intricate set of winding pathways takes one through the Blomquist Garden of Native Plants, containing c. 850 species and varieties. A highly regarded collection of southeastern wildflowers is tastefully displayed in a woodland setting.

The 20-acre Asiatic Arboretum, still under development, features c. 300 species and cultivars of trees and shrubs from the Far East. Most of the large trails through it and around the large pond in it are wheelchair accessible.

Smaller, but still charming, attractions include the rose garden, the rock garden and the iris garden. The diversity of plant material is considerable and something is at prime in all seasons. Visit any time.

Personal Impression. This is a mature, one-stop garden, containing something for virtually any taste. I was particularly intrigued with how the landscaping simultaneously accented feelings of openness and heavy forestation. And, of course, the Terraces are a gardening landmark for the entire east coast.

(18) Tanglewood Park

P.O. Box 1040
Clemmons, NC 27012
(910) 766-0591
Hours: open 24 hours a day, year round; new visitors not admitted after dusk.

Overview. This county-owned recreational complex in central North Carolina occupies 1150 rolling acres and offers a more diverse botanical dimension to family recreation than any other recreational complex in the Region. The Park accommodates both day visitors and overnight guests at the campground or motel. Gardens are principally informal and range from a small annuals bed to a sizeable Piedmont Arboretum.

Directions. Locate Winston Salem in central North Carolina. Taking I-40 west from it, take Exit 182 and follow signs to the nearby entrance.

Historical Profile. Settled in 1757 and farmed by William Johnson, the site was named after Hawthorne's Tanglewood Tales. The Reynolds (tobacco) family purchased it in 1921 and, 30 years later, deeded it to the people of Forsyth County for a recreational complex.

Ownership	Pet on leash	Brochure
pub., county	yes	yes

Size	Weddings	Ed. programs
1150 acres	yes	coming

Rest rooms	Sell plants	Spec. events
yes	no	no

Pay phone	Membership	Labeling
yes	yes	some

Visitor center	Gift shop	Volunteers
yes	yes	yes

Fees	Off street parking
yes, modest	yes

Library for public	Ext. photo limits
no	commercial

Garden clubs active	Food
yes	yes

Description. Campground, stables, motel, athletic fields, tennis courts, championship golf course, church, children's center, picnic areas, race track, concert hall--these are *some* of the attractions at Tanglewood Park. It is one of the few drive-through complexes in the Region, and one of the few places to offer bike rentals.

It contains an unusual arboretum, a place visitors can walk among Piedmont-hardy trees to decide what they want to purchase (elsewhere) to plant on their properties. There is a rose garden (800 plants) near the motor lodge, a hedged fragrance garden and a volunteer-kept annuals garden. Burning bush is found throughout the property as are ornamental grasses, flowering cherries, dogwoods, azaleas and rhododendron. There are three self-guided nature trails with audio stations for the sight-impaired. There is a wildlife viewing station.

At this writing, a beautification committee is working on a landscape theme for the whole park, so that there will be even more attractions in the future.

Personal Impression. Although I was only a day visitor, I can readily understand how a family could just disappear in there and never emerge. There is that much to do and see. A very unique place.

(19) Tryon Palace
c/o Tryon Palace Historic Sites and Gardens
P.O. Box 1007
New Bern, NC 28563
(919) 638-1560
Hours: the grounds are open 9:30-5 Mon.-Sat. and 1:30-5 Sun., year round; last entrance at 4 p.m.; same hours for Palace, Visitor Center and Gift Shop; closed Thanksgiving, Dec. 24-26 and Jan. 1.

Overview. A majestic, predominantly formal set of gardens in 18th century

English style nearly surround the regal Tryon Palace in New Bern's historic district. A very large, highly ornate parterre dominates the nearly 14 landscaped acres. The diversified flora provide the visitor with a stunning experience all year long. A premier garden complex!

Directions. Locate New Bern in southeastern NC. Proceeding south on Rte. 17 into town, turn left onto George St. (at the sign) and you are facing Tryon Palace one block away.

Historical Profile. New Bern is nestled on a pensinsula at the confluence of the Neuse and Trent Rivers. "... North Carolina's second oldest town was founded by Swiss and German settlers in 1710 and named for Bern, Switzerland." The elegant Palace, completed in 1770, reflects the world of Royal Governor William Tryon in North Carolina's first capital. Calamitously, it burned to the ground in 1798 and was reconstructed in the 1950s from the architect's original plans, along with adjacent structures in the historic district.

Without the original garden plans, an 18th century, formal, English-style garden was created predominantly with American period plants. In 1992, however, a copy of the original garden plan was found in Caracas, Venezuela; it had been acquired by visiting Francisco de Miranda in 1783. At this writing, it has not been decided whether modifications will be made in the current gardens based on the discovery.

Description. The parterre garden mentioned above is called the Maude Moore Latham (a restoration donor) Memorial Garden. Clipped yaupon holly edgings surround a seasonal procession of tulips, summer annuals and mums in the beds, and the whole is flanked with

Ownership	Pet on leash	Brochure
pub., state	no	excellent
Size	**Weddings**	**Ed. programs**
14 acres	no	yes
Rest rooms	**Sell plants**	**Spec. events**
yes	excellent	yes
Pay phone	**Membership**	**Labeling**
yes	yes	some
Visitor center	**Gift shop**	**Volunteers**
yes	excellent	some
Fees		**Off street parking**
yes		yes
Library for public		**Ext. photo limits**
no		commercial
Garden clubs active		**Food**
no		yes[1]

[1]Next to the cutting garden.

oleander, gardenia and dahoon holly. In size, style and maintenance, it is unsurpassed in the Region. Stunning.

One leaves the parterres for Hawk's Allee (includes a fine collection of statuary) and then to the Pleached Allee (holly over an archway) and to the Wilderness Walk (naturalized garden segments were innovative in 18th century England).

118

The Walk encircles the large, oval South Lawn which stretches away from the Palace and toward the Trent River.

Two formal privy gardens grace either side of the Palace. To the west is a small, yaupon holly parterre garden; to the east is the Kellenberger Garden, hedged by germander around seasonal beds. Further east of the latter is a very large kitchen garden with espaliered trees inside the wall.

Scattered throughout are lesser garden areas, a gift shop, a nursery, a blacksmith shop, a cannon, a darlington oak allee, a stately courtyard, a smoke house, a classical temple, gorgeous brickwork, fine ironworks, and *much* more. All around the magnificent Palace, which deserves its name. Along the northern perimeter are other restored houses and the museum shop. Across the street, one encounters other restorations and the visitor center. To the side of the center, one finds a cutting garden, a boxwood garden and a small parterre.

The description above merely highlights some principal features. Please be advised that this is a very large complex of attractions of consistently high quality and careful maintenance that will consume a full day to appreciate. Moreover, the complex is harmoniously beautiful--the gardens, Palace and other features complement each other tastefully.

Educational programs and special events proceed throughout the year. Call for a schedule of events. The selection of plants for sale is among the best in the entire region. Gift shops offer quality merchandise. Fees are staggered according to whether you want to see the gardens only, to tour the Palace as well or to enjoy the entire complex.

Personal Impression. Hopefully I will not sound repetitious, but this historic complex blends quantity and quality in a beautiful and tasteful manner. The complex depicts high society in the 18th century, and the exquisite gardens there enhance the regal ambience of the times. I recommend it highly.

---

(20) UNC at Charlotte Botanical Gardens

Biology Department
University of North Carolina at Charlotte
Charlotte, NC 28223
(704) 547-2555
Hours: the gardens open daylight hours, year round; the greenhouse complex opens weekdays 9-4 and closes for some holidays.

Overview. The Biology Department at UNC-Charlotte offers an outdoor garden complex featuring shrubs (esp. rhododendron) in a woodland setting; a greenhouse complex featuring orchids, various tropicals and pitcher plants; and an herbarium. Garden design is predominantly informal/natural, and winter plantings make it an all-seasons garden both indoors and outdoors.

Directions. Locate on a map Charlotte and I-85 entering it from the northeast. UNC-Charlotte is nestled at the confluence of I-85 and Rte. 49. Enter the campus from Rte. 49 and bear right immediately to Mary Alexander Rd. which passes between the outdoor gardens and the greenhouse complex. Park in lot #2 or on a meter.

Historical Profile. The Van Landingham Glen and the herbarium began in 1966; the Susie Harwood Garden began in 1979; the McMillan Greenhouse began in 1983.

Description. With donations from Ralph Van Landingham, the namesake Glen opened as a rhododendron garden in 1966. Under a high canopy of oaks, hickories, maples and poplars and a lower growth of dogwoods, sourgums, hemlocks and redbuds, the visitor finds one of the largest and most diverse rhododendron collections in the southeast. Two trails of different length take one through over 800 species of indigenous trees, shrubs and wildflowers, and more than 50 species of wild ferns. The rhododendrons number in the thousands. Excellent self-guiding brochures are available at the Greenhouse complex.

The Susie Harwood (Ralph's mother) Garden lies next to

Ownership	Pet on leash	Brochure
pub., univ.	no	several
Size	**Weddings**	**Ed. programs**
10[1]	yes	2
Rest rooms	**Sell plants**	**Spec. events**
yes	occasionally	2
Pay phone	**Membership**	**Labeling**
no	yes[2]	yes
Visitor center	**Gift shop**	**Volunteers**
no	no	yes
Fees		**Off street parking**
no		yes
Library for public		**Ext. photo limits**
in greenhouse		no[3]
Garden clubs active		**Food**
yes		coll. cafeteria

[1]The Glen, 7 acres; Harwood 3 acres; 4,000 sq. ft. greenhouse
[2]Although teaching and research are the principal purposes of the Gardens, there is a surprisingly high degree of community outreach. The best way to stay informed of upcoming events is to become a Garden Associate and receive the excellent quarterly newsletter.
[3]Give courtesy notice if you use a shot.

the Glen with more well-defined beds under a broken canopy, and parts of it feature a semi-Oriental motif. The international plant selection includes trees, shrubs, vines, annuals, perennials, bulbs, succulents and aquatic plants. Winter plantings (e.g., holly, witch hazel, camellias) yield to bulbs and other spring bloomers (e.g., azaleas, viburnums), then to summer annuals and crape myrtles, and finally to fall perennials and arboreal splendor. It truly is an all-seasons garden over about three acres.

The McMillan Greenhouse maintains five growing environments with 4000 sq. ft. under glass. Orchids adorn one entire compartment. The largest compartment features a simulated tropical rain forest containing c. 75 families and c. 400

120

species, including one of the largest epiphyte collections I have seen. Bromeliads, ferns, cacti and succulents are well-represented. The enclosed courtyard includes a world-class pitcher plant collection. Occasional plant sales are located here. It's a fascinating complex. A small library is available for on-site reference.

The herbarium in an adjacent building, open to the public on weekdays, contains over 20,000 preserved specimens of native and introduced plants.

The quarterly newsletter, *Gardens Associates Quarterly*, links the University with the community in a highly readable fashion. A recent issue, for instance, provides considerable detail on butterfly and hummingbird gardens.

Personal Impression. I have found in my travels a very rough correlation between how meticulously a garden is groomed and how relaxed I felt. It's an inverse relationship--I feel most comfortable in the casually maintained gardens. This is an exception. The grounds and greenhouses are hospital-clean, but the ambience is warm and inviting.

My visit there coincided with the overlapping bloom seasons of the azaleas, viburnums and rhododendrons. My wife and I had to force ourselves to leave. Magnificent!

---

(21) Wing Haven (Gardens & Bird Sanctuary)

c/o Wing Haven Foundation
248 Ridgewood Ave.
Charlotte, NC 28209
(704) 331-0664
Hours: open 3-5 Tue. and Wed. and 2-5 Sun., year round.

Overview. Both formal and informal gardens on this four-acre preserved estate offer delight to humans and food/shelter for birds. From the brochure: "In 1970, the Clarksons made a gift of the gardens to Wing Haven Foundation, Inc., so that the gardens would remain open to the public. The purpose of the Foundation is: 'to maintain and develop a sanctuary for wild birds and animals for the education of the general public; to establish and maintain gardens and grounds for the benefit and enjoyment of the community; to educate the public on horticultural and wildlife subjects and stimulate interest in the beautification of the geographic area.'" It's worth your attention any time of the year.

Directions. Locate Charlotte near the South Carolina border; I-77 runs north/south through the City; exit east onto Woodlawn, then left onto Selwyn, and left onto Ridgewood to Wing Haven.

Historical Profile. Elizabeth and Edwin Clarkson purchased for their residence little more than a red clay field in a newly developed section of town in 1927. Over the next 60 years, they created an intensely planted, formal and informal set of gardens for the dual purpose of human delight and haven for birds. The Foundation received the property in 1970 and has maintained it for the public since then. (The Clarksons continued residence there until 1989.)

Description. Two perpendicular axes divide the property into quadrants and provide two unobstructed views of the length and width of the garden, but these are the only unobstructed views. Tall hedging breaks each quadrant into a set of small, isolated "rooms" connected by a set of circuitous paths. A leisurely stroll through it all takes an hour and leaves the visitor feeling that there's *much* more than four acres there.

Garden design ranges from a herb parterre and a boxwood edged rose garden on the formal side to completely informal and naturalized in the far corner. In all cases, the planting is dense, in spite of the loss of dozens of trees and their undergrowth in a recent hur-

Ownership	Pet on leash	Brochure
private, NP	no	yes
Size	Weddings	Ed. programs
4 acres	yes	yes
Rest rooms	Sell plants	Spec. events
yes	yes	yes
Pay phone	Membership	Labeling
no	yes	yes
Visitor center	Gift shop	Volunteers
yes	yes	many
Fees		Off street parking
no		yes
Library for public		Ext. photo limits
yes		commercial
Garden clubs active		Food
?		no

ricane. The diversity of plant material is incredible for the size of the property, ranging from native wildflowers to introduced exotics such as the Chinese parasol tree. Every nook seems filled with statues, ponds and fountains, benches, pergolas, a sundial and other garden ornaments. Educational programs for children and a speakers bureau reach into the community, and spring/fall open houses concentrate festivities and plant sales. Group tours by prearrangement.

Personal Impression. Probably this is the most densely planted garden in the region, almost tropically dense but without a feeling of overcrowding. It is a lovely garden with a strong dose of something quite intangible. It is the home of a loving couple whose decades of birthday, anniversary and Christmas gifts to each other dot the garden. Volunteer guides tell of the bluebird that chose to live indoors with them for eight years. And there was the sick robin who recovered in winter, too late to continue its southerly migration; a newspaper plea for travel assistance was answered by an airline which released the bird in Florida. And there was Daphne the Rabbit ....

What happens when a couple dies after a lifetime of devotion to their garden and to their winged friends? A small army of volunteers keeps the garden open and maintained. Nine thousand visitors a year come from 45 states and 20 countries. And, on a typical day, 30-40 species of birds come for a visit! That's what.

Chapter 5
Pennsylvania

**Phipps Conservatory (16) and the Pittsburgh
Civic Garden Center (17) are in Pittsburgh in
the western part of the State (not shown).**

★ *(7)*
Harrisburg

(5)

(20) *(8)* *(15)*
(10) *(1)* *(2)* **Philadelphia**
(4) *(6)(9)(12)*
(13)(14)
(11) *(3)* *(19)* *(18)* *(21)*

(1) Appleford
*(2) Arboretum of the Barnes
    Foundation*
(3) Brandywine Conservancy
*(4) Colonial Pennsylvania
    Plantation*
(5) Delaware Valley College
*(6) Fairmount Park
    Horticulture Center*
(7) Hershey Gardens
(8) The Highlands
(9) Historic Bartram's Garden
(10) Jenkins Arboretum

(11) Longwood Gardens
(12) The Maxwell Mansion
(13) Morris Arboretum
*(14) Pennsylvania Horticultural
     Society*
(15) Pennsbury Manor
(16) Phipps Conservatory
*(17) Pittsburgh Civic Garden
     Center*
*(18) Scott Arboretum
     (Swarthmore College)*
(19) Tyler Arboretum
(20) Welkinweir Preserve
(21) Wyck

Pennsylvania has a highly varied, well-balanced set of gardens. Longwood Gardens and Phipps Conservatory are the State's mega-gardens. Colonial gardens include Colonial Pennsylvania Plantation, Historic Bartram's Garden and Pennsbury Manor. The Maxwell Mansion and Wyck are 19th century restorations. Twentieth century estate gardens include the Arboretum of the Barnes Foundation, Appleford and the Jenkins Arboretum. The Highlands represents emerging gardens. The Pittsburgh Civic Garden Center and Fairmount Park Horticulture Center lead urban-based beehives of activity. Intrinsically beautiful gardens are represented by Hershey Gardens and the Pennsylvania Horticultural Society. Academically-based gardens include Delaware Valley College, the Morris Arboretum (U.PA.) and the Scott Arboretum (Swarthmore College). And the Brandywine Conservancy, the Tyler Arboretum and Welkinweir Preserve present their attractions in the broader context of conservation and preservation.

American horticulture traces its roots to the greater Philadelphia area in general and to the Quaker influence in particular; consequently, there is an overloading of gardens from that area.

Note: some of the (215) telephone area codes for these gardens will be changing to (610) during the year following the publication of this guidebook.

---

(1) Appleford
(also known as the Parsons-Banks Arboretum)
770 Mt. Moro Rd.
Villanova, PA 19085
(610) 527-4280
Hours: open daylight hours every day, all year for grounds; house (visitor center) open only by appointment.

Overview. This preserved, 22-acre, twentieth century estate garden and bird sanctuary designed by Thomas Sears tastefully combines a variety of formal and informal/natural plantings which bloom from spring to fall in a fine, old, heavily wooded, moderately hilly suburb of Philadelphia. The property is publicly owned, but significantly managed and maintained by volunteers, and includes a restored, early Pennsylvania farmhouse.

Directions. Locate Villanova on the map, a half dozen miles west of the Philadelphia border. From Route 30 in Villanova (the major thoroughfare), turn northeast onto Spring Mill Rd. for about three blocks, then left onto Old Gulph Rd., then almost immediately right onto Mt. Moro Rd; the marked entrance is on your left shortly.

Historical Profile. Originally a land grant in 1682 from William Penn to James Moore, the estate underwent numerous changes in size and uses until 1928 when the Parsons family purchased the property, restored the old farmhouse and retained Thomas Sears to design the grounds and gardens. Willed to the lower Merion Township in 1973, the grounds opened to the public in the mid-1970s.

Ownership	Pet on leash	Brochure
public[1]	yes	yes
Size	**Weddings**	**Ed. programs**
22 acres	yes, for fee	no
Rest rooms	**Sell plants**	**Spec. events**
in house	annually	annual plant sale
Pay phone	**Membership**	**Labeling**
no	yes	some
Visitor center	**Gift shop**	**Volunteers**
house	no	extensive use
Fees		**Off street parking**
none for grounds		yes
Library for public		**Ext. photo limits**
no		no
Garden clubs active		**Food**
meet there		none; no picnicing

[1]*Significant private management.*

Description. Sears' design called for a set of formal gardens around the residence, yielding to a more natural landscape for the larger property accented by a rippling stream (with small falls) that feeds an upper pond (claimed by Canada geese in fall) and a lower pond (claimed by mallards).

Immediately around the house are a boxwood maze; a rose garden with statuary; an enclosed, small lawn with perennial borders; a terrace with shrub borders and a production greenhouse.

A seasonal border along the road leads to the larger property with stream and ponds, meadows and naturalized plantings of bulbs (especially daffodils), shrubs (esp. rhododendrons, azaleas and lilacs) and ornamental fruit trees. The overall diversity of genera, species and varieties is considerable. A sampler: wisteria, mums, dogwoods, lantana, hibiscus, pansies and wildflowers.

The house is available at reasonable cost for social and business meetings, and local garden clubs meet there; free tours are available by appointment. There is an annual plant sale.

Personal Impression. This is a cozy, casual, warm property that is very pleasant to visit and, perhaps, to meditate in such quiet surroundings.

---

(2) Arboretum of the Barnes Foundation

57 Lapsley Lane
Merion, PA 19066
(610) 664-8880
Hours: the grounds open 9:30-4:30, Mon.-Fri.; closed most holidays.

Overview. The Barnes Foundations maintains this 12-acre, preserved and enhanced, 20th century estate garden in support of its teaching program. It combines formal and informal landscaping and prides itself on its great diversity of all seasons genera and species.

Directions. From the intersection of Routes 30 and 1 on the border of Philadelphia west of the center of the City, proceed northeast on Rte. 1 to St. Joseph's University on your right; across the street from it, enter Lapsley Lane and you find the Arboretum in a block. The entrance to it is on the other side of the block.

Historical Profile. Joseph Lapsley Wilson owned the property from 1880 to 1922, introducing a variety of trees in the 1880s. When he sold the estate to Dr. and Mrs. Barnes in 1922, preservation of the trees was a condition of sale. Mrs. Barnes not only preserved them, but added more trees, shrubs, wildflowers and ferns within the overall design of Frank A. Schrepfer, Professor of Landscape Architecture at the University of Pennsylvania. Landscaping was essentially complete by 1933 and opened to the public in 1985.

The Barnes Foundation received its charter as an educational institution in 1922; the Arboretum School is across the street and uses the Arboretum in support of its courses of instruction.

Description. The centenarian trees, especially around the perimeter, provide a stately ambience for the largely open areas in the center.

The large number of small gardens and special plantings is mainly confined to the far half of the grounds from the entrance. There are collections of lilacs, peonies, dwarf conifers, woody vines and viburnums. The small gardens include a rose garden, shrub garden, rock garden, heath and heather garden, ornamental rosaceous shrubs, and the E.T. Wherry Memorial Garden--Appalachian herbaceous plants.

Ownership	Pet on leash	Brochure
public trust	no	yes
Size	**Weddings**	**Ed. programs**
12 acres	no	some
Rest rooms	**Sell plants**	**Spec. events**
yes	no	no
Pay phone	**Membership**	**Labeling**
no	no	yes
Visitor center	**Gift shop**	**Volunteers**
yes	no	no
Fees		**Off street parking**
no		no
Library for public		**Ext. photo limits**
no		prior approval
Garden clubs active		**Food**
no		no

The Arboretum prides itself on its diversity of attractions. From the brochure: "Among the notable trees are its specimens of *Cedrus atlantica, Cercidiphyllum japonicum, Davidia involucrata, Fagus sylvatica* cultivars, *Hovenia dulcis,* and

Ginkgo biloba. Genera well represented by large numbers of species include *Acer, Aesculus, Cornus, Ilex, Magnolia, Quercus*, and *Viburnum*. The Gymnosperms comprise twenty-four different genera ...."

A woodland area in the corner also contains a teahouse, a small pond and a profusion of wildflowers.

Personal Impression. The diversity of both design and specimens is exceeded only by the extraordinary degree of grooming. The grounds are kept in picturebook style, almost unrealistically beautiful.

(3) Brandywine Conservancy

P.O. Box 141
Chadds Ford, PA 19317
(610) 388-2700
Hours: the grounds are open daylight hours, year round; the Museum opens 9:30-4:30 daily, year round except Christmas; the restaurant opens 11-3 daily.

Overview. The Brandywine River Museum, a restored 19th century grist mill, displays works by three generations of Wyeths--Andrew, N.C. and Jamie. The five landscaped acres around the Museum contain informal and naturalized grounds with plants indigenous to the region to promote their use in home gardens and to preserve the natural history of the Brandywine Region.

Ownership	Pet on leash	Brochure
private, NP	discouraged	yes

Size	Weddings	Ed. programs
5 acres	no	occasional

Rest rooms	Sell plants	Spec. events
yes	in spring	plant sale

Pay phone	Membership	Labeling
yes	yes	some

Visitor center	Gift shop	Volunteers
yes	yes	many

Fees	Off street parking
not for grounds	yes

Library for public	Ext. photo limits
no	commercial

Garden clubs active	Food
no	yes (11-3)

Directions. The Museum is on Rte. 1 between Philadelphia and Longwood Gardens in Kennett Square. From the intersection of Routes 1 and 202, proceed 2.5 miles southwest to the entrance on your left.

Historical Profile. The Civil War-era grist mill on the banks of the Brandywine River was restored and expanded into an art museum featuring the Wyeths, opening to the public in 1971. The gardens started at that time and were dedicated in 1979 by Lady Bird Johnson.

Description. From the brochure: "... the gardens feature indigenous and some naturalized plants of the greater Brandywine region displayed in natural settings. Originally designed to screen parking areas and provide borders around the Brandywine River Museum, these demonstration gardens use wildflowers, trees and shrubs in landscaped areas. Plants are selected to provide a succession of blooms from early spring through the first killing frost. Each is located in a setting akin to its natural habitat: woodland, wetland, flood plain, or meadow." There also is a 1-mile nature trail with "tons" of wildflowers.

Some of the blooms by season:

Spring--bloodroot, creeping phlox, crested dwarf iris

Summer--sundrop, coneflower, trumpet vine

Fall--tupelo, New England aster, pink turtleheads

Winter--American holly, inkberry, northern bayberry.

Seeds are available in the gift shop. Group tours are by prearrangement.

Be sure to ask for the garden brochure at the visitor center; unless asked for, only the general museum brochure is given. It will call your attention to features that are otherwise not self-evident. For instance, there is a rainwater detention basin between the two paved parking areas that provides a wetlands habitat for several species and simultaneously contains river pollution from parking lot run-off.

Personal Impression. One has to be impressed with the Conservancy's native plant and habitat preservation role. In fact, its mission extends far beyond the Museum to thousands of acres in that region. Please inquire at the visitor center about how you can support the Conservancy's efforts.

(4) Colonial Pennsylvania Plantation

Ridley Creek State Park
Media, PA 19063-4398
(610) 566-1725
Hours: the Platation opens April-Nov., Saturday and Sunday only, 10-4; group tours by prearrangement during the week.

Overview. Public ownership and private management offer this authentically restored, 112-acre, "working-class" plantation which contrasts sharply with the genteel plantations of southern society. The grounds are completely realistic, in contrast to glamorized or romanticized, in reflection of an 18th century plantation, and reside in Pennsylvania's large Ridley Creek State Park.

Directions. Locate Media on Rte. 1 southwest of Philadelphia. Ridley Creek State Park is five miles north of Media at Rte. 1. Follow signs to the Park and, once in, to the Plantation.

Historical Profile. The enormous, state-owned Ridley Creek State Park opened in 1966. A local group of individuals, businesses and organizations formed the non-profit Bishop Mills Historical Institute in 1973 to express concern for the two-dozen historic buildings on-site. The State awarded it a lease of the current site, a farm before the Park with farming roots stretching back to the early 1700s. The Institute has managed the operation continuously to this time as a colonial, working-class farm.

Ownership	Pet on leash	Brochure
pub., state[1]	no	yes

Size	Weddings	Ed. programs
112 acres	no	general

Rest rooms	Sell plants	Spec. events
yes	occasionally	general

Pay phone	Membership	Labeling
no	yes	some

Visitor center	Gift shop	Volunteers
yes	yes	yes

Fees	Off street parking	
yes	yes	

Library for public	Ext. photo limits	
no	commercial	

Garden clubs active	Food	
yes	no	

[1]*Private management--see text.*

Description. Many colonial plantations in the South developed their stately gardens with the aid of slave labor, a considerable advantage in a labor-intensive field. In more northerly plantations such as Colonial, there simply was no potential for grandeur, and that is the type of plantation restored here, where survival supplanted affluence as the objective. Although preserved farms constitute a study population of their own, they do overlap with the garden population and Colonial balances my selection of more affluent, more southerly plantations.

Instead of attempting to restore the farm to one of the actual colonial farming families about whom little is known, the property was restored to the typical family in the area--Quaker parents, six children, a widowed grandmother, unmarried relatives, hired help--up to 15 people.

The large, stone farmhouse (authentically restored and furnished) is surrounded by a very large number of typical farm outbuildings. A pasture, sheepfold, chicken house, stable and pig pen accommodate a sample of typical farm animals.

A mixed-fruit orchard has survived foraging deer. The crop field yields corn, wheat, rye and flax for clothing. Ridley Creek creates a marshy habitat for native plants and wildlife.

The kitchen garden provides typical vegetables. Herbs for teas, dyes and medicines include mint, thyme, chicory, parsley and fennel. European imports that are now considered weeds include dock, stinging nettle and plantain. Decorative plants that also are useful include hollyhocks, columbines, nasturtiums, calendula and Queen Anne's lace.

This "living history museum" now supports itself with entrance fees, memberships and structured educational programs on the general lifestyle of the period. The larger Park provides many recreational opportunities such as picnicing, fishing, bicycling, horseback riding, tent camping and cross-country skiing.

Personal Impression. Although this is a highly interesting operation, it is also somewhat chilling to realize that the *average* family today has more time, money and plant selection for an ornamental environment than a typical colonial farming family. It makes one more appreciative of the enormous effort John Bartram must have made to rise above subsistence farming to his pioneering botanical enterprises.

---

(5) Delaware Valley College: The Henry Schmieder Arboretum

700 E. Butler Ave.
Doylestown, PA 18901
(215) 345-1500 (ext. 2244)
Hours: the Arboretum opens daylight hours, year round.

Overview. Delaware Valley College has converted its entire main campus into an arboretum, the landscaped areas covering about 60 acres. Formal and informal gardens dot the campus. The College is more receptive to visitors than most colleges in the Region.

Directions. Doylestown is due north of Philadelphia, north of the PA Turnpike. Exit the Turnpike north on Rte. 309 to Rte. 202 east to Doylestown and follow signs.

Historical Profile. Delaware Valley College was founded as the National Farm School in 1896. The campus-wide Arboretum grew steadily under the direction of Henry Schmieder, a faculty member from 1921 to 1964, and was named after him in 1962. Subsequent leadership has integrated the Arboretum into the surrounding community as fully as any educational institution in the Region.

Description. From the Summer-Fall 1993 newsletter: "Today the Arboretum serves as a center for horticultural study and design and as a teaching resource for the region. It covers approximately 60 acres of our main campus area and contains thousands of plant species, specialty gardens and landscape planting. The college also operates approximately 15,000 square feet of greenhouses."

Independent garden segments pepper the campus: the nuclear Henry Schmieder Arboretum (sassafras and sycamore trees); the Lois Burpee Herb Garden; a hedge demonstration garden; an ornamental grass collection; a rock garden; a conifer collection (dwarf); a woodland garden (azaleas and rhododendrons); a winter walk (by lake--witch hazel, etc.); a 1920s cottage garden; a "blue" garden; a "pink" garden; plus thousands of naturalized bulbs throughout the campus. Plus dogwoods. Plus various groundcovers. Plus wildflowers. Plus more.

Ownership	Pet on leash	Brochure
priv., coll.	no	coming

Size	Weddings	Ed. programs
60 acres	some	many

Rest rooms	Sell plants	Spec. events
yes	yes	yes

Pay phone	Membership	Labeling
yes	yes	good

Visitor center	Gift shop	Volunteers
no	campus	yes

Fees	Off street parking
no	yes

Library for public	Ext. photo limits
campus	none

Garden clubs active	Food
yes	campus

The calendar of educational events is as interesting as the gardens. A recent newsletter for members of the Arboretum includes lectures on fall-blooming shrubs, daylilies, rock gardening, growing perennials, rhododendrons and azaleas; it also included information on landscape exhibits, a plant sale, an advisory board to-be-formed, indoor plants, a membership drive. Additionally, annual events have drawn upwards of 50,000 people in spring. Clearly the College is not a retreat.

Personal Impression.
As this guidebook draws to a close, some general conclusions seem in order.

As a former university professor, I know that my academic peers would prefer to confine their professional activities to research and teaching pursuits that lead to rank promotion and tenture. In the botanical and related sciences, however, both teaching and research careers require a living laboratory for success, which frequently exceeds a realistic academic budget. "Community involvement" is frequently the only answer to the problem in the form of financial support, student recruitment, volunteer services and sales of plants and gifts.

As a state, only North Carolina recognizes this and, consequently, sports the finest collection of college- and university-based gardens in the Region, possibly the nation. In Pennsylvania, Delaware Valley College leads in community involvement and, possibly consequentially, has an imposing, campus-wide arboretum.

Community involvement "works"--to the benefit of college and community alike. It's a wonderful campus. Visit it.

(6) Fairmount Park Horticulture Center

P.O. Box 21601
Philadelphia, PA 19131
(215) 685-0096
Hours: grounds--7-6, seven days a week; closed for about a dozen City holidays (call to confirm).
   visitor center--7-3, seven days a week (closed holidays)
Japanese House--May - Aug., Wed.-Sun., 11-4
            --Sept. - Oct., Sat.-Sun., 11-4

Overview. The 23-acre Horticulture Center and centennial arboretum reside within the enormous, multi-purpose, 8900-acre Fairmont Park Commission complex, the largest municipally-owned park complex in the world. The Center's management not only offers a botanical facility for the public, but also hosts (and collaborates with) various other horticultural groups which, in turn, offer many on-site programs for the public. Combined indoor and outdoor attractions provide an all-seasons opportunity for interested visitors.

Directions. Locate the Schuylkill River in northwest Philadelphia with I-76 running alongside it; exit I-76 onto Montgomery Dr. heading west; the first left takes you to the fenced Horticulture Center.

Historical Capsule. In 1812, the City Fathers purchased five acres along the Schuylkill River for a reservoir and public gardens. From this humble beginning, Fairmount Park has grown to nearly ten thousand acres including recreational complexes, historic and cultural treasures, and both botanical and zoological centers.

The current Horticultural Center began as the 1876 Centennial Exhibition around the Centennial Horticultural Hall. In 1958, a Japanese house and garden were added. Finally, in 1979, the current Center opened to the public and the total 23-acre area has been continuously refined since then.

Description. The surviving plantings from the 1876 Centennial Exhibition (mainly trees of Asian, European and North American origin) are distributed principally along the fenced perimeter.

The Center buildings house the visitor center and the greenhouse complex (c. 10,000 square feet). This complex is dynamic, constantly changing for seasonal displays and very numerous special events; the functions are divided between display and production.

Immediately outside the Center, one encounters a set of small demonstration gardens. The most unique of these is Penn State's Accessible Garden. Designed, planted and maintained by visually impaired volunteers, the raised beds (wheel-chair accessible) contain "over 50 types of culinary, ornamental and medicinal herbs, perennials and annual flowers and shrubs. Signage is in large-type and braille."

Down the road is the Japanese House in the style of a late 16th to early 17th

Ownership	Pet on leash	Brochure
public--city	yes	yes
Size	**Weddings**	**Ed. programs**
23 acres	yes	yes
Rest rooms	**Sell plants**	**Spec. events**
yes	yes	yes
Pay phone	**Membership**	**Labeling**
yes	yes[1]	yes
Visitor center	**Gift shop**	**Volunteers**
yes	no	yes

Fees	Off street parking
no[2]	yes
Library for public	**Ext. photo limits**
no	no
Garden clubs active	**Food**
yes	picnicing

[1]*There are many memberships, some of which are (i) Friends of the Horticulture Center, (ii) Friends of the Japanese House and Garden, and (iii) Gift for All Seasons (plant a tree).*

[2]*There is a modest fee for the Japanese House.*

century Japanese scholar, with formal tea complex and the Shofuso Garden. The garden, collaboratively maintained by the Friends of the Japanese House and Garden, includes a bamboo grove, many traditional Japanese plants harmonized with local species, and a pond with island (stocked with koi--Japanese carp). The Friends have a full calendar of cultural and educational events throughout the year.

Scattered throughout the premises are picnic areas, an oblong reflecting pool, fountains, statuary, a one-mile woodlands walk, and various blooming beds and borders.

Interestingly, the management of the total operation is shared with many public and private groups, including sponsorship of many educational programs in addition to those above.

Plants are sold in late May and in early December. Group tours are by pre-arrangement. Call to obtain a schedule of special events throughout the year. This is a much-used facility.

So also is the larger Fairmount Park complex. A very partial list of attractions on thousands of acres includes dozens of athletic fields, miles of bridal paths and hiking trails, the zoo, the Mann Music Center, the Rodin Museum, the Philadelphia Museum of Art and what many experts consider the finest chain of restored early-American houses in the country.

Subjective Impression. The sheer size of the Fairmount Park complex is both stimulating and a little intimidating; a full day's visit will just get you started.

(7) Hershey Gardens
170 Hotel Rd.
P.O. Box 416

Hershey, PA 17033
(717) 534-3492
Hours: the gardens are open 9-5 daily, mid-April through October.

Overview. The M.S. Hershey Foundation offers the public this 23-acre, predominantly formal set of modern gardens. It is a fully diversified and meticulously groomed garden complex with spectacular blooms throughout the open season. One of the most colorful gardens in the Region.

Directions. Hershey is located due east of Harrisburg in central PA. From Harrisburg, take Route 322 east, turning north on Rte. 39 on the outskirts of Hershey and onto Hersheypark Dr. The marked access road to the Garden is on your left. The huge chocolate manufactory and nearby recreational complex are known to everybody for miles around. Once in the general vicinity, detailed directions are easily obtained.

Historical Profile. Mrs. Hershey's personal rose garden was planted in 1907. Milton Hershey transplanted it to its present site on 3.5 acres and opened it to the public in 1937. Pleased with

Ownership	Pet on leash	Brochure
private; NP	no	excellent
Size	**Weddings**	**Ed. programs**
23 acres	--	school kids
Rest rooms	**Sell plants**	**Spec. events**
yes	yes	no
Pay phone	**Membership**	**Labeling**
yes	yes	some
Visitor center	**Gift shop**	**Volunteers**
yes	yes	no
Fees		**Off street parking**
yes		yes
Library for public		**Ext. photo limits**
yes		none
Garden clubs active		**Food**
no		no

the amount of public interest, Milton expanded the site to its present size by 1941, and additions and refinements have continued to the present. Ownership and operation were placed under the M.S. Hershey Foundation in 1989.

Description. The Gardens sit near the top of a large hill and offer an infrequently encountered sense of openness. The specimen trees are widely dispersed as are the numerous horticulturally-themed gardens. Nowhere on site is there a feeling of overcrowdedness.

The self-guiding tour brochure takes the visitor past nearly a dozen garden stops: the Plant Doctor's Vegetable Garden (planted by TV's Noel Falk); the garden of shrubs (featuring summer bloomers); the Japanese garden (Shinto bridge and "gurgling" stream); the ornamental grass garden (these range in height from six inches to 20 feet); the rock garden (dwarf evergreens and over 70 varieties of holly); the herb garden (27 varieties of medicinal and culinary herbs); the hemlock room (a lawn enclosed by sheared eastern hemlocks); a memorial garden (for service men and women); a seasonal display garden (bulbs, annuals, mums--very large and *very* colorful); rose gardens (at two locations, Mrs. Hershey's 1907 roses and 8,000 additions).

Specimen trees include giant sequoia, blue atlas cedar, bald cypress, oriental spruce, copper beech and many more.

Again, everything is well spaced so that each garden stands by itself, like a museum-piece. Each garden features beauty for the sake of beauty, and does so exquisitely.

Personal Impression. I think this is the type of enormous garden the average person would love to create with Lottery winnings. Unfortunately, the average Lottery pot would not cover the expenses of six gardeners who toil endlessly to give the gardens a manicured look. (My wife and I have found these gardeners to be especially responsive to questions.) If you like formal, beautiful, colorful gardens, you can't go wrong here.

---

(8) The Highlands

7001 Sheaff Lane
Fort Washington, PA 19034
(215) 641-2687
Hours: the grounds are open daylight hours, year round; the estate house is open 9-4, Mon.-Fri.; closed major holidays.

Overview. The Commonwealth of Pennsylvania and local volunteers are collaborating on the restoration and preservation of this 200 year-old estate and its grounds. The somewhat formal gardens reflect the cumulative tastes of a succession of owners and will be refined upon the completion of a landscape master plan.

Directions. Fort Washington is northwest of central Philadelphia, just north of the PA Turnpike. From the intersection of Routes 202 and 73, go south on Rte. 73 for 3.9 miles, turning left onto the property at the sign.

Historical Profile. Anthony Morris, a wealthy Quaker lawyer, purchased the original property in 1794 and built the still-standing mansion and outbuildings by 1801. George Sheaff, the third owner in 1813, made many improvements including the crenelated stone walls, a grapery, the large pleasure garden to the east of the house, and a gardener's cottage, now called the Pink Palace, making the total estate a widely recognized showcase by the mid-19th century. Under new ownership, Philadelphia architect Wilson Eyre refined the garden plan for a pleasure garden of the 20th century. Finally, ownership of the last 44 acres passed to the Commonwealth of Pennsylvania in 1970. The Highlands Historical Society was organized in 1975 and works with the State on the restoration and preservation of the property. In 1992, a landscape firm began work on a plan that will guide further restoration and enhancement.

Description. In the summer of 1992, the Board of Trustees hired Andropogon Associates, Ltd. to prepare a landscape master plan for the Highlands, which is due about the time this guidebook is published. This means that interested viewers can watch the restoration process at work--a rare opportunity.

The large garden east of the house features herb and boxwood parterres and two rose arbors. Annuals supplement surviving perennials, bulbs (daffodils), rhododendron, fruit trees and stately hardwoods. Restoration probably will include a kitchen garden near the spring house.

The restoration challenge here differs from, for instance, Woodlawn Plantation that was beautifully created by one distinguished family and then deteriorated under unappreciative ownership, so that restoration clearly was to the original state. At the Highlands, several waves of owners contributed to the refinement of the estate and these enhancements appear as preservation-worthy as the original status. At the time I visited, preservation was leaning toward an early 20th century restoration of the grounds.

Ownership	Pet on leash	Brochure
pub., state	discouraged	general
Size	**Weddings**	**Ed. programs**
44 acres	yes	pending
Rest rooms	**Sell plants**	**Spec. events**
yes	in May	yes
Pay phone	**Membership**	**Labeling**
--	yes	pending
Visitor center	**Gift shop**	**Volunteers**
yes	no	yes
Fees		**Off street parking**
no		yes
Library for public		**Ext. photo limits**
no		commercial
Garden clubs active		**Food**
history clubs		no

Personal Impression. I have included the Highlands because it provides the viewer with an opportunity to see the restoration *process,* in contrast to the finished product. I find that exciting. Very similar to the new North Carolina Arboretum in excitement.

---

(9) Historic Bartram's Garden
54th and Lindbergh Blvd.
Philadelphia, PA 19143
(215) 729-5281
Hours: group tours (minimum of 10) may be scheduled 9-5, seven days a week, year round; for drop-in visitors, 12-4 Wed.-Fri., Nov.-April, and 12-4 Wed.-

Ownership	Pet on leash	Brochure
[1]	yes	excellent

Size	Weddings	Ed. programs
44 acres	yes	yes

Rest rooms	Sell plants	Spec. events
yes	in April	yes

Pay phone	Membership	Labeling
no	yes	some

Visitor center	Gift shop	Volunteers
yes	yes	yes

Fees		Off street parking
only for tours		yes

Library for public		Ext. photo limits
by app't		none

Garden clubs active		Food
yes		no

[1]*Publicly owned, privately managed; see text*

Sun., May-Oct.; closed major holidays.

Overview. Colonial Quakers John and William Bartram did more to popularize North American native plants both here and in Europe than anyone else in U.S. history. They established one of the first commercial nurseries in colonial America, offered the first printed catalogue, propagated more than 4000 species, filled orders from George Washington's Mount Vernon and Thomas Jefferson's Monticello, corresponded internationally, introduced hundreds of species to Europe, wandered all over the eastern half of North America collecting seeds and plants, and received international recognition from Linnaeus and King George III. Their garden is the oldest, continuously surviving botanical garden in the U.S., a premier shrine to the birth of gardening in America. Significant and meticulously accurate restoration and preservation continue to this day.

Directions. Locate on a map of Philadelphia I-95 which runs through it parallel to the Delaware River; locate also the intersection of I-95 with the Schuylkill River. Bartram's garden sits on the west bank of the river. Exit I-95 onto Island Ave./291 West, then turn right onto Lindbergh Blvd. for about three miles to the entrance on your right. Use a detailed map to get there from other directions.

Historical Profile. John Bartram (1699-1777) and son William (1739-1823) were the earliest colonial "botanists" to leave an indelible imprint on American horticulture.

John purchased 102 acres with fieldstone farmhouse from a Swedish farmer in 1728, and immediately enlarged the house. The many known species he brought back from his travels throughout the East, his international correspondence and his standard-setting nursery earned him and his traveling son international recognition.

The family maintained the gardens and the business until c. 1850, when Andrew

Eastwick purchased it for preservation. It was purchased by the city of Philadelphia in 1891 and found a permanent ownership home in 1917 in the Fairmount Park Commission. The John Bartram Association founded itself in 1893 in an advisory capacity that expanded to hiring staff during the City's financial crises in the 1970s; in 1981, the Association leased the property from the City and has managed it continuously since then. Its first accomplishment consisted of rescuing a 15-acre meadow next to the historic core from an industrial complex; the meadow contains a profusion of the daisies that allegedly interested John in his career in the first place.

Thus, the gardens never experienced a period of total neglect like so many other historic gardens. However, time and nature do take their toll and restoration must continuously accompany preservation. About 76% of the structures are fully restored at this time and most of the garden areas. Officials told me that additional restoration will be continuous into the future.

Description. John Bartram's fairly detailed 1758 sketch of his grounds has guided preservation and restoration.

Next to the house was a set of relatively small gardens in which he grew vegetables, herbs, perennials and some shrubs. The Upper Kitchen Garden today features raised beds with 78 different vegetables and herbs, re-created with period-appropriate plants. Next to it, the Common Flower Garden contained Bartram's personal favorites and included bulbs and herbaceous plants; it was and is the most colorful garden segment on the grounds, which are "greener" than most modern gardens. And next to it, the New Flower Garden functioned as a trial garden and has not yet been restored. Proceeding away from these garden segments toward the river, one encounters the Lower Garden which once contained root crops, possibly some fruits and a mix of vegetables that probably changed annually; this also awaits restoration.

The remaining, large plot of ground all the way down to the river contains over 82 different trees and shrubs. A sampler: sugar maple, indigo bush, pawpaw, Carolina allspice, atlas cedar, eastern rosebud, flowering dogwood, common fig, fothergilla, franklinia, common witch hazel, white oak, flame azalea, flowering raspberry, Canada hemlock, American wisteria. Some of these survive from the Bartrams' time, some are direct descendants and some have been re-introduced.

Educational programs include an ongoing program for schoolchildren and irregularly scheduled lectures for anyone interested. Annual events include a green sale in December and a plant sale the last weekend in April. One field trip a year explores a part of the continent the Bartrams visited. Consider becoming a supporting member; as a publicly owned operation, fees can be charged only for services such as guided tours, and the resultant limited finances constrain the rate at which the full restoration of this national treasure can proceed. Guided tours of the gardens proceed regularly.

Personal Impression. I've always thought of John Bartram as Johnny Appleseed in reverse. Instead of wandering all over the land scattering seeds, he wandered all over *collecting* seeds and plants, toting them home by the thousands and sharing them with the world. Just standing on such a significant historical site gave me an eerie feeling. Perhaps someone can convince Walt Disney to do a movie about the Bartrams so that the general public can appreciate the fact that they lived much more adventurous, lively and significant lives than even the fictional characters we've immortalized.

---

(10) Jenkins Arboretum

631 Berwyn-Baptist Rd.
Devon, PA 19333
(610) 647-8870
Hours: the grounds are open daylight hours daily, year round; the visitor center has no fixed hours.

Ownership	Pet on leash	Brochure
private; NP	no	very good
Size	**Weddings**	**Ed. programs**
46 acres[1]	yes	some
Rest rooms	**Sell plants**	**Spec. events**
yes	occasional	some
Pay phone	**Membership**	**Labeling**
no	yes	yes
Visitor center	**Gift shop**	**Volunteers**
yes	no	yes
Fees	**Off street parking**	
no	yes	
Library for public	**Ext. photo limits**	
no	commercial fee	
Garden clubs active	**Food**	
yes	no	

[1] *16 acres are for public access.*

Overview. Sixteen acres of 44 combined acres from two estates offer a variety of habitats in this heavily wooded, highly naturalized garden. A worldwide azalea and rhododendron collection sets the grounds ablaze in spring, supported by a profusion of dogwoods and wildflowers.

Directions. Devon is due west of north-central Philadelphia. Exit Rte. 202 south onto Rte. 252 (Valley Forge Rd.); shortly, Route 252 bears right sharply, but you continue straight on Valley Forge Rd. for 0.4 miles; at the fork, bear right for a block and then turn right onto Berwyn-Baptist Rd. to the entrance on your left.

Historical Profile. The Jenkins family lived on the 20-acre nucleus of the Arboretum until their deaths in 1968. Mr. Jenkins directed that a non-profit foundation be established in memory of his wife. In 1971, the Browning family added her 26 acre, adjoining property. Formal planting of the 16 naturalized areas began in 1975 and the Arboretum opened to the public in 1976.

Description. From the brochure: "The Jenkins Arboretum is located in an existing remnant of Southeastern Pennsylvania's hardwood forest. This consists predominantly of a canopy of oaks with tulip-poplar, hickory, beech, maple and other species. The shrub layer consists chiefly of members of the heath ... family including mountain laurel, pinxterbloom azalea, huckleberry and blueberry. The herb layer is composed of many different woodland wildflowers and ferns .... The stream and pond also provide habitat for a variety of flora and fauna not normally found in a woodland setting."

In July, over 350 varieties of daylilies light up the otherwise "green" season. Witch hazel and hollies provide winter color.

Personal Impression. The very dense canopy and the well-maintained grounds combine a bit of enchanted forest with a bit of "dark" forest that authors of children's books would love. I did not visit during the spring bloom of azaleas and rhododendron, but the plants are so numerous that it must be spectacular.

---

(11) Longwood Gardens

P.O. Box 501
Kennett Square, PA 19348-0501
(610) 388-6741
Hours: the outdoor gardens and conservatories open at 9 a.m. and 10 a.m., respectively, every day of the year; they close at 6, April-Oct. and at 5, Nov.-March; both frequently remain open after dark for special events and holiday displays such as summer fountain festivals and the Christmas display. Call for schedule of events.

Overview. The Region's premier garden--800,000 visitors per year can't be wrong! Pierre du Pont's early 20th century country estate garden offers an incomparable blend of indoor and outdoor, formal and informal, day and evening, internationally reknowned, all-seasons displays. It takes 175 full time and 150 part time staffers to operate the facility, plus students and volunteers, on 1050 acres. It is truly a horticultural extravaganza.

Directions. From the brochure: "Longwood Gardens is located on US Route 1, three miles northeast of Kennett Square, PA, and 30 miles west of Philadelphia in the museum-rich Brandywine Valley."

Historical Profile. The Quaker Peirce family purchased the original property from William Penn, built the Peirce house in 1730 and began planting an assortment of trees in 1798. When development threatened the trees, Pierre du Pont purchased the property in 1906 for a country home, modernized the house, introduced the flower garden walk in 1907, the open air theatre in 1913, the main conservatory in 1921, and the Italian water garden in 1931.

Mr. du Pont entertained lavishly at his estate. His gardening tastes were completely eclectic in pursuit of beauty for its own sake. He seems not to have minded having strangers drop in to see the gardens, which accelerated after the completion of the main conservatory. He created the currently managing Foundation in 1937, well before his death in 1954. Since then, the Foundation has preserved the du Pont gardens and has added to them "... in the spirit and beauty of the early twentieth century gardens of Pierre S. du Pont."

Growth and refinement have been continuous since du Pon't death. In the 1950s, the waterlily pools were added; in the 1960s, the visitor center; in the 1970s, the east conservatory; in the 1980s, the Terrace Restaurant. The 1990s have been a period of consolidation, including major renovations of the fountains and modifications in the consevatory complex.

Ownership	Pet on leash	Brochure
priv; NP	no	excellent
Size	**Weddings**	**Ed. programs**
1050 acres	no	many
Rest rooms	**Sell plants**	**Spec. events**
yes	some	many
Pay phone	**Membership**	**Labeling**
yes	no	yes
Visitor center	**Gift shop**	**Volunteers**
large	large	yes
Fees		**Off street parking**
entrance fee[1]		yes
Library for public		**Ext. photo limits**
by appointment		tripods; commercial
Garden clubs active		**Food**
yes		very good

[1]*Some special events have an add-on fee; there is a frequent visitor pass for those able to visit regularly.*

Description. About a third of the 1050 acres is devoted to public-access gardens, the remainder being devoted to service areas and to a surrounding buffer zone. After leaving the large visitor center, which contains an orientation theatre and excellent gift shop, one may turn either east or west.

To the east, one encounters the open air theatre, the Peirce-du Pont house (regular tours), Peirce's Park (200 year old trees), the large, oblong flower garden walk (April-Oct. blooms), the Italian water garden (600 jets--recently refurbished), a sizeable lake, a wisteria garden (May blooms), a peony garden (peonies and irises in spring) and a rose arbor (June blooms).

To the west, one encounters the restoration complex, the conservatory complex, the waterlilies (hardy and tropical, summer blooms), an idea garden (flowers, roses, vegetables), the main fountain garden (daily jet displays, May-Sept.), a hillside garden (March-Oct. blooms), the chimes tower/waterfall (panoramic overlook), a heath and heather area (spring and summer), a conifer knoll, a rose garden, a very large topiary (shaped hedge) garden, and a strange "eye of water" patterned after a Costa Rican structure.

On the far side of the grounds from the visitor center, natural areas provide oppotunities for a forest walk or viewing field flowers.

The conservatory complex is a world unto itself, with over *3.5 acres* under glass--a "crystal palace." The three largest rooms--the east conservatory, the main conservatory and the exhibition hall contain almost constantly-changing seasonal displays. The Christmas display (starting Thanksgiving Day) draws up to 200,000 visitors into January. Many published photos of Longwood feature these seasonal displays which are almost hypnotically beautiful. All told, there are 20 gardens under glass featuring tropicals, palms, bonsai, roses, orchids, a children's garden and more. The cascade garden and the Mediterranean garden are the newest additions. For special events, there is a ballroom and a music room, with possibly the world's loudest organ. Surrounded on three sides by the conservatory, the outdoor waterlily displays includes Victoria hybrids whose platters can attain seven feet across and support a 150 pound person.

A short write-up cannot do justice to the extraordinary diversity of species at Longwood or the sheer quantity of attractions. Fortunately Colvin Randall has done that in his 104-page book, *Longwood Gardens: the Ultimate Garden Treasure* (1987, York Graphic Services, Inc.). In addition to describing the horticultural wonders for all to see, Randall also describes the production process. In 1986, for instance, Longwood began a 5-year plan to increase the number of bulbs by more than one million. "Total time for outdoor bulb planting in 1986 was 2,092 hours or 299 employee days, or .51 minute per minor bulb, .93 minute per tulip, and 1.05 minute per daffodil." That type of detail is found throughout, and is not available elsewhere.

Incredibly, Longwood averages more than one special event per day year round. There are over 400 performing arts events (concerts, plays, dance groups) per year. Peppering the calendar are such events as bonsai lectures, plant shows, talks on mushroom magic and gingerbread houses, demonstrations on pruning, workshops on culinary herbs, constantly changing children's programs and more. The summer-long Festival of Fountains (every evening after dark from Memorial Day weekend through September) draws thousands to the multi-color illumination of the fountains. And most popular of all are the occasional evening summer fireworks displays accompanying the other attractions; purchase your tickets in advance because attendance cannot exceed the 1,250-space parking lot. Call for a seasonally updated calendar of events.

Five educational opportunities are offered: a continuing education program (certificate); a professional gardener training program (a two year program for high school graduates); an internship program (3-12 months for college students); a Master of Science in Public Horticulture Administration (collaboratively with the University of Delaware); and an international gardener training program (12 months for students from other countries).

Personal Impression. The litany of features above speaks for itself. Longwood Gardens is an *experience!*

I like the way it is landscaped for openness; there are several parcels of high ground from which one may enjoy a panoramic view of the premises. The staff, busy as they are, take time to answer your questions. Most of all, the gardens are tastefully designed and meticulously groomed.

I recommend at least two trips to Longwood. The visitor spends the first trip in a bit of a daze, trying to comprehend that there really *is* that much there. It's during the second trip that one finds time to savor the individual delights. Between trips, read Randall's book to understand what it takes to offer such an attraction.

Longwood Gardens is an *experience!*

---

(12) The (Ebenezer) Maxwell Mansion

200 West Tulpehocken St.
Philadelphia, PA 19144
(215) 438-1861
Hours: the grounds open daylight hours, year round; the mansion opens April through Dec., 1-4 Thurs.-Sun.--other times by appointment; closed Christmas, Easter and Thanksgiving.

Overview. " A Victorian house museum, garden and restoration resource library in Philadelphia." The grounds provide a re-creation of a mid-to-late 19th century period garden--graceful, tasteful, informal and Victorian--beautiful.

Directions. Follow instructions to Wyck and walk; the two attractions are only a couple blocks from each other and are ideally seen at the same time.

Ownership	Pet on leash	Brochure
private; NP	no	yes
Size	**Weddings**	**Ed. programs**
corner lot	yes	no
Rest rooms	**Sell plants**	**Spec. events**
yes	no	no
Pay phone	**Membership**	**Labeling**
no	yes	no
Visitor center	**Gift shop**	**Volunteers**
in house	no	many
Fees		**Off street parking**
not for grounds		no
Library for public		**Ext. photo limits**
yes		no
Garden clubs active		**Food**
yes		no

Historical Profile. Ebenezer Maxwell, a Philadelphia dry goods merchant, built his Victorian home c. 1859 in the old Germantown section of town. After experiencing significant deterioration in the 1950s and 1960s, it was restored in the 1970s and opened to the public in 1975.

"It is the anchor for the Tulpehocken Station National Register Historic District, a six-block designation of Victorian housing. It is a charter member of Historic Germantown Preserved, an association of thirteen museums in Germantown which jointly depict three hundred years of life in Philadelphia."

Description. The Industrial Revolution created a burgeoning middle class that lived comfortably, but not grandiosely, in this Germantown neighborhood.

The original iron fence still surrounds the two period gardens. In front, a pond, rock garden, annuals, clusters of mixed evergreens, a small lawn and cast iron deer were created from Alexander Jackson Downing's writings of the mid-1800s. To the side, climbing roses, annuals, a grape arbor and a comely collection of trees and shrubs were created from the 1870 suburban landscape plans of Frank J. Scott.

The furnishings of the house are period-appropriate and the restoration library is open to the public at no cost.

Personal Impression. Grounds like these defy meaningful written description; they haved to be seen. It's the total effect of the landscaping that impresses. Although individual plants and beds are well cared-for, it's the way they are clustered and distributed tastefully over the graded terrain that commands attention.

Given that the mansion, really a medium-size house by today's standards, is equally well-maintained, the uninformed visitor would likely only take notice of the very attractive place on the corner, without realizing that it looked that way a century and a half ago. Victorian architecture and landscaping do not suffer in comparison to more modern standards. In fact, some people prefer them.

---

(13) Morris Arboretum

100 Northwestern Ave.
Philadelphia, PA 19118-2697
(215) 247-5777
Hours: the Arboretum opens at 10 a.m. every day except Thanksgiving, Christmas and New Year's Day; it closes at 4 Nov.-March and at 5 April-Oct.

Overview. The Morris Arboretum of the University of Pennsylvania, the official arboretum of the Commonwealth of Pennsylvania, offers public view gardens over 92 of its 166 acres in both formal and informal design. About 7000 plants are accessioned, with emphasis on trees and shrubs. The rose parterres are unsurpassed in the Region. Tree collections contain 30 State Champions. The University's mission accents reseach, teaching, conservation and display.

Directions. The Arboretum sits astride the City limits in the northwest corner of Philadelphia in the Chestnut Hill area. Take Germantown Ave. to the city limits from downtown, then turn right onto Northwestern Ave. to the marked entrance.

Historical Profile. The Arboretum began in 1887 as Compton, the estate of John and Lydia Morris, brother and sister in a prosperous, iron-manufacturing family. In the general context of Victorian landscaping, the keystone of the grounds, both then and now, was the large, formal rose garden, laid out in 1888 and renewed in the 1970s.

Most of the Arboretum's 7000 accessioned plantings were introduced after 1932 when Compton became the Morris Arboretum and opened to the public.

Description. The Arboretum's 166 acres feature alternating open meadows and widely scattered clusters of trees, collections and garden areas on hilly terrain and bordered by Wissahickon Creek.

Ownership	Pet on leash	Brochure
pub., state	no	yes
Size	**Weddings**	**Ed. programs**
166 acres[1]	yes	many
Rest rooms	**Sell plants**	**Spec. events**
yes	in spring	yes
Pay phone	**Membership**	**Labeling**
no	yes	excellent
Visitor center	**Gift shop**	**Volunteers**
yes	no	many
Fees	**Off street parking**	
modest	no	
Library for public	**Ext. photo limits**	
no	commercial	
Garden clubs active	**Food**	
no	no	

[1]Of the 166 acres, 92 are display and 74 are for research.

Near the center, the Marion W. Rivinus Rose Garden contains four very large parterres, each of which subdivides into at least six sections, each section having a slightly different central or peripheral configuration. Hybrid teas dominate numerically, with significant numbers of floribundas, grandifloras and miniatures, and with a scattering of climbers and shrubs. Additionally, this is an All-America Rose Selections garden. Almost perfectly square, the garden resembles a rainbowed oasis in a sea of green from the hilltop near the visitor center.

Tree selection includes both native and introduced species. A small sampler: Greek fir, white oak, Chinese elm, weeping hemlock, trident maple, sweet bay magnolia, Japanese sapium, ginkgo. The Arboretum also features the only Victorian estate fernery in the nation. Rhododendrons, azaleas and hollies dominate the taxa. Witchhazels, crabapples and viburnums are also well represented.

The Arboretum also demonstrates a commitment to the fine arts that is unsurpassed in the Region. At least a dozen sculptures dot the landscape, including grazing sheep, lifesize bronze portraits of John and Lydia Morris, a kinetic sculpture and the classical "Mercury at Rest."

An extraordinarily diverse educational program includes (from the brochure): "teacher training; internships; school tours; adult and professional courses in arboriculture, landscape and horticulture; university programs; publications and exhibits; lectures and workshops; plant clinic; urban forestry; and community outreach." A recent fall catalogue lists 39 courses available to the general public and to professionals. The basic Morris Arboretum Member fee of $40 may be recovered quickly by taking member-discounted courses. A seasonal newsletter documents the successes and problems of the Arboretum, such as the significant damage a tornado did to the oak allee.

Personal Impression. This seems to be a garden complex without a weakness: everything it does, it does well. I was particularly impressed with the diversity of educational programs. If I lived nearby, I'd be there all the time.

---

(14) Pennsylvania Historical Society

325 Walnut St.
Philadelphia, PA 19106
(215) 625-8250
Hours: the grounds are open daylight hours, year round; the visitor center opens 9-5 Mon.-Fri.; closed major holidays.

Overview. "Founded in 1827, the Pennsylvania Horticultural Society (PHS) is the oldest horticultural society in America ...." Headquartered within the downtown historic district, the Society has created a garden typical of an 18th century fashionable part of town. It contains a formal parterre garden; a small orchard; and an area with mixed herbs, vegetables and perennials. It is a delightful garden, and the only one in this guidebook to feature a garden in a "row house" neighborhood.

Ownership	Pet on leash	Brochure
private, NP	yes	general
Size	**Weddings**	**Ed. programs**
1 acre	only photos	yes
Rest rooms	**Sell plants**	**Spec. events**
yes	no	yes
Pay phone	**Membership**	**Labeling**
no	yes	some
Visitor center	**Gift shop**	**Volunteers**
yes	no	many
Fees		**Off street parking**
no		no
Library for public		**Ext. photo limits**
yes, large		no
Garden clubs active		**Food**
many		no

Directions. You *must* have a street map of Philadelphia. Locate the historic area downtown, then Walnut Street within it. Drive to the address above.

Historical Profile. Philadelphia is the historical epicenter of horticulture in America. The Quaker tradition in general, and John Bartram in particular, started it. In 1763, the University of Pennsylvania (in Philadelphia) created the first botany department in a university in the nation. Expectedly, the PHS was also the first of its type in the nation. It occupies structures within the Independence National Historic Park and introduced a period-appropriate, small garden in the 1960s that was dedicated by Lady Bird Johnson in 1966. The garden serves as an appropriate show-and-tell for the Society's burgeoning activities.

Description. Shielded from busy Walnut St. by a brick and iron fence, the parterres--100 sq. ft. each--are edged with barberry and boxwood, enclosing seasonal bloomers. It is as neat, tidy, manicured and beautiful as any parterre garden in the Region. Judging from its appearance during my visit, the grape arbor is carefully pruned and well-fertilized. Similarly, the small orchard displayed the end product of hours of care, as did the mixed annual, vegetable and perennial garden. Only experienced gardeners can appreciate that this lovely little garden represents untold hours of toil to render it picture-perfect.

One expects nothing less from the Society that sponsors the world-famous Philadelphia Flower Show, that has spearheaded the "greening of Philadelphia," and that generally leads horticultural initiatives in the area.

Personal Impression. The State of Delaware characterizes itself as a "small wonder." That characterization aptly describes this garden. Considerable additional verbage would do little to reinforce the *fact* that this is perhaps the most carefully groomed little garden in the Region. I absolutely loved it, have returned twice and recommend it without reservation. It is a work of art. Enough said.

---

(15) Pennsbury Manor

400 Pennsbury Memorial Rd.
Morrisville, PA 19067
(215) 946-0400
Hours: Pennsbury opens 9-5 Tue.-Sat. and 12-5 Sun., year round; closed Mondays and major holidays except Memorial Day, July 4 and Labor Day.

Overview. Pennsbury Manor, the 17th century colonial estate of William Penn, has been restored by the Pennsylvania Historical and Museum Commission with the assistance of the Pennsbury Society. In the absence of information on the precise nature of Penn's garden, it has been restored to period designs and plants in Colonial Revival style.

Directions. Pennsbury Manor is located northeast of Philadelphia on the banks of the Delaware River. From Route 1 at Morrisville, turn south on Rte. 13; shortly turn left (east) onto Tyburn Rd. and, at the light, right onto New Ford Mill Rd.; turn right at the dead end, then left onto Pennsbury Memorial Rd. From a recent telephone conversation, I understand that they have recently added many road signs to the Manor as many as five miles away.

Historical Profile. William Penn, founder of Pennsylvania and America's best known Quaker, arrived in the colony in 1682 and work began on his estate the following year--home, outbuildings and gardens. With neglect (Penn spent most of his time in England), the house collapsed and his descendants ultimately sold the property in 1792. In 1932, the Charles Warner Co. gave the 10 nuclear acres of the current 43 acres to the Commonwealth of Pennsylvania. The first restoration garden was designed in 1942 by landscape architect Thomas Sears, and it is still the master plan for the property.

Description. Although business interests and ill health kept Penn away from his estate most of his life, Pennsbury was a working plantation and undoubtedly contained the field crops and kitchen garden in vogue at that time, and restoration has been to that style and substance.

The typical kitchen garden in 17th century England (books of the period were found in Penn's library and served as guides) was far more than a vegetable garden. It was walled against intruding animals and employed raised beds to extend the growing season, and it was very densely planted. Typically, fruit trees bordered the garden and were densely underplanted with shrubs, flowers, herbs, berry bushes

Ownership	Pet on leash	Brochure
pub., state[1]	yes	excellent
Size	**Weddings**	**Ed. programs**
43 acres[2]	yes	yes
Rest rooms	**Sell plants**	**Spec. events**
yes	occasionally	yes
Pay phone	**Membership**	**Labeling**
no	yes	no
Visitor center	**Gift shop**	**Volunteers**
yes	yes	many
Fees		**Off street parking**
yes		yes
Library for public		**Ext. photo limits**
yes		no
Garden clubs active		**Food**
no		no

[1]With the assistance of the Pennsbury Society.
[2]The gardens occupy 1.5 acres.

and more. The vegetable core also was interplanted with blooming plants, herbs and berry-bearing plants. Consequently, in Penn's "kitchen" garden visitors will also find roses, violets, bayberry, lavendar, hollyhocks, oregano, asters, hyacinths, iris, raspberries and an assortment of apple, plum and peach trees.

There also is a separate orchard and a vineyard--the imported French grapes in Penn's time all died. A small flowering garden and a large courtyard lie on either side of the manor house, which was more resplendent than typical Quaker residences but less elegant than the residences of many colonial contemporaries. Working outbuildings dot the landscape.

Personal Impression. I think "plantation" best describes Pennsbury. This is more than a gentleman's country estate and is far more than a family farm. It is an impressive complex designed for self-sufficiency and graceful living combined. It does not provide a rainbow of colors such as a Reynolda Gardens, but it is nonetheless attractive in the style of the times. It takes at least a half day to savor its many attractions. If possible, obtain and read the brochures before you go; they are highly informative.

(16) Phipps Conservatory

Schenley Park
Pittsburgh, PA 15213
(412) 622-6914
Hours: the outdoor grounds open daylight hours, year round; the Conservatory opens 9-5, Tue.-Sat., year round, with longer hours for special events.

Ownership	Pet on leash	Brochure
pub, city[1]	no	yes
Size	**Weddings**	**Ed. programs**
2.5 acres	yes	many
Rest rooms	**Sell plants**	**Spec. events**
yes	yes	many
Pay phone	**Membership**	**Labeling**
yes	yes	yes
Visitor center	**Gift shop**	**Volunteers**
yes	yes	yes
Fees		**Off street parking**
yes for indoors		no
Library for public		**Ext. photo limits**
no		commercial
Garden clubs active		**Food**
yes		not yet

[1]Privatized management.

Overview. Located in Pittsburgh's large Schenley Park, this Victorian glass house offers both indoor and outdoor gardens. Throughout 2.5 acres under glass, seasonally changing shows and permanent exhibits provide informal and formal, all seasons attractions. The spring-through-autumn outdoor gardens help make the Conservatory one of the Region's premier garden complexes.

Directions. Locate the University of Pittsburgh on a map and Forbes Ave. running by it. As you approach the Cathedral of Learning (a tall columnar building visible for miles around) on Forbes Ave., turn south onto Schenley Dr. and park at a meter near the Conservatory.

Historical Profile. Henry Phipps, a nineteenth century Pittsburgh industrialist and twentieth century philanthropist, financed the conservatory that bears his name. It opened in 1893 as a magnificent Victorian glass house and has undergone several periods of refinement and renovation. Ralph Griswold designed the exterior gardens in the 1930s; after a period of neglect in the 1960s

149

and 1970s, the Garden Club of Allegheny County restored them. Garden clubs and volunteers are still a mainstay of interior and exterior garden management.

The Conservatory is celebrating its centennial at this writing. The City of Pittsburgh has recently privatized management, so that significant changes may be realized in the years ahead.

Description. The outdoor gardens and interior displays are independent attractions.

The exterior gardens feature two lily ponds, a perennial garden, a collection of dwarf conifers, summer beds of annuals, a semi-shade garden (azaleas, rhododendron, ferns, various ground covers), a medieval herb garden (culinary and medicinal; espaliered dwarf fruit trees), a rose garden (Men's Garden Club of Pittsburgh), and various blooming borders. Garden color proceeds from spring tulips to fall foliage. There are several open lawns with wooded borders. Benches are strategically placed.

Graceful and decorative as the exterior grounds are, the Conservatory has traditionally provided the principal attractions. Thirteen rooms under glass exhibit permanent and seasonal displays over 2.5 acres. The procession of seasonal shows includes winter (Nov. 26-Jan. 9), spring (March 19-April 17) and fall (Sept.-Oct.); themed displays include the Parterre de Broderie with embroidered patterns in Louis XIV-style (a favorite for wedding pictures), the palm court (up to 45 feet high), cacti in a desert environment, rare tropical collections, succulents, orchids, an economic room (plants of significance to the economies of society). A major Bonsai collection was added recently in the Conservatory's open courtyard.

Interior tours proceed at pre-determined times--call to determine. A full calendar of educational programs and special events is conducted throughout the year. Volunteers and garden clubs provide a full range of services.

Personal Impression. I visited on a weekday when visitors were few and was surprised at the contemplative ambience there in such a well-used urban facility. The grandeur of the Victorian house of glass, the charm of the new parterre, the comeliness of the exterior gardens--all combine to make it difficult to leave. It's one of those complexes well worth going far out of your way to see.

---

(17) The Pittsburgh Civic Garden Center
1059 Shady Avenue
Pittsburgh, PA 15232
(412) 441-4442
Hours: the grounds are open daylight hours, year round; the visitor center opens 8:30-4:30 and the gift shop opens Mon.-Sat. 10-4; closed all major holidays.

Overview. The Garden Center occupies 17 acres in Mellon Park for a diversified set of educational gardens and an imposing collection of educational programs and special events. Beginning with spring daffodils, there is a continuous procession of attractions year round, displayed both formally and informally.

Directions. See the directions to Phipps Conservatory and locate on a street map 5th Avenue which is north of Phipps and runs east-west. Proceed east on 5th Avenue to Shady Avenue and turn right to the Mellon Park.

Ownership	Pet on leash	Brochure
priv, NP	yes	no

Size	Weddings	Ed. programs
17 acres	yes	many

Rest rooms	Sell plants	Spec. events
yes	year round	many

Pay phone	Membership	Labeling
yes	yes	yes

Visitor center	Gift shop	Volunteers
yes	yes	many

Fees	Off street parking
no	yes

Library for public	Ext. photo limits
yes	commercial

Garden clubs active	Food
many	no

Historical Profile. The Pittsburgh Civic Garden Center has been in continuous operation for 59 years. Since the 1940s, it has headquartered itself in the old carriage house on the former Mellon estate, now Mellon Park. Gardens and educational programs have steadily grown and diversified to the present.

Description. Mature hardwoods dot the landscape, both native (oaks, tulip poplars) and introduced (e.g., ginkgo). Over a dozen, small educational gardens are widely distributed over the 17 acres, including a dogwood (and shrub) garden, a rock garden, an herb garden, a native plant garden, a groundcover (c. 70 varieties) garden, and an ornamental grass garden. A daffodil (70 varieties) trial garden has recently been introduced. Both trees and plants are labeled, and the greenhouse is one of the few in the Region to sell plants virtually year-round.

If anything, the activity-set of the Center is more diversified than the gardens. The 1993 summer calendar included special programs (e.g., a session on bulb care), tours (e.g., to nearby nurseries), certificate courses in horticulture (e.g., diagnosing plant problems), non-certificate courses (e.g., practical composting), floral design (e.g., "Dry It, You'll Like It"), children's classes (e.g., summer salads), school programs (for teachers) and short courses (e.g., "Bulbs for All Seasons"). Additionally, the Center offers: art exhibits, a master gardener program, a horticultural therapy program, a large lending library, a quality gift shop and a "greenline" for troubled gardeners.

151

Personal Impression. This is a lively place. The people in Pittsburgh are *very* fortunate to have an operation like this is driving distance. All populous areas need something like this, and all don't!

---

(18) The Scott Arboretum of Swarthmore College
500 College Ave.
Swarthmore College
Swarthmore, PA 19081-1397
(610) 328-8025
Hours: the grounds are open daylight hours, year round; the visitor center opens 8:30-4:30, Mon.-Fri. and is closed for major holidays and Christmas week.

Overview. Many consider Swarthmore College to have the finest, campus-wide arboretum in the Region. The Scott Arboretum occupies 110 of the campus' 330 acres and features formal, informal and natural areas. Over 5000 different types of ornamental plants are displayed in specialty and theme gardens, and in collections. It is an all-seasons garden that provides a catalogue of ideas for the home garden.

Directions. Swarthmore College is 11 miles west of Philadelphia. From the intersection of Rtes. 1 and 320, take Rte. 320 south to College Ave. and turn right for a block to the Scott offices on your left. You have passed the offices if you encounter a rose garden on your left. If there are no street parking spaces, ask for directions to the visitor parking lot.

Historical Profile. Founded in 1864 by the Society of Friends, Swarthmore College has a student population of c. 1300. The Arboretum was established in 1929 in memory of Arthur Hoyt Scott and has grown steadily over the ensuing decades.

Description. An extraordinarily diverse set of collections pepper the rolling terrain. The James R. Frorer Holly Collection (1974) has been designated an official Holly Arboretum by the Holly Society of America.

Ownership	Pet on leash	Brochure
priv, college	yes	excellent
Size	**Weddings**	**Ed. programs**
110 acres	yes	many
Rest rooms	**Sell plants**	**Spec. events**
yes	occasionally	several
Pay phone	**Membership**	**Labeling**
no	yes	excellent
Visitor center	**Gift shop**	**Volunteers**
yes	no	many
Fees		**Off street parking**
no		yes
Library for public		**Ext. photo limits**
yes		commercial
Garden clubs active		**Food**
yes		nearby

152

Other collections are distributed throughout the campus: spring bulbs, flowering cherries, corylopsis, crabapples, lilacs, maples, magnolias, rhododendrons, native azaleas, roses, wisteria, viburnum, conifers (a pinetum and dwarf conifers), hydrangeas and tree peonies.

The specialty and theme gardens, many to home scale, include: the Terry Shane Teaching Garden (1989--mixed trees, shrubs and perennials); the Suzanne Schmidt Memorial Garden (a canopy of flowering cherries which are under-planted with azaleas, rhododendrons and mountain laurel which, in turn, are underplanted with bulbs and herbaceous plants); the Dean Bond Rose Garden (designed by Gertrude Wister in 1956; over 650 plants bloom from June through October); the Theresa Long Garden of Fragrance (1986); the Harry Wood Memorial Garden (evergreens and deciduous plants); the Entrance Garden (a mix of perennials, bulbs and groundcover at the visitor center); and the Winter Garden (evergreens and shrubs).

Remember, this large assortment of tasteful gardens is distributed throughout the campus--leave enough time.

The natural areas include the Scott Outdoor Amphitheater (built into a mature tulip poplar woods) and the Crum Woods (several miles of pathways).

Various lectures, workshops and tours, and festivals in spring and fall, are distributed throughout the year. Group tours are by prearrangement. The benefit package of the Associates of the Scott Arboretum is unusually large.

Personal Impression. Words alone cannot describe this incredibly beautiful campus. You simply *must* go see it.

---

(19) Tyler Arboretum

515 Painter Rd.
Media, PA 19063
(610) 566-5431
Hours: the grounds open 8 a.m. to dusk, year round; the gift shop opens 10-3 in July & Aug., and until 4 the rest of the year; call for hours of other attractions.

Overview. The Tyler Arboretum offers a massive, 650-acre arboretum to the public with massive uncultivated areas and significant, informally cultivated grounds. It is an all-seasons arboretum that features native plants and enjoys an extraordinary volume of human use and contribution.

Directions. From Route 1 west of Philadelphia near Media, take Rte. 352 north for 1.8 miles; turn right onto Forge Rd. which becomes Painter Rd. in a block, and the marked entrance is on your left.

Historical Profile. Seven generations of the same family occupied this property from 1681 to 1944. Two brothers, Jacob and Minshall Painter started the arboretum in 1825 with a systematic planting of over 1000 kinds of trees and shrubs. In 1944, Laura Tyler, a direct descendant, bequeathed the property to the public as an arboretum. Cultivated expansion began in the 1950s and refinements have been continuous to this time.

Description. About two-thirds of this enormous, 650-acre property is devoted to native woodlands, a natural shrub undergrowth, a profusion of wildflowers and a pinetum. Twenty *miles* of hiking trails run through it.

In the cultivated areas, one finds entrance perennial borders, a fragrant herb garden, a butterfly garden, a bird garden and Pink Hill (wildflowers). Significant tree-and-shrub collections include magnolias, lilacs, rhododendrons, hollies, flowering cherries and crabapples.

Snowdrops, azaleas, dogwoods and bulbs support the collections in the resplendent spring; annuals support the themed gardens through

Ownership	Pet on leash	Brochure
priv, NP	yes	excellent
Size	**Weddings**	**Ed. programs**
650 acres	yes	many
Rest rooms	**Sell plants**	**Spec. events**
yes	occasionally	many
Pay phone	**Membership**	**Labeling**
yes	yes	yes
Visitor center	**Gift shop**	**Volunteers**
yes	very good	many
Fees		**Off street parking**
yes		yes
Library for public		**Ext. photo limits**
yes		commercial
Garden clubs active		**Food**
many		no

summer to the awesome fall display; witch hazels complement the hollies and conifers in winter. One may enjoy a visit any time of the year.

Throughout, native plants are emphasized.

Several buildings greet the visitor. The Barn houses the gift shop and the education center; Lackford Hall (museum and administrative offices); a library; a springhouse; production greenhouses; maintenance and residence buildings. The gift shop contains a superior collection of books and horticulturally-related items.

The "human network" of the operation is as impressive as the Arboretum. In a recent annual report: membership exceeded 2,200; 50 teachers were trained; the educational programs served 7,500 children and adults; volunteers contributed over 5,000 hours in 13 specified roles.

Personal Impression. I did not need an annual report to recognize that the Tyler Arboretum is a lively place. During my three visits there in three different seasons, there was a constant procession of people in, around and through the various attractions. I'm not sure how, but massive conservation and massive use seemed compatible.

---

(20) Welkinweir Preserve

R.R. 7, Box 309
Prizer Rd.
Pottstown, PA 19464
(610) 469-6366
Hours: the grounds are open daylight hours year round, except from Thanksgiving through the first week of December--the policy on hours is under review; call in advance; the reception area opens irregularly but brochures are left outside.

Ownership	Pet on leash	Brochure
priv, NP	no	yes

Size	Weddings	Ed. programs
165 acres	[1]	yes

Rest rooms	Sell plants	Spec. events
no	no	yes

Pay phone	Membership	Labeling
no	yes[2]	expanding

Visitor center	Gift shop	Volunteers
yes[3]	no	yes

Fees	Off street parking
no	yes

Library for public	Ext. photo limits
no	none

Garden clubs active	Food
no	no

[1]Policy under review.
[2]In the National Lands Trust.
[3]It may be locked on open days if the staff person is elsewhere on the grounds.

Overview. The Natural Lands Trust is preserving this 165-acre, mid-twentieth century estate-arboretum in both natural and informally landscaped forms. Although spring is particularly spectacular, this is an all-seasons arboretum that gracefully harmonizes natural and cultivated attractions.

Directions. From the Pennsylvania Turnpike west of Philadelphia, take Exit 23 north on Rte. 100 for about 7.5 miles to Prizer Rd. on your left (it is not well-marked; if you intersect Rte. 23, you have gone one mile too far); continue on Prizer for a mile to the entrance on your left. (Note: there are two entrances. Take the second one for off-street parking.)

Historical Profile. Grace and Everett Rodebaugh purchased this 165-acre estate in the 1930s in seriously neglected condition. Over the ensuing decades, they diversified habitats for plants and wildlife alike, improved the general landscaping and introduced a broad selection of trees, shrubs and perennials to complement the considerable native flora. Mrs. Rodebaugh, who still lives on the estate, conveyed the property to the Natural Lands Trust in 1986, whereupon it opened to public visitation.

"The Natural Lands Trust protects open space throughout the greater Delaware Valley and Mid-Atlantic Region, in 54 preserves covering 13,000 acres. Our properties include saltmarshes, working farms, arboreta, and woodland trails, creating a network of open space that enhances the quality of our lives."

Another Trust property that seems to meet my acceptance criteria is the Taylor Memorial Arboretum (1-610-876-2649). Unfortunately, I discovered its existence too late for inclusion here. For general information on the Trust's work (including volunteer opportunities), call 1-610-353-5587.

Description. The area around the Preserve is quite rural and the terrain in it is quite hilly. Open meadows alternate with natural woodlands (predominantly white oak and tulip poplar), five ponds (the largest is 6 acres), and modified landscapes.

The introductions in the latter include a quaint dwarf conifer pinetum, a sundial-rock garden (perennials, candytuft and various alpine plants) and a still-developing springhouse garden (ostrich ferns, Japanese primroses, irises). The holly and magnolia collections are distributed throughout the grounds. Ivy, periwinkle and pachysandra provide ground cover.

Spring explodes across the estate in massive numbers of wildflowers, daffodils, azaleas, rhododendrons, dogwoods, redbuds and more. Lilies, annuals and perennials continue the blooming season into the resplendent fall. Witch hazel and pyracantha support the hollies and conifers through the winter. And, expectedly, wildlife abounds.

Educational programs are customized. That is, instead of calling the Preserve to participate in on-going events, state your interests and, if feasible, an education program will be tailored to your needs. Additionally, the Trust sponsors special events throughout the year which change annually--call for an up-to-date list.

The property's generous donor still resides there, so appropriate courtesy is expected.

Personal Impression. In addition to the informal and natural beauty across the property--there are two miles of trails--I most distinctly remember the quiet. Chirping birds in the canopy and hedgerows have little competition in this remote area.

It also was reassuring later on to learn that the Natural Lands Trust was engaged on such a large scale in essential conservation and preservation efforts. Future updates of this guidebook will accord attention to this work.

---

(21) Wyck
6026 Germantown Ave.

Philadelphia, PA 19144
(215) 848-1690
Hours: Wyck opens April 1-Dec. 15, 1-4 Tue., Thurs. and Sat.; open by appointment at other times; closed major holidays.

Overview. Nine generations of the same family lived continuously at Wyck for nearly 300 years. The gardens, on 2.5 of the original 50 acres, contain both a formal rose parterre and informal areas, restored mainly to its 1820s status.

Ownership	Pet on leash	Brochure
priv, NP	no	yes

Size	Weddings	Ed. programs
2.5 acres	pictures	--

Rest rooms	Sell plants	Spec. events
yes	no	yes[1]

Pay phone	Membership	Labeling
no	yes	roses, yes

Visitor center	Gift shop	Volunteers
yes, house	small	yes

Fees		Off street parking
yes		10 cars

Library for public	∘	Ext. photo limits
yes		none

Garden clubs active		Food
yes		no

[1]*A Garden Open House is generally held in June each year.*

Directions. Germantown is in north Philadelphia, north and a little west of the historic center of town. Germantown Ave. runs northwest/southeast through it. From the intersection of Rte. 1 and Germantown Ave., proceed northwest nearly two miles to Wyck on your left at the address above.

Historical Profile. From the brochure: "Wyck, a National Historic Landmark located in the Germantown section of Philadelphia, was home to nine generations of the same Quaker family, the Wistars and Haineses ..." from 1690 to 1973. The gardens, as restored today, began in the 1820s, featuring old roses. The property was transferred to Foundation ownership in 1973 and opened to the public in 1974.

Interestingly, the family mistakenly named the homestead Wyck after its English ancestral home. By the time the mistake was recognized, it was too late--everyone knew it as Wyck.

The garden restoration is mainly period-appropriate.

Description. Eighteen of the 37 types of roses in or near the parterres date back to the 1820s design of June Haines, none of them having been first cultivated after 1827. A small sampler: cabbage rose, white rose of York, bella donna, old blush, rosa mundi and pink leda. (Ask for the separate rose brochure.)

Grape vines over the house-long arbor are descendants of the originals.

The ample selection of trees includes horsechestnut, dogwood, tulip poplar, saucer magnolia (150 years old), franklinia and princess tree. Fruit trees include pears, quinces, apples. A vegetable garden on the far side (not period) includes herbs.

Viburnums, hollies, crape myrtles, buckeyes, daylilies, wisteria, pachysandra, ferns, tree peonies and a large selection of hosta add color and texture throughout the year.

Overall, there is an incredible diversity of species on such a small corner lot. The garden is history over time--the cumulative expression of the gardening interests of multiple generations of the same family.

Tours proceed regularly of the house. A very large collection of family papers is available for research.

Personal Impression. Like the Maxwell Mansion a couple blocks away, I just liked the house and grounds at Wyck, which is older and more casual and more relaxed--more comfortably lived-in. The garden is a personal garden, a loving garden. Its historical significance just amplifies its intrinsic appeal.

If you have a 35mm camera body that uses interchangeable lenses, I recommend using a 35-75mm zoom lens. In many gardens you are confined to pathways that leave you too close to, or too far from, your subject for your fixed focal length lens. A 35mm setting has the effect of moving you away from your subject and expanding your field of view; a 75mm setting has the effect of moving you closer to your subject and narrowing your field of view; a 50mm setting gives you an image the same size as your eye sees. It's the most useful single lens you can use in a garden.

Chapter 6
Virginia

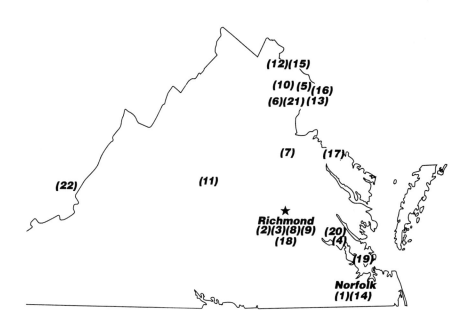

(12)(15)

(10) (5)(16)
(6)(21)(13)

(7)   (17)

(22)   (11)

★
Richmond
(2)(3)(8)(9) (20)
(18)   (4)

(19)

Norfolk
(1)(14)

Virginia is a Regional leader in at least three respects. Most visibly, it has the largest number of fine historic estate gardens in the Region. Additionally, the garden-set provides a shopper's paradise: over half of the gardens maintain gift shops with distinctive merchandise, especially of a horticultural nature--a greater proportion than any other state. And lastly, there has been a longer and broader groundswell of volunteer support for gardens: individual volunteers, garden clubs, historical societies and other organizations all over the State have an unsurpassed, 1.5-century track record of significant garden creations and restorations.

The gardens cluster into four parts of the State. The largest cluster is found along or near the Potomac River. West of D.C., one finds Morven Park, Oatlands, Meadowlark Gardens Regional park outside the Capital Beltway, and Green Spring Gardens Park inside. Southeast of D.C., one finds River Farm, Mount Vernon, Woodlawn Plantation, Gunston Hall and Stratford Hall Plantation.

In the north-central and west-central parts of the State, one finds Kenmore and Monticello. Also, just over the Virginia border sits the Greenbrier. (West Virginia is not an Atlantic state, but the Greenbrier is close enough and unique enough to warrant inclusion.)

In the Richmond area, one finds Agecroft Hall and its next door neighbor, Virginia House, Maymont, Bryan Park and the relatively new Lewis Ginter Botanical Garden.

In the southeast corner of the State, one finds Williamsburg, Carter's Grove, the Virginia Living Museum, the Norfolk Botanical Garden and the Adam Thoroughgood House.

---

(1) Adam Thoroughgood House

1636 Parish Rd.
Virginia Beach, VA 23455
(804) 627-2737
Hours: the grounds are open daylight hours, year round; the visitor center and house open 12-5 Tue.-Sat., Jan. 1-March 31; 10-5 Tue.-Sat. and 12-5 Sun., April 1-Dec. 31; closed July 4, Thanksgiving, Christmas and New Year's Day.

Overview. Owned by the City of Norfolk and managed by the non-profit Chrysler Museum, the Adam Thoroughgood House and grounds feature a very pleasant formal garden, a daylily extravaganza in June and a tasteful assortment of year-round attractions throughout its 4.5 acres. It is a gentleman's pleasure garden, 17th century English style, around a 17th century structure.

Directions. Locate Norfolk/Virginia Beach in southeastern Virginia. From I-64, exit north onto Rte. 13 until you see the Thoroughgood sign; turn right at it onto Pleasure House Rd.; turn left almost immediately at the sign and continue 1.6 miles, following signs all the way.

Historical Profile. Adam Thoroughgood arrived in the Virginia Colony in 1621 as an indentured servant; with time, he was awarded 5350 acres along the Lynnhaven River and a descendant built the 1.5 story estate house c. 1680, which was restored in 1957. The Garden Club of Virginia completed the period garden in 1960 and its design has undergone modifications from time to time.

Ownership	Pet on leash	Brochure
public, city[1]	no	general
Size	**Weddings**	**Ed. programs**
4.5 acres	yes	some
Rest rooms	**Sell plants**	**Spec. events**
yes	no	some
Pay phone	**Membership**	**Labeling**
no	yes	some
Visitor center	**Gift shop**	**Volunteers**
yes	yes	yes
Fees		**Off street parking**
not for grounds		yes
Library for public		**Ext. photo limits**
no		none
Garden clubs active		**Food**
yes		no

[1]Privately administered by the Chrysler Museum.

Description. This 4.5-acre site in a pleasant Virginia Beach neighborhood along the Lynnhaven River contains the restored house, a separate gift shop/visitor center and formal gardens behind the house, along with a lawn bordered with shrubs, punctuated with deciduous and evergreen trees (e.g., dogwoods and magnolias) and surrounded by a quaint, red picket fence. Although little is known of the original garden design, garden characteristics of the period were incorporated.

The formal garden, which is the principal attraction, features two tasteful parterre gardens with centered topiaries, separated by espaliered pear trees and framed by two yaupon holly arbors. There is a small herb garden to the side of the house.

There is a good selection of perennials, shrubs and trees, groundcover (ivy) and wildflowers. In June, 5000 daylilies break into awesome bloom.

Personal Impression. I found it fascinating to see how well this historic site blends with its modern rancher neighborhood and its open lawns, azaleas and scattered beds of annuals; the area's tall, horizontally-fulfilled trees seem to unite the two entirely different structures and landscape styles. Also, I enjoyed the very large diversity of botanical attractions on a property this size without any feeling of overcrowding. I stop by every chance I get; it's a very pleasant place.

(2) Agecroft Hall

4305 Sulgrave Rd.
Richmond, VA 23221
(804) 353-4241
Hours: year round, Agecroft opens 10-4 Tue.-Sat. and 2-5 Sun.; closed major holidays.

Overview. One of a kind! Agecroft Hall is an actual 15th century Tudor mansion from England on a 23-acre estate in northwest Richmond. The formal grounds surrounding it contain formal pleasure gardens in 17th century English style. All three--the mansion, the grounds and the gardens--are equisitely done and meticulously kept in a fine Richmond neighborhood.

Directions. Proceed south on I-95 into Richmond, exit southwest on I-195, then exit onto Cary St.-west (Rte. 147) turning left almost immediately at the light (there's a sign also) onto Canterbury Rd.; in half a dozen blocks it merges with Sulgrave Rd. and the entrance is on your left after the Virginia House.

Historical Profile. Built in 15th century Tudor England, the manor house was saved from destruction in 1926 by Richmond businessman T.C. Williams who transported it to Richmond, lived in it and ultimately established an endowment in support of the present museum and grounds. The gardens were developed

Ownership	Pet on leash	Brochure
private, NP	no	several
Size	**Weddings**	**Ed. programs**
23 acres	no	yes
Rest rooms	**Sell plants**	**Spec. events**
yes	in future	yes
Pay phone	**Membership**	**Labeling**
no	not yet	yes
Visitor center	**Gift shop**	**Volunteers**
yes	not yet	yes

Fees	Off street parking
yes	yes
Library for public	**Ext. photo limits**
no	commercial
Garden clubs active	**Food**
no	no

according to landscape architect Charles Gillette's plan and have been continuously maintained to the present.

Description. Although this guidebook emphasizes the botanical attractions at historic estates, one's visit to Agecroft Hall appropriately begins with a film and guided tour of the mansion. It has been wonderfully restored and authentically furnished, providing a fascinating glimpse into affluent lifestyles in the Tudor period. I have found nothing like it in the Region.

Actually your visit begins with a mesmerizing view of the picturebook grounds--the surrounding holly hedge, immense magnolias and elms, gently sloping lawns, and the commanding architectural style of the mansion, almost unrealistically stately. You may want to sit in your car awhile and stare.

On a continuous axis one finds the pleasure gardens, the mansion and a brick-tiered cutting garden. Seventeenth century English publications guided the design and plant selection.

Boxwood-edged pathways lead to and around the pleasure gardens, the largest component of which is the rectangular sunken garden. The centered pond, with lilies and irises, is bordered by seasonally changed beds. At the far end of the axis is a true knot garden and a period herb garden, one or both of which may undergo transformation as a result of a gift from the John Tradescant (c. 1570-1638) Society. The cutting garden, predominantly perennials, occupies the other end of the axis, slopes gently down from the mansion and occasionally provides a nourishing meal for the local deer.

Interesting features dot the landscape--potted topiaries, tasteful brickwork, crape myrtles, spring bulbs, the layout for a maze, espaliered pears, a woodlands walk, statuary and much more, all in fine taste.

The educational programs and special events are sufficiently numerous to warrant brochures and printed circulars. Call to obtain.

Personal Impression. I like everything about Agecroft Hall--it's a first class operation. The fact that it is also historically unique makes it an irresistible attraction.

---

(3) Bryan Park Azalea Gardens

Dep't of Parks
City of Richmond
900 E. Broad St.
Richmond, VA 23219
(804) 780-5712
Hours: daylight hours, year round

Overview. The City of Richmond offers an appreciative public tens of thousands of spring azaleas on 17 acres within the very large Bryan Park. It's one of the few drive-through (or park) gardens in the Region.

Directions. See directions to the Lewis Ginter Botanical Garden. Continue past Ginter on Lakeside Ave. (which becomes Hermitage Rd.) for 1.6 miles to the entrance; once in, keep bearing left to the Gardens. (Alternately, you may pass the entrance, continue over I-95, turn right at the light onto Bellevue, which takes you directly to the Gardens.)

Historical Profile. This previously undeveloped land began its conversion to a garden in 1952 and refinements have proceeded continuously since then.

Description. A one-mile perimeter road takes the visitor around a small, centered lake with several off-road parking areas for those who want to walk.

About 45,000 azalea bushes (over 50 species) are distributed informally throughout the park, providing a spectacular springtime extravaganza.

A large collection of dogwoods and scatterings of crabapples, magnolias, hollies, camellias and crape myrtles provides supplementary attractions, but *this* is an azalea garden.

Personal Impression.
I was fortunate enough to visit during peak azalea bloom, which was one of the most colorful experiences of my life. In addition to the drive-through alternative for the visitor, biking is permitted which allows a more intimate, stop-and-start meandering through the gardens. For sheer color, Bryan Park is hard to beat. Peak bloom usually falls in the latter half of April, but weather variations can have a significant impact.

Ownership	Pet on leash	Brochure
public, city	no	no
Size	**Weddings**	**Ed. programs**
17 acres	yes	no
Rest rooms	**Sell plants**	**Spec. events**
nearby	no	no
Pay phone	**Membership**	**Labeling**
no	no	no
Visitor center	**Gift shop**	**Volunteers**
no	no	no
Fees		**Off street parking**
no		yes
Library for public		**Ext. photo limits**
no		none
Garden clubs active		**Food**
no		picnicing

(4) Carter's Grove
c/o Colonial Williamsburg Foundation
P.O. Box 1776
Williamsburg, VA 23187
(804) 229-1000
Hours: the facility opens 9-5, Tue.-Sun., mid-March - late Oct.; 9-4 Tue.-Sun., November and December.

Overview. Although Carter's Grove is owned by the Colonial Williamsburg Foundation, it is physically separate from the historic district and deserves a separate write-up. It is a carefully restored 18th century plantation with gardens in which the mixed formal and informal, mixed vegetable/fruit/flowering garden segments support the overall lifestyle depiction of the period. The best viewing times of the 750 acres are spring through fall.

Directions. From Colonial Williamsburg, proceed southeast on Rte. 60 to the marked entrance on your right.

Historical Profile. English settlers arrived in 1619 and built Wolstonholme Towne which was largely destroyed in the great 1662 Indian uprising. The surviving, small, scattered farmsteads continued throughout the 17th century until gentleman planters began consolidating them into tobacco plantations with slave labor. Robert "King" Carter purchased the present site and his grandson built the standing brick mansion c. 1750. After the family moved west in 1792, the property changed owners regularly in a period of general deterioration until the McCrea family purchased it in 1928 and began restoration. The Colonial Williamsburg Foundation acquired the estate in 1964 and continued the restoration process. The period restoration of the grounds and gardens was largely completed by the mid-1970s.

Ownership	Pet on leash	Brochure
private, NP	yes	yes
Size	**Weddings**	**Ed. programs**
750 acres	--	no
Rest rooms	**Sell plants**	**Spec. events**
yes	occasionally	no
Pay phone	**Membership**	**Labeling**
yes	no	some
Visitor center	**Gift shop**	**Volunteers**
yes	yes	no
Fees		**Off street parking**
yes		yes
Library for public		**Ext. photo limits**
no		tripods; commercial
Garden clubs active		**Food**
no		box lunches

Description. Distributed throughout the 750 acres are the large reception complex, the restored plantation mansion, the stable, the Archaeology Museum (with some nearby institutions of Wolstonholme Town), the slave quarters and the garden areas. These include the large, rectangularly segmented garden south of the mansion and below it on a separate level (mixed vegetables and ornamentals); a vegetable garden and orchard areas, especially apples, near the slave quarters; an 8-mile private, one-way road back to the historic district that "traverses marshes, tidal creeks, wooded hills, and open fields." The diverse period plantings include fragrant lavender, pomegranates, crape myrtle, English ivy, English and American boxwood, some wildflowers and a mixture of bedded annuals, perennials and herbs appropriate for the period.

Personal Impression. This is a first class, but not romanticized, re-creation of the total lifestyles of an 18th century tobacco plantation. The garden areas, not flamboyant by modern standards, are most fully appreciated in that context.

(5) Green Spring Gardens Park

4603 Green Spring Rd.
Alexandria, VA 22312
(703) 642-5173
Hours: the grounds are open daylight hours, year round; the Horticultural Center opens 9-5 Mon.-Sat. and 12-5 Sun., year round; closed for national and local holidays.

Overview. Fairfax County provides its citizens with this user-friendly garden complex that caters to the needs of the home gardener. Yard-size display gardens, a display greenhouse, a native plant trail and educational programs contribute to the beautification of the County and the enjoyment of its residents. This relatively new and still-growing complex occupies 27 acres in a densely populated area.

Ownership	Pet on leash	Brochure
pub., co.	yes	several
Size	**Weddings**	**Ed. programs**
27 acres	yes	many
Rest rooms	**Sell plants**	**Spec. events**
yes	occasionally	yes
Pay phone	**Membership**	**Labeling**
no	yes	yes
Visitor center	**Gift shop**	**Volunteers**
yes	yes	many
Fees	**Off street parking**	
no	yes	
Library for public	**Ext. photo limits**	
yes	none	
Garden clubs active	**Food**	
many	no	

Directions. A map really helps here. If you are proceeding north on I-95 from Richmond and intersect the Capital Beltway, you can either continue north toward D.C. on I-395 or proceed west on the Beltway (I-495). Little River Turnpike runs east-west between the two and you can access it from either Interstate. You turn north from Little River Turnpike onto Green Spring Rd. which takes you immediately into the Park. It is a small road and you may more easily find Braddock Rd., which runs parallel to it.

Historical Profile. Formerly Green Spring Farm with an 18th century farmhouse, the property was donated to the County in 1970. About a third of the property is still natively wooded and the cultivated areas are still in process of refinement.

Description. A large, circular lawn near the center of the property provides a park-like atmosphere. Most of the structured and botanical gardens are distributed immediately around it.

The principal structures include the manor house (horticultural and natural art on the first floor, offices on the second), a gazebo (a favorite place for weddings) and the Horticulture Center (classroom, library, restrooms and a 1000 sq. ft. display greenhouse).

Surrounding the Horticulture Center are an iris collection, a rock garden, seasonal displays, a butterfly garden, a cutting garden, a garden of everlastings (for dried arrangements) and interesting beds of native plants rescued by the Virginia Native Plant Society.

Proceeding counter-clockwise around the lawn, one encounters a vegetable garden, a fruit garden (50 cultivars of trees and also grapes, blackberries, raspberries and strawberries), and a sycamore bed (shrubs of extended seasonal interest and companion herbaceous plants). This set of gardens lies between the circular lawn and native plant and pond area, a predominantly naturalized area with path.

Continuing around the center lawn, one encounters an herb garden (medicinal, culinary, dye and fragrance plants in a formal, four-quadrant design), a mixed border (using Gertrude Jekyll color schemes against a boxwood background), a rose garden (both heritage and modern roses with companion plants), the Manor House, a witch hazel collection, the gazebo and blue garden and a meadow (grasses and woody plants).

That is a rather formidable list of discrete attractions.

Through lectures, workshops, guided tours, a newsletter, a library, twice-a-month guided (seasonal) tours and twice-a-year plant sales, staff and volunteers together create a significant educational environment for an appreciative public.

Personal Impression. I was surprised to find a flurry of activity during my mid-week, off-season visit. This is more than a showcase garden (which it is); it's a working garden complex that seems well-used and highly appreciated by the County's residents who also generously donate their time. I also was impressed with the variety of educational literature around. It's a lively place!

(6) Gunston Hall

Lorton, VA 22079
(703) 550-9220
Hours: the buildings open 9:30-5 daily, year round; the grounds are open an hour longer; closed Thanksgiving, Christmas and New Year's Day.

Overview. The Commonwealth of Virginia has restored Gunston Hall, the 18th century plantation of George Mason, the Father of the Bill of Rights and a framer of the U.S. Constitution, on 550 of the estate's original 5000 acres. The garden features perhaps the Region's finest and most formal, very large boxwood garden and an impressive natural trail with excellent brochure.

Directions. Gunston Hall is located about 20 miles south of D.C. between I-95 and the Potomac River, not far from Mount Vernon and Woodlawn. Take

Exit 161 or 163 to Route 1 and follow signs. From the intersection of Routes 1 and 242, take Rte. 242 3.6 miles to the entrance on your left.

Historical Profile. George Mason built Gunston Hall in 1755 on 5000 acres on the Potomac River for his tobacco and grain plantation, and it remained in the family until 1866. In 1912, Louis Hertle purchased it and began the restoration that was continued under the ownership of the Commonwealth of Virginia and the administration of the National Society of the Colonial Dames of America, opening to the public in 1950. The Garden Club of Virginia restored the boxwood garden in 1950, and general landscape restoration has continued to the present.

Ownership	Pet on leash	Brochure
public, state[1]	yes	yes
Size	**Weddings**	**Ed. programs**
550 acres	yes	yes
Rest rooms	**Sell plants**	**Spec. events**
yes	twice a year	yes
Pay phone	**Membership**	**Labeling**
yes	yes	limited
Visitor center	**Gift shop**	**Volunteers**
excellent	excellent	yes
Fees		**Off street parking**
yes		yes
Library for public		**Ext. photo limits**
yes, on site		commercial
Garden clubs active		**Food**
yes		picnicing

[1]Private management.

Description. One enters the estate on a curving road informally lined with late-May-blooming mountain laurels, and then onto a straight road formally tree-lined and in sight of majestic Gunston Hall, the exquisite reception complex and open meadows. Other structures on the grounds include an old schoolhouse, a chicken house, kitchen, dairy, laundry and smokehouse.

Behind the house one finds two long, rectangular boxwood parterres separated by a scenic allee. The English boxwoods in the formal garden are original, thus being more correctly preserved than restored. Deer permitting, annuals add color and dogwoods cheerfully greet the spring. A long trail down to the River introduces the visitor to native flora (including a spring profusion of wild-flowers) and surprisingly diverse wildlife, with the aid of an excellent brochure.

Gunston Hall participates in Historic Virginia Garden Week in late April and has recently introduced a new annual seminar on historical gardening.

Personal Impression. This is a first-class preservation and restoration effort that has the visitor's comfort and education clearly in mind. The reception complex does an unsurpassed job of preparing the visitor for a tour of the beautiful brick mansion with exquisite period furnishings, the several outbuildings and the grounds that simultaneously blend formal, informal and natural areas. Leave enough time to enjoy it all.

(7) Kenmore

1201 Washington Ave.
Fredericksburg, VA 22401
(703) 373-3381
Hours: Kenmore opens 9-5 daily, March 1-Nov. 30; 10-4 daily, Dec. 1-Feb. 28; closed Thanksgiving, Dec. 24, 25, 31, and Jan. 1.

Overview. Public consciousness of decaying national historic treasures seemed to have stirred shortly after World War I, and the 1922 beginning of Kenmore's restoration was among the first in the nation. The 18th century colonial estate mansion and grounds occupy five of the original 1300 acres in a pleasant Fredericksburg neighborhood with casual landscaping and a hint of formality.

Ownership	Pet on leash	Brochure
private, NP	yes	yes

Size	Weddings	Ed. programs
5 acres	no	--

Rest rooms	Sell plants	Spec. events
yes	no	yes

Pay phone	Membership	Labeling
no	yes	--

Visitor center	Gift shop	Volunteers
yes	yes	no

Fees	Off street parking
not for grounds	no

Library for public	Ext. photo limits
no	none

Garden clubs active	Food
no	no

Directions. Fredericksburg lies between D.C. and Richmond, just east of I-95. Take Exit 130 (Rte. 3) east from I-95 for 2.1 miles, then turn left at Washington Ave. (by the graveyard) to Kenmore in three blocks, on your right.

Historical Capsule. Colonel Fielding Lewis began the construction of Kenmore for his wife, Betty--George Washington's only sister, just before the American Revolution. During the Civil War, it was caught between Union and Confederate lines, and an unexploded cannon ball was found between the floors during restoration. The Garden Club of Virginia sponsored a fund-raising Garden Week in 1929 to restore the grounds with period-appropriate material; Garden Week continues to this day. Stated simply, the grounds are beautiful.

Description. Except for a colorful cutting garden, the grounds are virtually seamless with expansive lawns under immense hardwoods, and tastefully distributed boxwood, rhododendron, bulbs, ground cover, camellias and even some wildflowers in a wilderness area. It is not the species that provide the principal attraction, however, it is the way they are harmonized into a graceful landscape that needs to be seen to be appreciated. It's picture-perfect.

The brick mansion and fusnishings are also impeccably restored and maintained. The ornate plasterwork, reportedly designed in part by the frequently visiting George Washington and probably enhanced somewhat after the Civil War, is the finest I have seen. The gift shop is widely known for its distinctive merchandise. (And they serve gingerbread and tea.)

Personal Impression. I happened to visit during the height of the dogwood bloom, which made meticulously-groomed Kenmore even more stunning. If I could choose any historic estate in the Region for my personal residence, I would choose Kenmore. It has a unique blend of casual stateliness and graceful quality.

---

(8) Lewis Ginter Botanical Garden (at Bloemendaal)

1800 Lakeside Ave.
Richmond, VA 23228
(804) 262-9887
Hours: the grounds open 9:30-4:30 daily, year round; the visitor center opens mornings and afternoons Mon.-Sat. and Sun. afternoons; closed Christmas and New Year's Day.

Overview. This 80-acre garden complex in north Richmond has its implementation of a masterplan for a premier garden in high gear. The completed components already place it among the mid-Atlantic region's finer gardens, and the full completion will place it in the top 10. It is worth viewing now both to savor the highly diversified formal and informal displays and also to share in the excitement of an odyssey in progress.

Directions. The Garden is located in north Richmond just off I-95. Take Exit 83B from I-95 onto Parham Rd. West, *immediately* turning left onto Rte. 1 (Brook Rd.) for 0.9 miles, then right onto Lakeside Ave. (there's a Ginter sign) and proceed 0.8 miles to the entrance on your right.

Historical Profile. Originally a Powhatan Indian hunting area and once owned by Patrick Henry, the area escaped serious development until Richmond entrepreneur Lewis Ginter purchased it in the 1880s and converted it into the bustling Lakeside Wheel Club. Grace Arents, Lewis' neice, inherited the property and built Bloemendaal (Dutch, meaning Flowering Valley) House, which initially served as a hospice for invalid children. "Incorporated in 1984, the Lewis Ginter Botanical Garden has a three-fold mission of horticultural display, botanical research and public education...," thus fulfilling Grace Arents' dream of the final disposition of her property.

Description. The large, centered lake and the confinement of mature trees mainly to the periphery of the property gives the garden a feeling of vast openness, quite similar to Hershey Gardens' ambience--quite atypical of most mid-Atlantic gardens.

Ownership	Pet on leash	Brochure
private, NP	no	several
Size	**Weddings**	**Ed. programs**
80 acres	yes	yes
Rest rooms	**Sell plants**	**Spec. events**
yes	yes	yes
Pay phone	**Membership**	**Labeling**
no	yes	yes
Visitor center	**Gift shop**	**Volunteers**
yes	yes	many
Fees		**Off street parking**
yes		yes
Library for public		**Ext. photo limits**
yes, on-site		commercial
Garden clubs active		**Food**
yes		yes

The initially cultivated areas resemble a boot. From the parking lot at the tip of the toe, one enters the mounded, informal Henry M. Flagler Perennial Garden, one of the largest perennial gardens in the east. It contains 12,000 plants (650 cultivars) across three acres, interplanted with trees, shrubs, annuals, bulbs and ornamentals for all-seasons appeal. It is nearly brand-new.

Proceeding toward the heel, one encounters the Grace Arents Garden, restored by the Garden Club of Virginia in 1990. The quadrant design features seasonal inner beds, rose and peony outer beds and a boxwood enclosure.

The visitor center and Victorian manor house with period furnishings complete the heel.

The ankle is composed of a set of small annual and perennial test beds and borders, production greenhouses and an 850-variety daffodil collection.

A children's garden, teahouse (Japanese style), a woodlands walk, a daylily collection, a significant ivy collection, a narcissus collection and flowering shrubs round out the attractions.

All of these are beautifully harmonized over the developed half of the 80 acres.

Group tours are by prearrangement. Educational programs and special events are presented regularly throughout the year--call for an up-to-date list.

Personal Impression. During all three of my trips to the Garden, I have been impressed with the boundless energy and good will the staff and volunteers bring to their tasks. Enormous strides have been made over the past three years and I saw no inclination to stand pat. It's beautiful now and it's headed for the top ten.

(9) Maymont

c/o The Maymont Foundation
1700 Hampton St.
Richmond, VA 23220
(804) 358-7166
Hours: the grounds are open daily from 10 to 5, Nov. 1 - March 31, and 10-7
April 1 through Oct. 31; indoor attractions are closed Mondays and have seasonal hours.

Overview. Richmond offers this 100-acre recreational and cultural complex
that includes an ornately furnished Victorian mansion, a children's farm, a carriage collection, a nature center, a gift shop and a combination of formal and
informal gardens. From formal to informal, the principal garden areas are an
Italian garden, an herb garden, an English courtyard garden, a Japanese garden,
an international arboretum and a daylily collection. Careful plant selection
makes this an all seasons garden.

Directions. One may enter this very large complex either from the west or
from the east. Since the main garden areas occupy the southeast corner, I recommend the latter. See directions to Agecroft Hall. Instead of proceeding west
on Cary St. to Agecroft Hall and Virginia House, proceed east on it for 1.5
miles, turning right on Meadow St. for one mile, then right onto Pennsylvania
Ave. for a block to the entrance.

Historical Profile. James Henry Dooley purchased this original dairy farm
in 1886, naming it Maymont after his wife. The 33-room Victorian Romanesque
mansion was completed in the 1890s; childless, the Dooleys willed the property
to the City of Richmond in 1925 and it opened to the public the following year.
The Italian and Japanese gardens were completed c. 1910 and the herb garden,
in the 1960s; management has been privatized.

Description. Soon after entering through the Hampton (east) Gate, the
visitor encounters the herb garden by the nature center (circular design;
labeling; centered sundial). From there one passes the English courtyard garden
(annuals, perennials) by the Carriage House on your way down to the stunning
Italian garden. This features a magnificent 200-foot long, colonnaded and wisteria-covered pergola with adjacent pool, statuary, seasonal plants in parterres
and roses. This is one of the few Italian gardens in the Region and it is, indeed,
a stunning attraction.

From the Italian garden there is a *very* steep descent to the Japanese garden,
with multi-level cascades and a 42-foot waterfall. The garden occupies six acres
on either side of a stream and includes a teahouse, an arched bridge, a bog area,
a medication area and sculpture--all tastefully harmonized in the most secluded
section in the complex. A strong contemplative ambience.

The daylily collection (over 100 varieties) is on the far side of the property and
the large, amply spaced collection of native and exotic trees pepper the landscape (over 200 species).

Color begins with a spectacular springtime explosion (wildflowers, thousands of bulbs, dogwoods, azaleas, rhododendron), continues through summer (roses, daylilies, annuals, crape myrtles), into fall (perennials, arboreal splendor), and even into winter (witch hazel, camellias, pansies, the greenery of conifers and boxwood). Interesting groundcover includes periwinkle and dianthus. Overall, the botanical diversity is very considerable and tastefully displayed.

Ownership	Pet on leash	Brochure
pub., city[1]	no	general
Size	**Weddings**	**Ed. programs**
100 acres	yes	some
Rest rooms	**Sell plants**	**Spec. events**
yes	no	some
Pay phone	**Membership**	**Labeling**
yes	yes	some
Visitor center	**Gift shop**	**Volunteers**
yes[2]	yes	yes
Fees		**Off street parking**
not for grounds		yes
Library for public		**Ext. photo limits**
no		courtesy notice
Garden clubs active		**Food**
some		yes

[1]Private management.
[2]There is no one place to start from; probably the best place is the Emporium (gift shop).

The non-botanical attractions are equally diversified and well-kept. My personal interests, of course, took me to the nature center, which includes a large assortment of educational displays. The gift shop (Emporium) offers distinctive merchandise. The carriage collection is considerable. The elegant Maymont House and outbuildings are "on the only intact Victorian estate in Virginia." The Children's Farm includes a large selection of domestic animals and wildlife. And one may traverse the considerable grounds by foot, by carriage or by tram (in season for a modest fee). There are selected educational and annual events throughout the year, such as a rose pruning workshop at the end of February.

Personal Impression.

There is a pleasant, cheerful atmosphere at Maymont even when it rains, which it did during my first visit. And the imposing blend of quality and quantity makes for a full day of enjoyment. It's a family place.

(10) Meadowlark Gardens Regional Park

9750 Meadowlark Gardens Court
Vienna, VA 22182
(703) 255-3631
Hours: the gardens open daily at 10 a.m., year round, and close at seasonally changing hours; closed on Thanksgiving, Christmas and New Year's Day.

Overview. The Northern Virginia Regional Park Authority owns and manages this 95-acre property which features alternating lakes, open meadows, natively-wooded areas and cultivated areas from a large, modern visitor's center. Not far in travel time from Green Spring Gardens Park, the Regional Park is much larger and much more naturalistic. "Serene" best describes the ambience of this relatively new addition to the set of mid-Atlantic gardens.

Directions. Locate northern Virginia outside and west of the Capital Beltway. "From the Beltway: take exit 10B onto Route 7 towards Tysons Corner. Drive 3 miles west on Route 7, turn left onto Beulah Road and drive 2 miles to park entrance."

Historical Profile. Gardiner and Caroline Means purchased this farmland in 1935 and, to preserve it, deeded it to the Northern Virginia Regional Park Authority in 1980. It opened to the public in 1987 and has been in a continuous mode of refinement to this time.

Description. The impressive visitor's center sits on the high ground just off Beulah Rd. sequentially overlooking the ever-refined herb garden, the Great Lawn, Caroline Lake with its far-side gazebo, and native woodlands replete with wildlife. This long, continuous natural axis provides one of the most beautiful, most serene vistas in the Region.

The brochure summarizes the attractions almost too succinctly: "More than two miles of paved trails take visitors around three lakes, through acres of mature woods and grassy hills. Seasonal displays of bulbs, annuals, perennials, and chrysanthemums dot the landscape with their color at different times of the year, while permanent collections of flowering cherries, Siberian irises, hostas, lilacs, azaleas, daylilies, herbs and evergreen trees welcome visitors all year long."

Additionally on the property are three gazebos (one specializing in weddings) and an early 19th century log cabin. Monthly tours of the garden are given on Saturday mornings. The set of regularly scheduled educational programs has already grown to the degree that it warrants a separate brochure. Plant sales are periodic. The volunteer program is approaching sophistication.

Ownership	Pet on leash	Brochure
pub., regional	in sections	several
Size	**Weddings**	**Ed. programs**
95 acres	yes	many
Rest rooms	**Sell plants**	**Spec. events**
yes	occasionally	yes
Pay phone	**Membership**	**Labeling**
yes	yes	yes
Visitor center	**Gift shop**	**Volunteers**
large	growing	many
Fees	**Off street parking**	
donations	yes	
Library for public	**Ext. photo limits**	
on-site only	none	
Garden clubs active	**Food**	
yes	no	

The catchment area of the Northern Virginia Regional Park Authority is Alexandria, Arlington, City of Fairfax, Fairfax County, Falls Church and Loudoun. Membership in the Park is being actively sought.

Personal Impression. The problem with the description above is that it is obsolete even as it is written. There is a dynamic human energy field surrounding this serene property that is continuously expressing itself in improvements, and no "snapshot" description can capture that. I do, indeed, enjoy visiting the emerging gardens, repeatedly. As the brochure says, "Come watch us grow!"

---

(11) Monticello
P.O. Box 316
Charlottesville, VA 22902
(804) 295-8181
Hours: open daily year round except Christmas, 8-5 March - Oct. and 9-4:30 Nov. - Feb.

> *Thomas Jefferson, third President of the United States, author of the Declaration of Independence, literate in seven languages and recognized in architecture, inventing, science, history and music, wrote to C.W. Peale in 1911: "No occupation is so delightful to me as the culture of the earth, and no culture comparable to that of the garden .... But though an old man, I am but a young gardener."*

Overview. The Thomas Jefferson Memorial Foundation owns and manages 2000 of the original 5000 acres of Jefferson's late 18th/early 19th century estate, including his restored, incomparable house, outbuildings and garden areas where he grew just about everything. Restoration is exactingly accurate in honor of one of America's most broadly talented forefathers.

Directions. Locate Charlottesville northwest of Richmond. Exit I-64 onto Rte. 20 where the Tour Center for Monticello is located. From the Tour Center, take Rte. 53 1.6 miles to the entrance on your left. (Directional signs are everywhere.)

Historical Profile. Thomas Jefferson (1743-1826) inherited Monticello from his father at age 14. Only marginally successful as a farm because of Jefferson's long and frequent absences, the gardens and grounds received increasing attention as he aged and became a highly regarded, innovative botanical enterprise.

The estate deteriorated badly following Jefferson's death until the currently owning Foundation acquired the property c. 1926 and began restoration of the house. The Garden Club of Virginia began restoring the gardens in the 1930s, fortuitously aided by Jefferson's detailed notes, correspondence and drawings, and the refinement of gardens and grounds continues to the present.

175

Jefferson's gardens, then and now, are described in detail in Peter Hatch's *The Gardens of Monticello*, recently published by the Foundation.

Description. The continuous procession of masses of visitors to Monticello requires a fair degree of organization which begins at the Tour Center just off I-64 nearly two miles from the entrance. One may view a film, ask questions and purchase fine merchandise at the gift shop.

After parking at the Monticello lot, one purchases a ticket for the short shuttle ride to the house which regulates the rate at which new visitors enter the grounds. If you have to wait for the shuttle, you may purchase light fare at a small stand or picnic in designated areas. You may also visit the plant shop (open from late March into November) of the Thomas Jefferson Center for Historic Plants (opened in 1987) which sells historic plants hard-to-find elsewhere.

The shuttle deposits visitors at the East Portico of the graceful, red brick house to await a group tour. Those whose interests are limited to horticulture are urged to take

Ownership	Pet on leash	Brochure
private, NP	no	yes
Size	**Weddings**	**Ed. programs**
2000 acres	no	yes
Rest rooms	**Sell plants**	**Spec. events**
yes	yes	yes
Pay phone	**Membership**	**Labeling**
yes	no	yes
Visitor center	**Gift shop**	**Volunteers**
yes	excellent	no
Fees		**Off street parking**
yes		yes
Library for public		**Ext. photo limits**
no		commercial
Garden clubs active		**Food**
in 1930s		some

the house tour because nothing else so fully reflects the creative genius of Jefferson, who designed it.

From the parlor of the house, one overlooks a large oval lawn with a perimeter path bordered on either side by seasonally changing beds. The house and west lawn sit on the high ground of the estate's hilly, heavily wooded terrain. In contrast to traditional, geometric, enclosed garden designs, the "roundabout" features the openness and informality that English gardeners had recently adopted, thereby helping to "modernize" American landscape design. There are about 100 ten-foot beds around the oval with up to three plantings a year, beginning with many tulip varieties. (Many of Jefferson's bulbs survived to help outline the original contours of the lawn and path.)

Small, oval beds surround the house--the original plan called for 20. These are seasonally planted with tulips, roses, native cardinal flowers, the "Columbian Lilly" from the Lewis and Clark expedition, sweet William, *Jeffersonia diphylla* and more.

If Jefferson had a favorite, it was the tree, both native and exotic. He planted allees of mulberry and honey locust, masses of sugar maples and pecans, peach tree borders for his fields and, overall, introduced over 160 species to his property. Only a few have survived. Restoration of the Grove began in 1977 and continues today.

On an 80 by 100 foot terraced shelf south of the house, Jefferson grew over 250 varieties of vegetables and herbs in 27 beds, the restoration of which began in 1979. The English pea was his favorite, nearly 20 varieties having been grown. Below the vegetable terrace lies a 400-tree, 7-acre orchard and an assortment of vineyards, berry squares, a nursery and submural beds. Restoration began in the early 1980s.

The invisible dimension of Jefferson's gardens is the careful research which has accumulated over the decades to an imposing degree and in a fast-growing literature. If you do not stop at the Tour Center, there is an on-site gift shop north of the house which contains many works of interest. Tours of the garden proceed regularly in season. Call to determine the current status of Saturday educational programs.

Personal Impression. One needs binocular vision to appreciate Jefferson's gardens--one eye on the gardens and one on the memory of the man who contributed so greatly to our national heritage. A visit to Monticello is really a pilgrimage.

---

(12) Morven Park

Route 3, Box 50
Leesburg, VA 22075
(703) 777-2414
Hours: the facility opens 12-5 Tue.-Sun., April 1-Oct. 31; group tours by pre-arrangement in winter months.

Overview. Located in Virginia's rolling hunt country 30 miles from D.C., Morven Park is still a working farm and features seven acres of formal gardens with "the largest stand of boxwood on the east coast from the 1930s." A private foundation oversees the 1200-acre estate, a carefully preserved relic from a gracious past.

Directions. Locate Leesburg west-northwest of D.C. From the intersection there of Routes 7 and 15, take Rte. 7 (Market St.) west for 0.5 miles, then right onto Morven Park Rd.

Historical Profile. The current mansion on the estate evolved from a field-stone farmhouse built in 1781. Thomas Swann, a Maryland governor, lived there in the 19th century and Westmoreland Davis, Virginia's reform governor, lived there the first half of the 20th century, giving it the still-preserved, turn-of-the-century look. Marguerite Davis supervised the furnishing of the elegant mansion and the creation of the current gardens. After a short period of neglect, the gardens were restored in 1967 and have been continuously maintained to the present.

Description. One enters the large estate on a mile-long, tree-lined road that suggests to the visitor that a casual, genteel experience lies ahead, a movie-like ambience of gracious southern living that is soon reinforced by the appearance of a glistening white mansion. The farmed fields and spacious lawns with occasional, well-spaced, native hardwood trees provide a feeling of openness.

The predominantly formal Marguerite Davis Boxwood Gardens contains a very attractive reflecting pool, spring bulbs, June dahlias, summer annuals and breathtaking fall splendor. Tree selection includes Japanese cherry, crabapple, dogwood, crape myrtle and southern magnolias. Two self-guiding nature trails wander through woods peppered with wildflowers. And, of course, masses of boxwood.

"Tourists enter the mansion through a Greek Revival portico to see a Renaissance great hall, a Jacobean dining room, a library and a display highlighting the life and times of Governor Davis." The mansion also includes the Museum of Hounds and Hunting. Separately housed is a very large coach and carriage museum--the largest of its type I have seen.

Ownership	Pet on leash	Brochure
private, NP	no	yes
Size	**Weddings**	**Ed. programs**
7 acres	yes	no
Rest rooms	**Sell plants**	**Spec. events**
yes	no	1
Pay phone	**Membership**	**Labeling**
no	no	no
Visitor center	**Gift shop**	**Volunteers**
yes	coming	no
Fees		**Off street parking**
not for grounds		yes
Library for public		**Ext. photo limits**
yes[2]		commercial
Garden clubs active		**Food**
no		picnicing

[1]There are race meets in spring and fall, a wine festival in the summer and a Civil War re-enactment is in planning.
[2]Particularly strong in material related to hounds and hunting.

Personal Impression. "Gracious" is the word I overuse to describe Morven Park. It is a quiet and relaxing place to be alone with your thoughts.

(13) Mount Vernon
Mount Vernon, VA 22121
(703) 780-2000
Hours: "Mount Vernon is open to the public every day of the year from 9 a.m.

Overview. The Mount Vernon Ladies' Association has restored and preserved George Washington's 18th century estate at Mount Vernon by the
Potomac River in northern Virginia. The several, predominantly formal gardens
on the 500-acre grounds have been restored as closely as possible to the design
and composition of 1799 Mount Vernon.

Directions. Mount Vernon lies southeast of D.C. on the Potomac River
outside the Capital Beltway. From the Beltway, take the Mount Vernon
Parkway 9.4 miles to the entrance on your left. One may also access the
grounds by boat on the Potomac.

Historical Profile. The Mount Vernon homesite was acquired in 1674 by
John Washington, George's great grandfather, but the nucleus of the house was
not constructed until c. 1735. George first leased the property from his half-
brother's widow in 1754 and fully inherited it in 1761, expanding the house (14
rooms are open for public viewing), the outbuildings (ten have been restored),
the property (2100 acres) and the gardens. George died in 1799 (restoration
targets the estate's status at that time), Martha died in 1802, and the Mount
Vernon Ladies' Association purchased the site from the Washington family in
1858 for preservation in perpetuity.

During the nearly six decades after George's death, the ill-fortunes of the
Washington family resulted in serious deterioration, presenting the Association
with a significant restoration task (in contrast to preservation), complicated
somewhat by the poorly documented changes the family had made in the structures and gardens. Restoration priority for the first five decades was accorded to
the structures, especially the mansion which has continuously been the principal
viewing attraction.

The most careful and surviving restoration of the gardens did not begin until the
1930s and refinements are still made as new information is found. The garden
restoration is not embellished: the Ladies' Association is the nation's oldest
preservation society and also a standard-bearer for accurate restoration. The
structures and 500-acre grounds today approximate as closely as possible their
status in 1799. Over one million visitors annually make Mount Vernon the
nation's most visited historic estate.

Description. Mount Vernon in George Washington's time was a much more
highly developed complex than most of its contemporaries and has been
restored as such. I heard many surprised visitors comment on how many more
structures there were than on other historic estates they had visited. Even the
reception area outside the grounds is more complex, containing a post office,
food outlets, a large gift shop and an information section.

An aerial view shows that most of the features are arranged within a large oval.
On an axis beginning at the Potomac River, one encounters the mansion, a
sundial-centered courtyard, and then the very large bowling green that is

sequentially flanked on either side by stately trees (some surviving from Washington's time), large garden areas and various outbuildings--all within and along on the oval's perimeter road. The principal restored gardens are the Upper Garden, the Lower Garden and the Botanical Garden.

Ownership	Pet on leash	Brochure
private, NP	yes	yes
Size	**Weddings**	**Ed. programs**
¹	no	no
Rest rooms	**Sell plants**	**Spec. events**
yes	some	yes
Pay phone	**Membership**	**Labeling**
yes	yes	yes
Visitor center	**Gift shop**	**Volunteers**
large	excellent	some
Fees		**Off street parking**
yes		yes
Library for public		**Ext. photo limits**
by appointment		commercial inside
Garden clubs active		**Food**
no		very good

¹Only 60 of the 500 acres are exhibited.

The large "Upper Garden," walled against intruding animals, greets the visitor not far from the entrance and offers the most formal and most flowering gardens on the estate. Sparse records suggest that nut-bearing, fruit and ornamental trees were introduced first, as well as some vegetables in boxwood-lined, rectangular beds. Curiously, records and correspondence indicate only the presence of flowering plants, not their names. The overly colorful nature of early restoration began yielding in the 1930s to a substitution of only late 18th century American plants such as "heliotrope and fox-gloves, pansies, violets, canterbury bells, blood root, corn flowers, larkspur, and in their season, tulips, daffodils, lilies, iris ..." interplanted with various vegetables. Roses were probably culti-vated as much as for their hips, rose water and medicinal uses as for their orna-mentation and fragrance. Even though brilliance for the sake of flowering bril-liance has been sacrificed for historical accuracy, I found the garden as orna-mentally pleasing as any modern garden. Between it and the greenhouse are dwarf box parterres in *fleur de lis* design. The brick greenhouse burned in 1835 and has been exactly reproduced, having probably served mainly as a winter storehouse for tubbed plants.

Equally as large as the Upper Garden and parallel to it on the other side of the expansive bowling green is the "Lower Garden" for fruits, vegetables and herbs--a kitchen garden. Surprisingly few details about its design and composition have survived, so that period-appropriate designs and plantings have supple-mented known features, delaying the exposure of the garden to public view until 1937. Espaliered fruit trees line an inner wall. Figs, nut trees, cherries, apples, pears, peaches. Strawberries, gooseberries, raspberries and currants. The list of vegetables sounds quite modern--onions, beets, turnips, cabbage, asparagus, carrots, etc. The known presence of mint and parsley is supplemented with period-appropriate herbs such as lavender, thyme, rue, sage.

The "Botanical Garden" adjacent to the Upper Garden was used to test the adaptability of imported seeds and plants and to start plants for later transplant. The small "Vineyard Enclosure" near the Lower Garden also was used for experimentation and for starting boxwood for later transplant; restoration is not yet complete. Washington dearly loved trees and brought many back from his travels (e.g., buckeyes), and these are distributed throughout the property.

An excellent source of more detailed information is Elizabeth Kellam de Forest's *The Gardens and Grounds at Mount Vernon*, published by the Association in 1982. It is for sale in both gift shops (one outside the grounds and one inside, near the Upper Garden).

Personal Impression. The enormous number of visitors makes efficient management a necessity, and Mount Vernon has it. I have found the best viewing time to be immediately after opening; the other visitors mainly rush to the buildings to be the first ones in, leaving the gardens relatively undisturbed and quiet. But the number of on-site and off-site attractions is so large that even seasonal crowds are well-distributed. George would be quite proud of his estate today.

---

(14) Norfolk Botanical Garden
Azalea Garden Rd.
Norfolk, VA 23518
(804) 441-5830
Hours: the gardens open 8:30-sunset daily, year round; the gift shop and restaurant open 10-3 weekdays, 10-4 Sat. and 12-4 Sun., with reduced hours in mid-winter; the Administration Building opens business hours on weekdays and 10-5 on weekends/holidays.

Overview. Formerly known as Gardens by the Sea, this publicly owned, privately managed megagarden offers throughout 175 acres a premier, highly diversified, formal and informal, international, indoor and outdoor, all-seasons garden complex that AAA has ranked among the top ten gardens in the *country*, and major expansion is planned for the immediate future. By virtually any set of evaluative criteria, this is a "must-see" extravaganza.

Directions. Locate Norfolk in southeastern Virginia and I-64 running through it. From I-64, exit north onto Norview Ave. (the airport exit) and, just before the airport, turn left at the light onto Azalea Garden Rd. and, shortly, right into the clearly marked entrance.

Historical Profile. The Garden began in 1938 as a WPA project with 4,000 azaleas planted on the original 25 acres. Subsequent azalea plantings (now about a quarter million) and diversification (e.g., 700 varieties of camellias, 150 varieties of rhododendron) led to the first annual International

Azalea Festival honoring NATO in 1954. A second growth spurt began in 1958 with a general diversification of theme gardens over the full 175 acres and ended with the opening of a tropical plant pavillion recently. Effective January 1, 1993, privatized management (the Norfolk Botanical Garden Society) assumed control from the City of Norfolk, adopted a 1991 growth masterplan, and is currently in a fund raising campaign that may enable work to begin in late 1994 on a new Visitor Reception and Orientation Building and an Education Complex. Sometime after that, work may begin on a grand conservatory for exotic and endangered species.

Description. The visitor immediately notices the ample supply of water (especially the large Lake Whitehurst) with a duck feeding area, a fishing island, a fishing pier and a picnic area near the entrance. On no part of the grounds is the visitor far from a pond, a lake or a lake-fed canal. One soon passes beneath a thick canopy with an extraordinary, informal azalea/camellia/rhododendron undergrowth--it is dazzling during peak blooms. Then past the administrative office building (with information booth and library), restrooms and the restaurant/gift shop building to the large parking area.

Ownership	Pet on leash	Brochure
public, city[1]	no	yes
Size	**Weddings**	**Ed. programs**
175 acres	yes	many
Rest rooms	**Sell plants**	**Spec. events**
yes	occasionally	many
Pay phone	**Membership**	**Labeling**
yes	yes	yes
Visitor center	**Gift shop**	**Volunteers**
yes	excellent	many
Fees		**Off street parking**
yes, modest		ample
Library for public		**Ext. photo limits**
for members		commercial
Garden clubs active		**Food**
many		yes

[1]*Privatized management.*

Most visitors will exit the parking area to return to the building complex from which one may access the 12 miles of pathways by foot, by trackless train or by canal boat, the latter two being offered together by no other garden in the Region. Return visitors, however, may prefer to venture directly into the 3.5 acre Bicentennial Rose Garden which displays over 4000 rose plants (over 250 varieties) with continuous blooms that rise and fall from mid-May through October--over a million blooms at the peaks. Awesome. The area also contains a pedestrian terrace, overlooks, rest areas, fountains and a sculpture garden.

From the building complex, one immediately encounters the 3600 sq. ft. Tropical Pavilion featuring over 100 varieties of plants from Earth's tropical belt and, to its side, the quaint and charming Japanese Garden which honors

Norfolk's sister city, Kitokyushu, and which follows the classic Japanese hill and pond design.

By car and by foot, you have now seen less than half of the grounds which contain most of the more than 20 theme gardens. As a sampler, there is a holly garden, a conifer garden, a flowering arboretum, a perennial garden, a wildflower garden, a desert garden, a fragrance garden, a bog garden and a dozen more, with a central observation tower from which one may scan the imposing panorama.

Those who like statuary and stonework will enjoy two acres across the canal from the tower. In classic 16th century Italian Renaissance-style, a symmetrical area is outlined with ornate stone fences, with cornered statues, a coronation court and a reflecting pool that my toddler son waded into 20 years ago when I wasn't looking. Near it is the Statuary Vista, an incomparable row of "eleven, seven foot, heroic sized statues ... carved from Carrara marble by Moses Ezekiel in Rome between 1879 and 1884 ..." depicting artistic overachievers such as Rubens, Durer and DaVinci.

This description focuses only on the magnitude and diversity of some of the garden attractions, which does an injustice to the cleanliness of the grounds and structures, and to the degree of manicuring both staffers and volunteers perform. Also, the gift shop, tasteful in its own right, is one of the few shops in the Region that stocks almost exclusively books and other items of horticultural relevance.

Special Events. On-going weekly educational programs, seminars, workshops, children's programs, extensive labeling, occasional plant sales and special events take the operation far beyond the status of showcase garden. A quick review of the Society's newsletter recently revealed a scope of programs that included: a plant doctor panel, summertime nature discovery weeks for children, plant society meetings, holly days, a pruning workshop, off-site tours of other gardens, a workshop on wetlands landscaping, an entire set of programs by the Virginia Camellia Society, various guest lecturers, a volunteer appreciation night, garden tours, book reviews, butterfly night--and *much* more. This is a lively place. Call for an up-to-date list of events.

Personal Impression. Only Longwood Gardens in PA, the National Arboretum in DC, the Biltmore Estate in NC and the Norfolk Botanical Garden blend quality and quantity on such a scale as to tax my comprehension. A single visit in one season just isn't enough. I have regularly visited the gardens in all seasons for nearly 25 years and still have not seen it all. Without equivocation, this is a must-see garden complex. Any day of the year.

(15) Oatlands
Route 2, Box 352
Leesburg, VA 22075

(703) 777-3174

Hours: Oatlands is open from April through late December, 10-4 Mon.-Sat. and 1-4 Sun.

Overview. Owned by the National Trust for Historic Preservation, Oatlands features four acres of predominantly formal gardens on a 261-acre historic estate and a magnificently restored pre-Civil War plantation mansion. The use-history of grounds and mansion differs uniquely from other historic estates in Virginia.

Directions. Locate Leesburg west-northwest of Washington, D.C. and the intersection in it between Routes 7 and 15. From that intersection, take Route 15 south for 4.9 miles to the marked entrance on your left.

Historical Profile. Oatlands today reflects the cumulative expression of two entirely different historical periods, two entirely different family lifestyles and two entirely different types of garden restoration.

In its antebellum period, Oatlands was a thriving plantation of c. 3000 acres which, at its height, included a sawmill, gristmill, brick foundry, blacksmith shop, school, church and store. The nucleus of the plantation mansion was built in 1803 from bricks fired on the property and wood milled from the surrounding forest, and it was embellished in the 1830s in the Greek Revival style popular at that time. By 1810, the owning Carter family built a terraced garden with a southern exposure, the single feature that has changed least over nearly two centuries.

Following the Civil War, the Carter fortunes declined steadily as did the maintenance of the estate. Its deterioration accelerated after the property's 1897 sale to an absentee owner.

Ownership	Pet on leash	Brochure
private, NP[1]	no	yes
Size	**Weddings**	**Ed. programs**
261 acres	yes	occasionally
Rest rooms	**Sell plants**	**Spec. events**
yes	in season	yes[2]
Pay phone	**Membership**	**Labeling**
yes	yes	no
Visitor center	**Gift shop**	**Volunteers**
yes	very good	yes
Fees		**Off street parking**
yes		yes
Library for public		**Ext. photo limits**
no		no interior flash
Garden clubs active		**Food**
no		picnicking

[1]*Oatlands is a co-stewardship property of the National Trust for Historic Preservation and is administered by Oatlands, Inc.*
[2]*The annual Garden Fair is held the last weekend in September.*

In spite of its poor condition, Mr. & Mrs. William Corcoran Eustis, wealthy Washington socialites, purchased the property in 1903 for a summer home, and

Mrs. Eustis maintained ownership until 1964. Considerable improvements were made to house and grounds to ready them for the gala entertainment of DC's urban socialites, in sharp contrast to the less glittering life on an antebellum plantation. Carter's terraced gardens had largely produced fruits, vegetables and herbs for the resident plantation families. Mrs. Eustis, however, "... enlarged the flower beds, extended the boxwood parterres, designed a rose garden, and added statuary and garden ornaments" in the garden's first restoration. A classical tea house was added and a reflecting pool. Overall, Mrs. Eustis' renovation moved the garden away from its kitchen characteristics and toward classic English garden design.

Upon her death in 1965, Oatlands became the property of the National Trust for Historic Preservation, and in the 1980s, serious renovation began for the second time--pruned boxwood, a redesigned rose garden, replenished flower beds and an introduced herb garden. These changes have occurred in the context of a balance between "historical accuracy and practical recognition of the improvements offered by selected modern hybrids."

Description. The large, brilliantly white mansion seems equally well-suited for an antebellum plantation's graciousness or an early 20th century socialite's country playground. Open meadows over the rolling terrain alternate with an exceptionally diverse collection of mature trees: red oak, white oak, dogwood, blue atlas cedar, empress tree and many more. The ginkgo, European larch and English oak are the largest of their species in Virginia. And a new boxwood garden by the mansion bodes well for the future.

However, the four-acre garden dominates the grounds, the stone and brick walls and terrace steps providing a season-extending windbreak for the Carter family and a charming accent to the formality of a classic English-style garden for the Eustis family. A single, square shaped path takes the visitor along the principal features: an herb garden, the reflecting pool and the Carter tomb, the exquisite rose garden, a boxwood edged bowling green, the tea house, the perennial garden, the very formal sundial parterre and the meditation terrace. The overall effect is one of stately and beautiful harmony, enhanced by the peace and quiet of Virginia's hunt country. The plant composition of spring bulbs and shrubs, summer annuals and roses, and fall perennials and arboreal splendor provides continuous color during the open season.

Group tours are by prearrangement. The gift shop offers a fine selection of books and other merchandise of quality.

Personal Impression. For me, the grounds as a whole have the ambience of a southern plantation and the formal garden has the ambience of genteel high society. Fortunately, they seem as compatible as graciousness and charm.

---

(16) River Farm
c/o American Horticultural Society

7931 East Boulevard Dr.
Alexandria, VA 22308
(703) 768-5700
Hours: from May 1 through Oct. 30, 8:30-5 Mon.-Fri.; call to verify Saturday openings and openings Nov.-April; closed major holidays.

Overview. The American Horticultural Society owns and maintains historic River Farm on the banks of the Potomac River southeast of Washington, D.C. The 27-acre property contains formal, informal and natural garden features with significant collaboration with many plant societies. On-site structures are mainly used in support of the Society's multi-dimensional national agenda. The very large collection of demonstration and trial gardens constitutes the distinguishing characteristic of the garden complex.

Directions. Refer back to the directions to George Washington's Mount Vernon. Exit the Capital Beltway onto Mount Vernon Parkway, but turn left at the sign into River Farm before you reach Mount Vernon. The entrance is clearly marked.

Historical Profile.
George Washington purchased this property in 1760 and converted it into one of his five working farms. The surviving 1757 house has seen many changes in ownership over 2.5 centuries, none of which altered the rural quality of the property on the banks of the Potomac River, only a few miles from Mount Vernon. Finally in 1973, the Enid A. Haupt Charitable Trust donated it to the American Horticultural Society, which headquarters itself there and has introduced the more formal gardens one finds today. The house and outbuildings are structurally preserved, but not for historic display.

Ownership	Pet on leash	Brochure
private, NP	yes	yes (two)
Size	**Weddings**	**Ed. programs**
27 acres	not yet	yes--call
Rest rooms	**Sell plants**	**Spec. events**
yes	periodically	yes--call
Pay phone	**Membership**	**Labeling**
no	yes	yes
Visitor center	**Gift shop**	**Volunteers**
yes	excellent	many
Fees		**Off street parking**
donations		yes
Library for public		**Ext. photo limits**
members only		none
Garden clubs active		**Food**
many		picnicing

Description. From the entrance to the River, there is a continuous procession of meadows interrupted occasionally by historic structures, young tree plantings, a walled garden complex and a ha-ha wall (to exclude animals without obstructing the view), with woodlands on either flank.

186

The brick-walled Ideas Garden principally features display gardens for area chapters of national plant societies, including the American Dahlia Society, the American Iris Society, the Old Dominion Chrysanthemum Society, the Herb Society of America and an integrated collection of the American Hemerocallis Society and North American Lily Society. The two rose gardens include an official display of All-American Rose Selections.

Other discrete areas include a shady border (with significant donations from the American Ivy Society), perennial borders (with significant donations from the Perennial Plant Association), a wildflower meadow, a dwarf fruit tree orchard, a new patio garden (with fountain), a kitchen garden, a wildlife habitat garden (with goldfish pool), and a perimeter woodland trail. A recent experiment with plots for children apparently will be continued. Considerable attention in recent years has been accorded to composting methods.

Tree selection includes trifoliate orange, tulip poplar, black walnuts, tamarisk, ginkgo, beech and many more. Tulips, Chinese wisteria, climbing hydrangea, English and American boxwood, hollies, ferns--species diversification is quite impressive.

Most of the considerable, on-site activities of the AHS are not visible to the public, but occasional lectures and special events are. The gift shop and book selection in the estate house are superior. Group tours are by prearrangement.

Personal Impression. These are grounds befitting a national horticultural association. I think of it as a Garden of Organizations because so many plant societies, garden clubs and other organizations contribute so significantly to its quality and diversity. Viewing Mount Vernon in the morning and River Farm in the afternoon makes for a very fine day, and there are benches for its conclusion.

---

(17) Stratford Hall Plantation
Stratford, VA 22558
(804) 493-8038
Hours: the grounds and other attractions open 9-4:30 every day except Christmas.

Overview. The Robert E. Lee Memorial Foundation has spent over half a century refining its restoration of General Lee's birthplace on 1600 of the original acres. Formal gardens dominate the grounds on this plantation, which is one of the oldest continuing agricultural operations in the nation.

Directions. Locate on your map the intersection of Routes 3 and 301 east of Fredericksburg (see Kenmore). From that intersection, proceed east on Rte. 3 to Route 214, turning left there and follow the signs to the plantation.

Historical Profile. Thomas Lee (1690-1750), founder of the Lee "dynasty," built the massive, H-shaped Stratford Hall in the late 1730s on the

187

banks of the Potomac River. Thomas' descendants include two signers of the Declaration of Independence and several revolutionary war heroes; a few hell-raisers who embarrassed the family and indebted it; and Robert E. Lee, the last surviving Lee to be born there and later the General in Chief of the Confederate Armies.

"Stratford passed from the Lee family in 1822 and was bought by the Robert E. Lee Memorial Foundation in 1929." Restoration began in 1931 and continues to this day. The formal garden designs are period-appropriate.

Description. When I asked a Plantation official what he was proudest of, referring in my own mind to the restoration that had been accomplished, I was surprised to hear: "It's the unobstructed view all the way down to the Potomac, at one of its widest spots." Although unexpected, the response does describe the vast, open meadows on the ample property that abruptly border ridge-top woodlands on this authentic representation of an early American plantation.

Ownership	Pet on leash	Brochure
private, NP	no	yes
Size	**Weddings**	**Ed. programs**
1600 acres	yes	no
Rest rooms	**Sell plants**	**Spec. events**
yes	some	no
Pay phone	**Membership**	**Labeling**
yes	yes	no
Visitor center	**Gift shop**	**Volunteers**
yes, large	yes	no
Fees		**Off street parking**
yes		yes
Library for public		**Ext. photo limits**
no		no
Garden clubs active		**Food**
no[1]		yes

[1]The Garden Club of Virginia started restoration in the 1930s in the East Garden.

The mansion faces north toward the River with a large formal garden on either side, appropriately called the East Garden and the West Garden. The East Garden features a boxwood maze and flower parterres--3200 boxwoods in all! The West Garden displays 18th century herbs, vegetables and flowers in orderly patterns.

Wildflowers, bulbs, espaliered fruit trees, dogwoods, heritage roses, summer annuals, crape myrtles and fall perennials contribute to the color, pattern and texture of the property in season, and immense hickories add a dimension of stateliness. There are several interlocking woodland trails.

The carefully restored mansion, reknowned for its tall Great Hall and elaborate paneling, exhibits a kitchen fireplace large enough to roast an ox--while sampling cider and ginger cookies. Corn, wheat, oats and barley are ground as they were centuries ago and may be purchased at the Stratford Store. The mill, near the Potomac, is the most impressive of the many restored outbuildings.

Tours proceed regularly. Large group tours may be prearranged.

Personal Impression. The awesome vista, I later learned, is one mile long. It is, indeed, impressive, but so is the working plantation as a whole. There is something there for everyone in the family.

---

(18) Virginia House
4301 Sulgrave Rd.
Richmond, VA 23221
(804) 353-4251
Hours: the grounds open 10-4 Tue.-Sun., year round; the house is still completing renovation and permanent hours have not been set; the policy on holiday closures is under review.

Overview. The Virginia Historical Society exposes the public to the wide diversity of native and exotic species on this 9-acre estate that should be introduced to American Gardens, in the framework of an aesthetically pleasing, mixed formal and informal garden and an historically significant house.

Directions. See directions to Agecroft Hall, which is next door.

Historical Profile. The stones of the "Virginia" House were quarried in 1125 A.D. for an English monastery. After centuries of roller-coaster fortunes, U.S. diplomat Alexander Waddell and wife Virginia saved the manor house from demolition in 1925, transporting it piecemeal to Virginia for their home until their accidental deaths in 1948. Landscape architect Charles Gillette designed and expanded the estate gardens in his reknowned picturesque style, blending elements of formal and informal designs, from 1928 to 1940. Willed to the Virginia Historical Society and opened to the public in 1948, the gardens have retained the basics of Gillette's design while expanding the garden area and complementing the original flora with modern hybrids and exotics not readily available in Gillette's time. Expansion and reconceptualization of the gardens continue to the present and into the projected future.

Description. Virginia House sits next to Agecroft Hall and enjoys several similarities with it. Both have ancient English houses that were rescued from destruction and transported to Richmond, and at about the same time; Charles Gillette designed both landscapes; and both operations collaborate on several events each year.

The dissimilarities, however, are more interesting. Virginia House's land is more elongated and more steeply sloped both from the house down to the James River and from side to side. This required considerably more terracing than at Agecroft Hall and smaller, but more numerous, garden segments. This, in turn, allowed Gillette to create perhaps his finest trademark vista. From the terrace behind the house, one has an unobstructed view of the James River. One overlooks the immediate set of terraced, formal gardens (with stonework, water and low plantings harmoniously blended) to the open meadow flanked by trees and

189

shrubs on either side, all the way down to the river. The total vista created is widely regarded as a landscaping masterpiece.

Intermediately, there are well over a dozen distinct garden areas that may be enjoyed independently, including: the canal garden (the initial Gillette garden with aquatic plants); a perennial border; a four seasons bed; an azalea garden; a rose garden (currently under renovation); a tea garden; a large wildflower meadow; the Sulgrave garden next to the house (two beds and a pond); a bog garden (125 species); a pergola; and much more--all in Gillette's mixed style. Throughout, there are many walls, statues, ponds and strategically located benches.

At a specimen level, the gardens are well diversified in annuals, perennials, bulbs (especially tulips and daffodils), shrubs, ornamental trees (e.g., cherries, magnolias, yellow poplars), groundcover, wildflowers, and more. Blooms are virtually continuous year round, with recent emphasis on fall-blooming plants. Plans include the lengthening of a woodlands trail. Wheelchair access is constrained by the terracing.

Ownership	Pet on leash	Brochure
private, NP	no	excellent
Size	Weddings	Ed. programs
9 acres	yes	yes
Rest rooms	Sell plants	Spec. events
no	occasionally	yes
Pay phone	Membership	Labeling
no	yes	yes
Visitor center	Gift shop	Volunteers
no	no	many
Fees		Off street parking
yes		no
Library for public		Ext. photo limits
no		commercial
Garden clubs active		Food
yes		no

Other dissimilarities are that the cultivated areas are more densely planted at Virginia House, the grounds overall are less formal, the plant material is more modern and more diversified, and the house is in an earlier stage of restoration and furnishing.

Personal Impression. The single most important attraction at Virginia House is the Gillettesque view from the rear terrace--it is incomparable. Also, the garden brochure does a superior job of describing the overall landscape, the plant composition and interesting features of individual garden segments--possibly the most informative brochure in the Region for my tastes. Together, Virginia House and Agecroft Hall make for a full day's enjoyment.

(19) Virginia Living Museum
524 J. Clyde Morris Blvd.

Newport News, VA 23601

(804) 595-1900

Hours: during the summer, 9-6 Mon.-Sat. and 10-6 Sun., and Thursday evenings; it closes an hour earlier in winter and opens 1-5 on Sunday. Closed Thanksgiving, Christmas Eve, Christmas, New Year's Day.

Overview. From the brochure of this 24-acre, southeastern Virginia operation: "The Virginia Living Museum in Newport News is a spectacular combination of the best and most enjoyable elements of a native wildlife park, science museum, aquarium, botanical preserve, and planetarium--all in one inspiring and beautiful setting! ... all native to America's eastern Coastal Plains Region ... see the rare combination of living native animals, plants, birds and even the land itself working together as a system." A quarter-million visitors annually go to view the attractions at this privately operated facility.

Directions. From Norfolk/Hampton Roads in southeastern Virginia, take I-64 west toward Richmond, exiting at Rte. 17 (Exit 258A), J. Clyde Morris Blvd., and proceed south for 1.7 miles to the marked entrance on your left.

Ownership	Pet on leash	Brochure
private, NP	no	yes
Size	**Weddings**	**Ed. programs**
24 acres	yes	yes
Rest rooms	**Sell plants**	**Spec. events**
yes	occasionally	yes
Pay phone	**Membership**	**Labeling**
no	yes	yes
Visitor center	**Gift shop**	**Volunteers**
yes	yes	many

Fees	Off street parking
yes	yes
Library for public	**Ext. photo limits**
no	commercial
Garden clubs active	**Food**
yes[1]	picnicking

[1]Mainly native plant societies.

Historical Profile. From the Museum's fact sheet: "The facility originally opened in 1966 as the Junior Nature Museum and Planetarium. It grew in 1974 to become the Peninsula Nature and Science Center; then a total $3.2 million expansion/renovation in 1987 transformed the center into the Virginia Living Museum, the first 'living museum' east of the Mississippi River."

Description. Zoos, nature centers, wildlife preserves and completely natural areas are sufficiently numerous in the Region to warrant their own guidebooks, and I have extracted from our living environment only cultivated gardens and arboreta. The Virginia Living Museum, however, uniquely and ingeniously re-integrates cultivated gardens into a total living environment. One hopes that this innovative approach is a harbinger of a new wave of facilities that emphasizes the living system as a whole.

The parking lot is separated from the large, two-story museum by a cultivated, labeled wildflower garden with perennials and shrubs that bloom from spring into fall. The building houses a planetarium, a gift shop, songbird aviary, beehive, a mountains-to-ocean series of exhibits, a "touch" tank, microscopes with slides, small living exhibits and a changing exhibition gallery; downstairs, a "Creature of the Night" set of exhibits. Over 24,000 square feet are devoted to living exhibits, plus a planetarium theatre and conservatory.

Outside, a boardwalk takes the visitor past a lake with adjacent labeled butterfly garden. Then a woodland path wanders past a large, wire-mesh wetlands aviary and enclosed natural areas with bald eagles, raccoons, foxes, deer, turkeys, river otters and more. A sign explains the uniqueness of the canopy, the understory, the forest floor, the underground. The path ends with the "Building a Backyard Habitat" section, which features labeled shrubs, bird feeders, a bird bath and a small pool. The 24 acres are devoted to wildlife exhibitry, the remainder being naturally and natively wooded and undergrown except for the parking lot and museum building. The emphasis throughout is on things natural and the living "system" as a whole.

Call for an up-to-date list of an impressive set of educational and other programs for all age groups, including an annual wildflower sale.

Personal Impression. For those who share my interest in the total living system, of which cultivated gardens are just a part, the Virginia Living Museum is a completely unique, first class, innovative establishment.

---

(20) (Colonial) Williamsburg
c/o Colonial Williamsburg Foundation
Williamsburg, VA 23187
(804) 229-1000
Hours: the grounds are open daylight hours, year round; hours vary among the considerable attractions and by season--call for current hours.

Overview. Colonial Williamsburg is a restored, 18th century colonial capital with restored gardens throughout its 175 acres. More modern gardens are found outside the historic area on property also owned by the Colonial Williamsburg Foundation. Especially the large, formal gardens behind the Governor's Palace have helped make Williamsburg one of the most popular tourist attractions in the nation. The "colonial revival gardens" are principally restored faithfully, but they are also partly interpretive.

Directions. Williamsburg is easily located on a map of southeastern Virginia just off I-64 between Richmond and Norfolk. Take Exit 238 (Colonial Williamsburg and Camp Peary) and follow the signs about two miles to the Visitor Center.

Historical Capsule. With financial support from the Rockefeller Foundation, the non-profit Colonial Williamsburg Foundation began planning the restoration and preservation of this 1699-1781, 175-acre colonial capital in 1926; 88 of the original structures had survived for restoration and many more have been rebuilt from surviving records. Ninety of the 170 acres are devoted to gardens and greens. From surviving records and from knowledge of gardens of the period, two dozen garden areas in the historic district have been restored with plants known to have been in use before 1776, and restoration has proceeded under expert interpretation of known garden designs in the historic district and at that time.

Ownership	Pet on leash	Brochure
private, NP	yes	general
Size	**Weddings**	**Ed. programs**
175 acres	yes	no
Rest rooms	**Sell plants**	**Spec. events**
yes	occasionally	yes
Pay phone	**Membership**	**Labeling**
yes	1	yes
Visitor center	**Gift shop**	**Volunteers**
yes	excellent	some

Fees	Off street parking
yes--see text	yes
Library for public	**Ext. photo limits**
yes, general	only indoor
Garden clubs active	**Food**
no	all types

1The Foundation welcomes, and needs, your support, but donations are not earmarked for the gardens alone.

Description. To appreciate the large scale of Colonial Williamsburg, it would be helpful to purchase the *Official Guide to Colonial Williamsburg* and to keep the detachable map in it close at hand. On this map, the historic district is green and its c. two dozen blocks resemble a high-top shoe, the sole facing south. Scattered throughout the area are the Governor's Palace, the Capitol, the courthouse, a magazine, and literally dozens of residences, taverns, specialty craft shops, and various other structures of historical interest. In dark green, 23 "exhibition gardens" are identified throughout the area.

At the upper left (northwest) of the green historic area is the Governor's Palace, the architectural and gardening pinnacle of the colonial capital. It was conceived by Governor Nicholson, financed by slave-trade taxes and actually built by Governor Spotswood. The original gardens followed the Dutch-English tradition introduced by William and Mary of parterre gardens and geometric topiary. The Palace's 10 acres contain the largest and most formal gardens in the historic area. Looking north from the Palace's ballroom, one first views the upper garden--symmetrical along its northward axis, consisting of 16 diamond-shaped parterres enclosing periwinkle and English ivy and 12 cylindrical yaupon holly topiaries. The central axis continues northward down to the lower garden between American beeches which are bordered by beds of red tulips in spring and perennials in summer. Beyond the lower garden and to its left is a large American holly maze patterned after the original at Hampton Court in England. The ample grounds also contain a kitchen garden, an orchard, a graveyard, terraces, a bowling green and a canal.

The remaining 22 exhibition gardens are distributed throughout the historic area, predominantly adjacent to residences. Compared to the Palace gardens, they are smaller, somewhat less formal and somewhat more devoted to herbs and vegetables. Boxwood, ivy, topiaries and seasonally blooming plants are found in abundance.

Interestingly, one finds a formal, enclosed, contemporary garden at the southwest border of the historic area next to the DeWitt Wallace Decorative Arts Gallery. The Lila Acheson Wallace Garden, named after a founder of the Reader's Digest, opened in 1986 and features a long, rectangular reflecting pool with perennial borders, statuary, container plantings and clipped hedges of yaupon holly. It presents an enchanting view from an east-side, tall pergola.

The world-class restoration by the Colonial Williamsburg Foundation has drawn criticism from some quarters for doing too good a job, better than the original. Irrespective of whether the criticism is warranted, the quality of the Foundation's undertakings is undisputed and extends far beyond the borders of the historic area. Property surrounding the historic area, and near it, contains lodging, conference facilities, a golf course, research facilities and more, all with landscaped grounds that are themselves worthy of visit.

For reading material, one may purchase in the Williamsburg bookstore Joan Dutton's *Plants of Colonial Williamsburg*. Additionally, a detailed treatise is due out shortly after the publication of this work.

From April to October, guided tours of the garden proceed twice a day with no advance itinerary. Usually gardeners conduct the morning tour and interpreters, the afternoon one; check at the Visitor Center for details. Group tours are by prearrangement.

Overall, the grounds are free to public viewers, the major exception being the Governor's Palace which requires a ticket and usually, in prime season, a wait to enter. (I recommend arriving at the Palace at least a half-hour before its scheduled opening.)

Shopping facilities at the Visitor Center and around the historic area are superior. Food selection is excellent, but dining within the historic area usually requires a reservation. Numerous special events throughout the year may fill all local motels; if so, accommodations are closer and more plentiful toward Norfolk than toward Richmond.

Personal Impression. The gardens in the historic area are not intended to be free-standing attractions, but an integral component of the overall restoration of a colonial capital, and are most completely enjoyed in that perspective. Like the Smithsonian Institution, the number of attractions is so great and spread over such a large area that advance planning is strongly advised. You may obtain a trip-planning kit by calling the number above. Even then, please start your visit at the Visitor Center and make the *Official Guide* your first purchase.

If you follow these simple directions, I doubt you can avoid enjoying your visit. I've averaged more than a visit per year for 25 years and intend to continue doing so.

---

(21) Woodlawn Plantation

9000 Richmond Highway
Alexandria, VA 22309
(703) 780-4000
Hours: open daily 9:30-4:30, except in January; closed major holidays; call to confirm current hours.

Ownership	Pet on leash	Brochure
private, NP	no	yes
Size	**Weddings**	**Ed. programs**
126 acres	yes	yes
Rest rooms	**Sell plants**	**Spec. events**
yes	planned	yes
Pay phone	**Membership**	**Labeling**
no	yes	yes
Visitor center	**Gift shop**	**Volunteers**
yes	yes	yes
Fees		**Off street parking**
yes		yes
Library for public		**Ext. photo limits**
no		commercial
Garden clubs active		**Food**
many		no

Overview. The National Trust for Historic Preservation has restored and is maintaining this 126-acre, early 19th century plantation. Originally part of George Washington's Mount Vernon, the plantation's original gardens were almost completely obscured, and the current informal/formal mix is period-appropriate, guided by surviving records.

Directions. See directions to Mount Vernon. Instead of stopping there, continue three more miles to Rte. 1; the marked entrance is across the intersection.

Historical Profile and Description. Unlike other garden narratives, history and description are combined here because Woodlawn, perhaps better than any other historic estate and garden, exemplifies the difficulties restoration faces. Consider the following chronology.

1799 - George Washington set aside 2000 acres on the far side of Mount Vernon as a wedding gift for his foster daughter, Eleanor Park Custis, and his favorite nephew, Lawrence Lewis.

1800 - William Thornton, first architect of the U.S. Capitol, was commissioned to design the Georgian-style mansion.

1802 - Eleanor (Nelly) Lewis moved into the nearly finished mansion and contributed to the development of the grounds.

1827 - A fierce windstorm downed 50 trees and generally devestated the grounds.

1846 - Quaker settlers bought the property, felled the trees for cordwood and ship timber, and subdivided the property for sale to other settlers.

1850 - The Mason family purchased the mansion and 500 acres.

1851 - Nelly Lewis visited her former home, writing: "You would not recognize it now--all the trees, the hedge, the flower knot, my precious Agnes's grove--all gone .... I will again like a poor exile visit my ruined home--"

1892 - A development company bought the Mason property.

1896 - A devastating hurricane's damage helped discourage development plans.

c. 1899 - Paul Kester purchased the property and moved in with mother, brother and 60 cats. He instituted some renovations and structural changes.

1905 - Elizabeth Sharpe bought the property, made some mansion alterations and introduced some formal gardens.

c. 1925 - Senator and Mrs. Oscar Underwood bought the property, both modernizing and restoring mansion and gardens.

1948 - Preservation-minded citizens purchased the property.

1951 - The National Trust for Historic Preservation leased the property--the first museum house in the Trust system.

1957 - The National Trust acquired the property. The Garden Club of Virginia was contacted re: restoration, with consultation from Alden Hopkins of Colonial Williamsburg. A surviving apple tree suggested the original location of the orchard. Nellie Lewis' correspondence was searched for clues to plant composition, design and location. Two boxwood-lined parterres with 36 beds of heritage roses were introduced. A long axial walk between rows of locust trees undergrown with peonies became the central feature of the garden. Additions and refinements continue to the present.

1963 - Frank Lloyd Wright's modernistic, 1940 home, threatened by highway construction, was moved onto the property.

Now - Funds are actively sought to maintain the exquisite mansion and grounds and to refine the restoration.

Personal Impression. Woodlawn, more so than any other single place, makes me understand that historic estates are not self-generating. Destructive nature, exploiting owners, self-serving owners--all combine to obscure the original plantation status. It makes me much more appreciative of the many restorations done in the Region.

---

(22) The Greenbrier
White Sulphur Springs, WV 24986
(304) 536-1110

West Virginia is not really an Atlantic state and has not been included in my definition of "mid-Atlantic." Nonetheless, the Greenbrier sits just over the Virginia line and visitors to Monticello may want to continue west on I-64 to visit it and possibly to stay. Beginning as a health resort in the early 1800s, it has grown into a fabulous recreational complex as diversified as Tanglewood Park in NC, but targets high society for its clientele. The guest book includes Dolly Madison, Andrew Jackson, Thomas Edison, Jack Kennedy, Judy Garland and 23 presidents. The grounds feature masses of rhododendrons and a Gillettesque mix of formal and informal landscaping. Accommodations are lavish; the food is exquisite; the shops are stunning; the recreational opportunities--unlimited.

If you *must* leave the mid-Atlantic region, go to Greenbrier. It lives up to its billing--"America's Resort."

Index

198

Mid-Atlantic Gardens

Detailed descriptions of over 100 public view gardens in DC, DE, MD, NC, NJ, PA and VA.　New for 1994; color photos.

16.95 each

Call Toll-free 1-800-553-5424
or send to: *Carolina Connections*

PO Box 2408, Kill Devil Hills,
North Carolina 27948
Fax: 919-441-1867

PAYMENT: ❏ **Check** ❏ **VISA** ❏ **MasterCard**

Card No. _____ **Exp.** _____

Name _____

Address _____

City/State _____ Zip _____

SHIPPING/HANDLING CHARGES

Please add $3.95 Shipping and Handling for the first book; 75¢ for books two and three; and 50¢ for each additional book through twenty. There is no handling charge for books number 21 and up. *North Carolina residents please add 6% sales tax.*

Number of books (x $16.95) : _____

Shipping and handling for *first* book : _____ $3.95

Shipping and handling for two books : _____ $4.70

Shipping and handling for three books : _____ $5.45

Add 50¢ each for the next 17 books : _____

NC residents only add 6% of total above : _____

TOTAL ENCLOSED : _____